THORSONS COMPLETE GUIDE TO

VITAMINS

AND

MINERALS

D0064459

THORSONS COMPLETE GUIDE TO

VITAMINS

AND

MINERALS

Leonard Mervyn

Thorsons Publishers, Inc.
Rochester, Vermont
Wellingborough, Northamptonshire

Thorsons Publishers, Inc.
One Park Street
Rochester, Vermont 05767

First U.S. edition 1987

Library of Congress Cataloging in Publication Data

Mervyn, Len.
   Thorsons complete guide to vitamins & minerals.

   Includes index.
   1. Vitamins—Dictionaries.   2. Minerals—
Dictionaries. I. Title.
QP771.M464   1987   615'.328   86-30087
ISBN 0-7225-1273-2 (pbk.)

Printed and bound in the United States
10 9 8 7 6 5 4 3 2 1

Distributed to the book trade in the
United States by Harper and Row

Distributed to the book trade in Canada by
Book Center, Inc., Montreal, Quebec

Distributed to the health food trade in Canada by
Alive Books, Toronto and Vancouver

INTRODUCTION

While Nature, in her wisdom, saw fit to include in our daily diets all of the vitamins and minerals—the micronutrients essential for health and indeed for life itself—that we need, we have in many cases, with our arrogant attitude toward how food should be grown and treated, demeaned what Nature has provided. Plants (including microorganisms), the ultimate source of all foodstuffs, are sprayed with toxic chemicals; animals destined for slaughter are injected with potent hormones and antibiotics; naturally grown food is refined, processed, and generally emasculated before being presented to the consumer as a pale shadow of its former self. Little wonder then that the more open-minded among our doctors and nutritionists are beginning to question what happens to the nutritive value of our food before it eventually ends up on our plates. Vitamins, particularly, are adversely affected by modern treatment of food; we should never forget that these substances are delicate, discrete, unstable chemical entities that will not stand up to many processing methods. Hence, while this book lists the food sources of our vitamins, it also warns of how these nutrients are lost or destroyed in cooking processes and refining. Minerals, too, are not exempt from losses in the transition of foods from the field to our mouths, and up-to-date information on these essential nutrients is also found here.

Vitamin and Mineral Supplementation

One of the more controversial subjects today is the role of vitamin and mineral supplementation. Do we need supplements and, if so, why and to what extent do we take these extra micronutrients? These questions are answered in the book under the appropriate headings but for simplicity we can divide vitamin supplementation into three categories, each of which demands a different level of potency. We can sum up the reasons for mineral supplementation in one category, since they are all based on deficiencies that occur for one reason or another.

Vitamin Supplements

The first category of vitamin supplementation is called the insurance category. We know that modern processing of foods reduces their vitamin content, and any losses in the factory are exacerbated in the kitchen. Certain segments of the population have also been pinpointed as being prone to deficiency of certain vitamins by virtue of their diets, age, sex, social and economic status, and general health. Hence people who fall into one of these segments or who are concerned about their diet may benefit from supplementation with all of the vitamins and minerals. Multivitamin and multimineral supplements for general use should ensure at least the minimum daily requirements of these micronutrients without reference to those in the diet. Fortunately, such preparations usually supply the recommended dietary intakes that are quantified elsewhere in this book.

A second category of supplementation may be required by those whose lifestyles increase their needs for certain vitamins. Stressful situations increase the requirements for the vitamin B complex and vitamins C and E, and extra amounts must be supplied to overcome the effects of stress. The habits of smoking tobacco and drinking alcohol strip the body of certain vitamins and some minerals by virtue of the poisons in tobacco smoke and alcoholic drinks that attack the body processes directly or produce metabolites that have similar deleterious effects.

Many medications can reduce absorption of vitamins or cause them to be excreted in abnormal quantities, so medical treatment can also contribute to decreased vitamin (and some mineral) body levels. Prime examples are antibiotics (vitamin B complex and vitamin K), corticosteroids (vitamins B_6, C, and the mineral zinc), diuretics (potassium and calcium), aspirin and other nonsteroidal anti-inflammatory drugs (vitamin C), and the ingredients of the contraceptive pill (vitamin B_6). In no case can diet supply all of the increased needs, and supplementation at up to five times the recommended dietary intakes is sometimes required.

The third category is that of therapeutic potencies of vitamins. Here the quantities of vitamins given are between ten and one hundred times those available even from a good diet and such amounts are needed because the vitamins appear to act as therapeutic agents. This approach represents the most controversial use of vitamins and argument still rages on the efficacy of such treatment. Among current uses are vitamin E in heart and blood circulatory disease; vitamin C in respiratory infections and cancer; pantothenic acid in rheumatoid arthritis, and vitamin A and zinc in the treatment of various skin conditions. While naturopathic practitioners continue to claim beneficial effects for the use of vitamins alone, an increasing number of medical practitioners are successfully using high-potency vitamin therapies to complement the medications deemed essential in some clinical conditions.

There the matter rests at present but the fact remains that therapies suggested in this book have had a measure of success in the hands of some practitioners and the beneficial results have been reported in medical and scientific journals. They can be undertaken in the knowledge that they are safe but, in cases where they best complement medical drug treatment, this is mentioned. The benefits of vitamin therapy are usually experienced by the person undergoing it. Who better to judge the efficacy of such treatment?

Mineral Supplementation

Mineral supplementation has no counterpart to that of vitamins. Minerals are needed only if they are deficient in the body and once that deficiency has been overcome there is little point in taking more. Poor diets and some clinical conditions are the main causes of mineral deficiencies and supplementation is often the only answer. There appears to be no justification for taking mineral supplements in massive doses comparable to those taken in vitamin therapy, and indeed such doses may even be harmful. Nevertheless, evidence is growing that, despite the stability of minerals, their poor absorption and their removal and immobilization during food processing contribute to their chances of deficiency in many individuals.

About This Book

This dictionary has been written to supply information on vitamins and minerals in a concise though comprehensive manner. All that we know about vitamins and minerals is summarized here in this dictionary in a form presented for easy reference. What vitamins and minerals do, where they are found, what happens when we do not have enough, what happens when we have too much, and what they can do to maintain or improve general health are all explained here.

This is the first time that a dictionary has been written supplying data on both types of essential micronutrients—vitamins *and* minerals. Information on each micronutrient is presented in a manner that allows the salient points about it to be easily and quickly seen. While the therapeutic uses of the vitamins and minerals are summed up

Figure 1: 100 percent of the minimum daily needs or desirable daily intakes

Vitamins minimum daily needs			Minerals minimum daily needs		Symbol
A			Calcium	1,000 mg	Ca
Carotene	750	µg (2,500 IU)	Magnesium	400 mg	Mg
D	10	µg (400 IU)	Phosphorus	1,000 mg	P
E	30	mg	Iron	18 mg	Fe
B_1	1.5	mg	Copper	2 mg	Cu
B_2	1.7	mg	Zinc	15 mg	Zn
Nicotinic Acid	19.0	mg	Manganese	5 mg	Mn
Pantothenic			Molybdenum	500 µg	Mo
acid	10.0	mg	Chromium	200 µg	Cr
B_6	2.0	mg	Selenuim	200 µg	Se
B_{12}	3	µg	Sulfur	800 mg	S
Folic acid	400	µg			
Biotin	300	µg	Minerals desirable daily intakes		Symbol
C	60	mg			
			Sodium	1,200 mg	Na
			Potassium	3,000 mg	K
			Chloride	1,800 mg	Cl

In all charts, B_3 is used for nicotinic acid; B_5 is used for pantothenic acid.

succinctly, more information is available under the entries for the relevant health problems or conditions.

The contributions of various foods to our vitamin and mineral needs are presented throughout the book, in chart form, as a percentage of what is generally recognized as the minimum requirements of adults in 100 g of food. This quantity is about 3.5 oz and, in most cases, represents an average portion. The percentage minimum daily needs or desirable daily intakes are not based on any particular government's recommendations, since these all differ, but are nearer the average of all the suggestions made by the authorities of different countries. They should not be confused with recommended daily allowances (RDAs), the main standard used in the US. For the purposes of the charts, 100 percent of the minimum daily needs or desirable daily intakes for the different vitamins and minerals are listed in Figure 1.

A

A, a fat-soluble vitamin. Known also as retinol, axerophthol, biosterol, and anti-infective vitamin. Present in supplements and used in food fortification as retinyl palmitate and retinal acetate. First isolated in 1913 by two American groups.

1 microgram retinol = 3.3 international units (IU).

Found only in foods of animal origin but its active precursor, beta-carotene, is present in fruits and vegetables.

Best Food Sources in μg per 100 g		Functions
Halibut liver oil	60,000	Sight
Liver	18,000	Skin
Margarine	800	Mucous membranes
Butter	750	Anti-infective
Cheese	385	Protein synthesis
Eggs	140	Bones
		Anti-anemia
		Growth

Recommended Daily Intake

should be at least 750 μg (2,500 IU).
See recommended daily intakes

Supplementary Daily Intake

should not exceed 2,250 μg (7,500 IU)

Stored

in liver and kidneys

Vitamin A cont.

Deficiency Symptoms	Deficiency Results in:
Spinal infections	Night blindness (unable
Respiratory infections	to see in the dark)
Scaly skin and scalp	Xerophthalmia
Poor hair quality	Kidney stones
Poor sight	Mild skin conditions
Burning and itching eyes	Inflamed mucous
Pain in the eyeballs	membranes
Dry eyes	
Eye ulceration	

Therapeutic Uses

Symptoms of Excess Intake

Therapeutic Uses	Symptoms of Excess Intake
Skin cancer	Loss of appetite
Gastric ulcers	Dry, itchy skin
Acne	Loss of hair
Eczema	Headaches
Psoriasis	Nausea and vomiting
Night blindness	

Stability in Foods

see losses in food
processing

Absorption

enhanced by fats and oils
reduced by liquid paraffin

Acetaldehyde, a toxic substance found in tobacco smoke and produced by the body from alcohol. Destroys vitamin B_1, vitamin C, and vitamin B_6. These vitamins plus the amino acid L-cysteine can overcome effects of acetaldehyde at these daily does levels: B_1—10 mg, B_6—10 mg, vitamin C—500 mg, and L-cysteine—100 mg.

Acetylcholine, a derivative of choline involved in the transmission of nerve impulses. Formulation depends on adequate vitamin B_1, pantothenic acid, and choline. Lack of acetylcholine leads to brain damage and may be a factor in senile dementia and Alzheimer's disease.

Achlorhydria, lack of production of hydrochloric acid in the stomach. Also known as hypochlorhydria. Believed to increase the chances of developing gastric cancer. A symptom of pernicious anemia specific to vitamin B_{12} deficiency.

Treat with betaine hydrochloride, also known as lycine hydrochloride; glutamic acid hydrochloride; or dilute hydrochloric acid (2 ml diluted to 200 ml with water and sipped through a straw during meals).

Acid-base balance, the balance between the amount of carbonic acid and bicarbonate base in the blood, which must be maintained at a constant ratio of 1 to 20 to ensure that the pH of the blood is kept between 7.35 and 7.45. In a healthy person, the blood is maintained within this narrow range of alkalinity. This pH value depends upon two mechanisms: the rate of excretion of carbonic acid (i.e., aqueous carbon dioxide) through the lungs in the expired air; and the ability of the kidneys to excrete either acid or alkaline urine. When the lungs and kidneys are diseased, these mechanisms may no longer function efficiently and an acidosis (excess acid) or alkalosis (excess alkali or base) results.

Dietary aspects of acid-base balance are less important than metabolic defects, but can still influence the acidity or alkalinity of the body and hence that of the urine. For example, a rabbit has a diet consisting mainly of green and other vegetables and normally excretes an alkaline urine. A dog, which is carnivorous or omnivorous, excretes an acid urine. Vegetarian human beings usually excrete a neutral or slightly alkaline urine; omnivorous human beings excrete a slightly acid urine; and large meat eaters excrete a more acid urine. This is due to the fact that protein is

high in sulfur, which the body converts to sulfuric acid
before excretion in the urine. The high phosphorus content
of meat ends up as phosphoric acid, which also contributes
to the acidity of the urine.

Dietary acids are organic acids present in fruits, vegetables,
and yogurt. Contrary to popular belief they do not produce
acid reactions within the body (acidosis) and are in fact
alkali-forming. Examples of such acids in the diet are:

1. Citric acid (citrus fruits, pineapples, tomatoes, most summer fruits). Citric acid is oxidized by the body in its normal energy-production cycle.
2. Malic acid (apples, plums, tomatoes). Malic acid is oxidized by the body in its normal energy-production cycle.
3. Benzoic acid (cranberries, lingonberries). Benzoic acid
is readily excreted by the kidneys (after combination with
the amino acid glycine) as hippuric acid.
4. Tartaric acid (grapes). This acid is hardly absorbed so
does not contribute to the acid-base balance of the body.
5. Oxalic acid (strawberries, green tomatoes, rhubarb,
spinach). Oxalic acid can combine with calcium to form insoluble calcium oxalate so it is not absorbed. However, excess oxalic acid can immobilize calcium and other minerals
to an extent that may cause mild deficiency. Any oxalic
acid absorbed is readily oxidized by existing metabolic
processes.
6. Lactic acid (yogurt). Lactic acid is metabolized by the
same body processes that dispose of lactic acid produced
from glucose.

Foods are either acid-producing or alkali-producing,
depending upon how the body metabolizes them. It is believed by some that an excess of acid-producing foods in
the diet is a factor in inducing arthritis. Treatment of the
condition is therefore aimed at switching to an alkali-
producing diet.

Acid-forming foods are: meats of all kinds; poultry; fish

and all sea foods; lentils; onions; brazil nuts; peanuts; walnuts; pearl barley; bread, all types of wheat, and other cereal flours; all types of pasta; oat flakes; rice; semolina; tapioca; cocoa powder; chocolate; eggs; and all cheeses.

Alkali-forming foods are: all fruits; all fruit juices; all vegetables (with the exception of lentils and onions); all vegetable juices; honey; molasses; cream; fresh milk or all types and treated milks (buttermilk, evaporated, condensed, dried); wine; and nuts (except brazil nuts, peanuts, and walnuts).

Acidosis, a condition in which the acidity of the body fluids and tissue is abnormally high, producing a low pH. Induced by a failure of the acid-base balance mechanism.

Lactic acidosis can be due to:

1. Accumulation of large amounts of lactic acid in the blood after severe muscular exercise. Rapid breathing during the recovery phase helps to restore the acid-base balance by removing excess carbon dioxide through the lungs.
2. Inadequate oxygenation of the tissues associated with certain diseases (e.g. heart failure).
3. Loss of sodium, potassium, and ketone bodies in the urine of those suffering from diabetes.
4. Some liver diseases.
5. Intravenous infusions of fructose.

Metabolic acidosis can be due to:

1. Kidney failure.
2. Lactic acidosis.
3. Poisons such as ethylene glycol or salicylates.
4. Acetoacetic acid, which accumulates in the blood of diabetics.
5. Excessive loss of alkali from the intestinal tract, as in diarrhea.
6. Ingestion of ammonium chloride.

Symptoms of acidosis include: increased depth and frequency of respiration; vague lassitude; nausea; and vomiting.

Apart from acidosis induced by severe muscular exertion, all other causes need medical management.

Acne, inflammation of the hair and sweat glands. Acne has been treated with oral vitamin A (2,272 μg or 7,500 IU daily) plus the mineral zinc (15 mg daily as amino acid chelate). It may also be treated with a cream containing vitamin A or retinoic acid, and may respond to oil of evening primrose (three 500 mg capsules daily) and to other polyunsaturated oils.

Premenstrual flare-up of acne responds to vitamin B_6 (50 mg daily for one week before and during menstruation).

Zinc appears to restore the hormone balance that may be upset at puberty. There is evidence of low body zinc levels at puberty.

Acrodermatitis enteropathica, a rare, inherited disorder characterized by psoriatic dermatitis; hair loss; infections of the nails; growth retardation; and diarrhea. Once fatal, it is now known to be due to malabsorption of zinc, leading to low levels in the blood plasma. Complete remission is obtained with daily doses of 35-150 mg zinc sulfate, which provides 8-34 mg zinc.

Addisonlan anemia, *see* pernicious anemia and B_{12} (vitamin).

Adrenal, a gland that produces anti-stress hormones (e.g., cortisol) from cholesterol. High concentrations of pantothenic acid and vitamin C are needed in the gland for production.

Aging, increases the need for all vitamins, particularly vitamin B complex, vitamin C, and vitamin E.

Supplementation is recommended as absorption and utilization of vitamins are impaired in old age.

Alcohol, drinking alcohol increases the need for whole vitamin B complex, particularly vitamins B_1, B_6, B_{12} (10 μg), and folic acid (200 μg). Chronic effects of deficiency are prevented by taking all vitamins plus oil of evening primrose (150 mg daily).

Aldosterone, a steroid hormone, elaborated by the adrenal cortex, that acts upon the kidney to regulate water balance by causing sodium retention and potassium loss. Used medically to treat deficient production and in the treatment of shock. Overproduction of aldosterone leads to excessive blood and tissue levels of sodium and loss of potassium, causing water retention and eventually high blood pressure. One class of diuretic drugs acts by inhibiting the action of aldosterone. *See* diuretic drugs.

Alkalosis, a condition in which the alkalinity of body fluids and tissue is abnormally high, producing a high pH. It is due to failure of the mechanisms that maintain a normal acid-base balance. It may be associated with: certain diuretic therapy; loss of acid through persistent vomiting; excessive sodium bicarbonate intake; deep breathing not associated with physical exercise.

Symptoms of alkalosis are muscular weakness or cramps.

Apart from that produced by abnormally deep breathing, alkalosis usually requires medical management.

Alopecia, baldness, loss of hair. A symptom of: pantothenic acid deficiency in animals; biotin deficiency in mink and fox; and polyunsaturated fatty acid deficiency.

May respond to: calcium pantothenate (100 mg); biotin (500 μg); wheat germ oil or safflower oil (3-5 g); nicotinic acid (35 mg); folic acid (200 μg); vitamin B_{12} (5 μg); or vitamin E (10 IU).

In addition, supplementary zinc (15 mg daily) may help restore hair growth.

Alpha-tocopherol,   *see* E (vitamin).

Alpha-tocopheryl acetate,   *see* E (vitamin).

Alpha-tocopheryl succinate,   *see* E (vitamin).

Aluminum,   chemical symbol Al. Atomic weight 27.0. The third most abundant element in the earth's crust at a level of 8.8 g per 100 g. Occurs mainly in combination with silica (aluminum silicates) and as aluminum oxide.

Present in trace amounts in plants, animals, and humans but it does not appear to act as an essential element.

Storage in the body is in the lungs, liver, thyroid, and brain. Later, most of the dietary aluminum is excreted.

In the diet, aluminum may be supplied by: aluminum cooking pots used to cook acid-containing foods or liquids; some baking powders; and food additives. Aluminum-containing preparations are widely used as antacids, which therefore represent another source. Water used in dialyzing solutions for those on kidney dialysis may also contribute aluminum.

Functions of aluminum in the body are not known but it is used in medicine:

1. As an antacid, to relieve the pain in gastric and duodenal ulcers and in reflux esophagitis (heartburn) by neutralizing hydrochloric acid in the gastric secretions. Aluminum salts used for this purpose include: aluminum glycinate;

aluminum hydroxide; aluminum phosphate; and aluminum sodium silicate.

2. As an astringent to form a superficial protective layer over damaged skin and mucous membranes. Preparations include: aluminum potassium sulfate (alum); aluminum acetotartrate; aluminum chloride; aluminum chlorhydrate; aluminum formate; aluminum subacetate; aluminum sulfate; and ammonia alum.

3. To reduce phosphate absorption in those with chronic kidney failure.

4. To treat disorders of the mouth. Preparations include aluminum lactate. The astringent properties of aluminum salts are also utilized in cosmetic preparations and in deodorants.

Toxic effects of aluminum on the skin include contact dermatitis and irritation in sensitive people. Internally, the mineral can cause phosphate depletion and skeletal demineralization, resembling osteomalacia, in those undergoing kidney dialysis; brain dysfunction in those undergoing kidney dialysis; brain degeneration characteristic of some types of senile dementia; slow learning in the young; epileptic-type fits in experimental animals; and exacerbation of osteoporosis.

Levels of 12 μg aluminum per g brain tissue give rise to brain deterioration in experimental animals. The same levels are found in the brains of human beings suffering from Alzheimer's disease or senile dementia. This suggests that aluminum may be a factor in these diseases of human beings.

Alzheimer's disease, occurs at any age and is characterized by loss of memory for recent events and an inability to store new memories. *See also* senile dementia. No medical treatment is available, but some cases respond to 25 g lecithin daily, increasing by 25 g weekly until side effects appear (nausea, abdominal bloating, and diarrhea), then returning to the previous dose.

A second line of treatment consists of 20 g choline chloride daily in four doses for eight weeks, six weeks' rest, then 100 g lecithin daily in four doses for eight weeks. Memory, language functions, and daily living usually improve. High-potency phosphatidyl choline (six capsules daily) can also be used in the early stages.

Amanitine,   *see* choline.

Amino acid chelates,   minerals that are organically bound to amino acids. They may occur in foods, or they can be produced within the small intestine from the binding of mineral salts with amino acids that are formed from the normal digestion of protein. It is also possible to produce amino acid chelates by mimicking the natural process under controlled laboratory conditions. Soy or other protein that is broken down by enzymes supplies the amino acids required; coupling with the mineral is carried out by adjusting the pH of the mixture and creating the ideal conditions for specific mineral chelates. Amino acid chelates may also be stabilized by buffering them to ensure they survive the acid/alkali changes of the digestive tract.

Many studies indicate that amino acid chelation of minerals is a natural process that: increases the rate and extent of absorption of the mineral compared with other mineral preparations (see Figure 2); enhances the retention of the minerals; improves the extent of utilization of the minerals; protects the mineral against precipitating factors like phosphate, oxalate, and phytic acid; and reduces the side effects of unabsorbed mineral on the gastrointestinal system.

Aminopterin,   an immunosuppressive agent that impairs folic-acid utilization.

Figure 2: The superior absorption of amino acid chelates

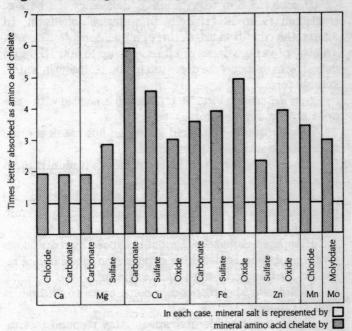

In each case, mineral salt is represented by ☐
mineral amino acid chelate by ▨

Ammonium chloride, a miscellaneous food additive that is used in yeast food and as a flavor. Provides 67.0 mg chloride per 100 mg.

In medicine, ammonium chloride is used to: acidify the urine when infection of the urinary tract is present; aid the excretion of certain drugs; increase the diuretic effect of mercurials; hasten lead excretion; supply chloride in chloride replacement therapy; and act as an expectorant in cough mixtures.

Amygdalin, *see* laetrile.

Anemia,   lack of production of normal red blood cells.

Hemolytic: due to vitamin E deficiency. In babies, treatment is 10-30 IU daily in water-soluble form. In adults, the condition arises through malabsorption of fats. Treatment is high doses of vitamin E (up to 600 IU daily) in oral form or moderate doses (up to 200 IU daily) in water-soluble form.

Iron-deficiency: Vitamin C (100 mg) is needed with each dose of iron supplement.

Megaloblastic: Folic acid is needed but medical diagnosis and treatment are essential.

Pernicious: Due to malabsorption of vitamin B_{12}. An injection of B_{12} is absolutely essential.

Pyridoxine-deficiency: Usually associated with taking the contraceptive pill. Prevented by taking 25 mg vitamin B_6 daily.

Riboflavin-deficiency: Probably caused by reduced activation of folic acid, which depends on riboflavin. Prevented by taking 10 mg vitamin B_2 daily.

Sickle cell: May respond in some cases to vitamin E (450 IU daily).

Thalassemia or Mediterranean: May respond to vitamin E (400-600 IU daily).

The iron-deficiency type of anemia, which is the most common, may be caused by:

1. Low dietary intakes of iron because of poor diet.
2. Poor absorption of dietary iron.
3. Inefficient incorporation into hemoglobin.
4. Pregnancy, because of the demands of the growing fetus for iron.
5. Lactation, because of loss of iron through breast milk.
6. Losses of iron being greater than dietary absorption as in: menstruation; gastric and duodenal ulcers; hemorrhoids (piles); and some drug treatments, e.g., aspirin.

A rare type of anemia where iron is adequate may be

due to a low intake of copper, which is needed for incorporation of iron into hemoglobin. Most iron-deficiency anemias respond to iron supplementation (up to 75 mg elemental iron daily), but small amounts of copper (up to 2 mg daily) and vitamin C (100 mg with each iron dose) will help the iron to be absorbed and utilized more efficiently. If the deficiency is due to malabsorption or greatly increased losses, professional help is needed to treat the underlying cause. *See also* iron.

Aneurin(e),   *see* B₁ (vitamin).

Angina,   full name angina pectoris. Characterized by severe pain in the chest usually radiating to the shoulder and arm. Treatment is high doses of vitamin E (800 IU and up, depending on response). Favorable response to lecithin (15 g daily) has also been reported. Preliminary results using polyunsaturated fatty acids from fish oils (eicosapentaenoic acid and docosahexaenoic acid, EPA, and DHA, 1500 mg total daily) has been promising. All vitamin therapy is compatible with existing drug treatments.

Animal galactose factor,   *see* orotic acid.

Anorexia nervosa,   a disorder characterized by a marked anxiety about body weight and weight gain, resulting in abnormal patterns of handling food, serious weight loss, and cessation of periods in women. The usual treatment is psychotherapy, but there is one case on record where zinc supplementation was successful in restoring loss of taste, increase in weight, and a return to normal eating habits. Treatment consisted of 15 mg zinc (as zinc sulfate) three times daily with meals. A good response was apparent after two weeks, but further progress was continued only after the dose was increased to 50 mg zinc (as zinc sulfate) three times daily. The main indications of zinc deficiency were loss of taste and loss of smell and these were used throughout to monitor the zinc status of the patient.

Antacids, gastric acid neutralizers. Prevent absorption of vitamins A and B complex.

Antagonists, substances that neutralize the action of vitamins or immobilize them. May be naturally occurring or produced synthetically. Used in research to quickly induce vitamin deficiency. Examples are:

Vitamin A: Mineral oil (liquid paraffin).

Vitamin B_1: Alcohol; the enzyme thiaminase, present in raw fish; antibiotics; and excess sugar.

Vitamin B_2: Alcohol; antibiotics; and oral contraceptives.

Nicotinamide: Alcohol; antibiotics; leucine, an amino acid in high concentrations in millet; niacytin, a bound, unabsorbable form found in corn and potatoes, and liberated only by alkali; and excess sugar.

Vitamin B_6: Deoxypyridoxine; isoniazid; hydralazine; penicillamine; and levodopa.

Folic acid: aminopterin; alcohol; oral contraceptives; phenytoin; and primidone.

Vitamin B_{12}: Oral contraceptives; intestinal parasites; excess folic acid; and vitamin B_{12} acids.

Biotin: Antibiotics; sulfonamides; and avidin, found in raw egg white.

Choline: Alcohol; and excess sugar.

Inositol: Antibiotics.

Pantothenic acid: Methyl bromide, used as fumigant in foods; and omega-methypantothenic acid.

Vitamin D: Mineral oil.

Vitamin E: Oral contraceptives; mineral oil; ferric iron; rancid fats and oils; and excessive PUFA.

Vitamin C: Aspirin; corticosteroids; indomethacin; tobacco smoking; and alcohol.

Vitamin K: Warfarin; and dicumarol.

Antibiotics,   drugs used to combat infectious diseases. Taken orally, they can destroy "friendly" intestinal bacteria that are providers of some B vitamins and vitamin K. Their ill-effects on the digestive system can be relieved by high doses of vitamin B complex, and vitamin K deficiency can be treated with acetomenaphthone.

Anti-gray-hair factor,   *see* para-aminobenzoic acid.

Antihemorrhagic vitamin,   *see* K (vitamin).

Antineuritic vitamin,   *see* B_1 (vitamin).

Antipellagra vitamin,   *see* niacin.

Antipernicious anemia vitamin,   *see* B_{12} (vitamin).

Antirachitic vitamin,   *see* D (vitamin).

Antisterility vitamin,   *see* E (vitamin).

Apples,   *eating varieties* supply carotene, vitamin E, and B vitamins (apart from B_{12}). Vitamin C levels are less than those of cooking apples (3 mg per 100 g). Carotene content is 30 μg per 100 g. Vitamin E content is 0.2 mg per 100 g. Levels of B vitamins (in mg per 100 g) are: thiamin—0.04; riboflavin—0.02; nicotinic acid—0.1; pyridoxine—0.03; and pantothenic acid—0.10. Folic acid present at 5 μg per 100 g, and biotin at 0.3 μg per 100 g.

Cooking varieties. Minimal losses of all vitamins present in raw state occur when baked or stewed. Carotene content (in μg per 100 g) for all three states respectively is 30, 30, and 25. Vitamin E content is 0.2 mg per 100 g. Levels of B vitamins (in mg per 100 g) for the raw, baked, and stewed states respectively are: thiamin—0.04, 0.03, and 0.03; riboflavin—0.02, 0.02, and 0.02; nicotinic acid—0.1; 0.1, and 0.1; pyridoxine—0.03, 0.02, and 0.02; and pantothenic acid—0.10, 0.09, and 0.08. Folic acid levels are only 5, 3, and 2 μg per 100 g, and biotin is constant at 0.2 μg per 100 g. Vitamin C levels are respectively 15, 14, and 12 mg per 100 g. Concentrations are slightly reduced if sugar is used in baking and stewing, due to a slight diluting effect of sugar.

Varieties differ in vitamin C levels, as shown in Figure 3. There is more vitamin C in the peel of the apples than in the flesh, so whole apples should be eaten.

Minerals

Apples are a low-sodium food that supply useful amounts of potassium and iron with only small quantities of the other minerals.

Eating varieties supply (in mg per 100 g): sodium—2; potassium—120; calcium—4; magnesium—5; phosphorus—8; iron—0.3; copper—0.04; zinc—0.1; sulfur—6; chloride—1.

Cooking varieties supply (in mg per 100 g) for raw, baked, and stewed states respectively: sodium—2, 2, and 2; potassium—120, 130, and 100; calcium—4, 4, and 3; magnesium—3, 3, and 3; phosphorus—16, 17, and 14; iron—0.3, 0.3, and 0.3; copper—0.09, 0.09, and 0.08; zinc—0.1, 0.1, and 0.1; sulfur—3, 3, and 3; and chloride—5, 5, and 4.

Arsenic, chemical symbol As. Atomic weight 74.9. Abundance in the earth's crust is 0.0005 percent. Occurs in

Figure 3: Vitamin C levels in apple varieties

	in mg Peeled	per 100 g Unpeeled
Cox Orange Pippin	2	5
Granny Smith	2	8
Golden Delicious	3	10
Sturmer Pippin	20	30

nature as the free metal and in combination with other metals.

Small amounts are present in most body tissues as a result of dietary intakes within the range of 0.4-3.9 mg daily. Most dietary arsenic ends up in the liver and muscle, which can have concentrations up to 49 and 195 μg per 100 g respectively. Excretion is fairly rapid, so toxic levels from the diet do not build up.

The richest food sources of arsenic are shellfish. Some meats contain organic arsenic, which was originally added to the animals' feeds. Poultry and pigs are given traces of arsenic to improve growth. Arsenic compounds are used as insecticides which find their way to the soil and hence to plants, which, when eaten, represent another dietary source. Water, too, contributes arsenic to the diet.

Traces of arsenic appear to be necessary for the health of animals but no specific functions have been assigned to the mineral. It is likely that it is also an essential trace mineral for man but such minute amounts are needed that a deficiency is highly unlikely.

Food and drink levels of arsenic are limited by law. Beverages may not contain more than 0.5 mg per liter. Dried herbs may not contain more than 5.0 mg per kg. Brewer's yeast is limited to less than 5.0 mg per kg. WHO (World Health Organization) recommends that drinking water should not exceed 50 μg per liter.

Excessive intakes of arsenic can be fatal.

Acute intoxication is indicated by: severe gastric pain; vomiting; profuse watery diarrhea; protein excretion in the urine; numbness and tingling in the hands and feet; intense thirst; and muscular cramps. Eventually nerve conditions, kidney disease, and brain damage result.

Chronic poisoning is characterized by: edema of the the face and eyelids; generalized itching; sore mouth; inflammation of the eyes and nasal membranes; loss of appetite; nausea; vomiting; and diarrhea. Continued administration for long periods leads to: dryness of the skin; dermatitis; pigmentation; and hardness. Loss of hair and nails usually follows. Late symptoms include: anemia; cirrhosis of the liver; jaundice; and neuritis.

Prolonged administration of sublethal amounts of arsenic may lead to cancer of the skin and lungs.

Lethal intake can be as low as 100 mg arsenic trioxide if taken in one dose.

Therapy with arsenic at oral doses of 1-5 mg arsenic trioxide was originally used for syphilis. It has been used externally to treat dermatitis, eczema, and syphilitic skin diseases. The therapeutic use of inorganic arsenic compounds is no longer recommended.

Arteriosclerosis, hardening of the arteries. Treated with lecithin (15-20 g daily), vitamin E (400 IU twice daily), vitamin C (up to 3 g daily), and vitamin A (7,500 IU daily). As a preventive treatment, particularly in diabetes, supplement the diet with lecithin (5 g), vitamin E (400 IU), vitamin C (500 mg), and vitamin A (7,500 IU) daily.

Arthritis, rheumatoid arthritis is an inflammation of the joints; osteoarthritis is a degenerative joint disease characterized by calcified outgrowths from cartilage.

Rheumatoid arthritis may respond to calcium pantothenate, with a regimen of: 500 mg daily for two days;

100 mg for three days; 1,500 mg for two days; and 2,000 mg per day thereafter for a period of two months, or until relief is obtained. Daily intake is then the minimum needed to maintain relief.

Rheumatoid and osetoarthritis may respond to vitamin C (4,000 mg daily in divided doses). Both types of arthritis may respond to high doses (3-6 g daily) of nicotinamide (preferred) or nicotinic acid. Supplementary preventive intakes are 100 mg calcium pantothenate, 500 mg vitamin C, and 100 mg nicotinamide daily.

Both types of arthritis have been reported as responding favorably to calcium supplementation at intakes between 500 and 1,500 mg daily. Reasons are not known, but even the calcified outgrowths of osetoarthritis, which are due to a high local concentration of the mineral, may disappear when low calcium levels elsewhere are remedied. These low levels may originate in the bone reserves, as in osteoporosis, which is associated with some cases of arthritis.

Localized copper deficiencies may also be a factor in arthritic conditions, particularly the rheumatoid type. Copper bangles may contribute copper through the skin (*see* copper bangles). Some oral copper complexes, e.g., those with aspirin, also appear to have an anti-inflammatory action greater than that of the aspirin itself. Organic forms of copper were more efficient than copper salts in relieving arthritic symptoms in experimental studies on animals.

Ascorbic acid, *see* C (vitamin).

Aspirin, an analgesic and temperature-reducing drug. Reduces vitamin C body levels by destruction and excessive excretion. Causes gastric bleeding, and impairs thiamin and folic-acid utilization. All side effects of aspirin can be reduced by taking 100 mg vitamin C with each tablet. Vitamin C also improves the absorption of aspirin.

Asthma, a respiratory disease characterized by attacks of difficult breathing with a feeling of constriction and suffocation. Treatment with vitamin B_6 is effective in some children and adults. The usual dose is 100 mg twice daily. Once relief is obtained (usually after one month), the maintenance dose can be lower depending upon the individual. This treatment is more likely to help B_6-dependent children, and can be taken with all antiasthmatic drugs. Vitamin C can also help some asthmatics by reducing the symptoms of the attack. The usual dose is 1 g orally every six hours.

Atherosclerosis, fat deposition within the walls of the arteries, causing constriction of the blood vessels.

Treatment is with vegetable oils, margarine (PUFA), and soy lecithin. Avoid saturated animal fats. Treatment can also include vitamin B_6 (25 mg daily) to ensure body synthesis of lecithin, plus vitamin C (100 mg) and vitamin E (800 IU) daily.

Prevention is by replacing animal fats with vegetable oils and margarines and daily intakes of: soy lecithin (5 g); vitamin B_6 (10 mg); vitamin C (500 mg); and vitamin E (400 IU). Recent studies indicate that fish oils containing polyunsaturated fatty acids in the form of the fatty acids EPA and DHA can prevent and treat atherosclerosis (900-1,800 mg daily).

Athletes, the combination of mental and physical stress associated with competition and training increases requirement for vitamins and minerals, as does high calorie intake. There is a particular requirement for extra vitamin B complex to: ensure full use of extra calories; ensure adequate supply of antistress hormones from adrenals; and supply the extra pyridoxine required by most female athletes. Vitamin C is also essential for the production of antistress hormones and to ensure the full potential of muscle energy. Vitamin E is essential to ensure adequate supply of oxygen to the muscles. A similar function is also attributed to pangamic acid.

Minimum needs can probably be met by up to 1,500 mg vitamin C, 1,000 IU vitamin E, 150 mg pangamic acid, and high-potency vitamin B complex.

Female athletes should take extra iron (10 mg daily) to ensure against anemia, and extra calcium (up to 1,000 mg daily) to prevent osteoporosis.

Autism, a personality disease in children who become withdrawn and cease to communicate with the outside world. Autism has been treated with megavitamin therapy including: vitamin C (1, 2, or 3 g); nicotinamide (1, 2, or 3 g); B_6 (150-450 mg); calcium pantothenate (200 mg); plus high-potency B complex daily, depending on the age of the child. Sometimes vitamin B_6 alone is sufficient. Medical monitoring is essential.

Avidin, a unique protein in raw egg white that binds biotin, rendering it unavailable for absorption. Cooking eggs destroys avidin and liberates biotin.

Axerophthol, *see* A (vitamin).

B

B_1, a water-soluble member of the vitamin B complex. Known also as thiamin(e) and aneurin(e). Supplied in supplements and in food fortification as hydrochloride or nitrate. First isolated from rice polishings in 1926 by Drs. B. C. P. Jansen and W. F. Donath.

Best Food Sources in mg per 100 g

Dried brewer's yeast	15.6
Yeast extract	3.1
Brown rice	2.9
Wheat germ	2.0
Nuts	0.9
Pork	0.9
Wheat bran	0.9
Soy flour	0.8
Oat flakes	0.6
Wheat grains	0.5
Liver	0.3
Whole wheat bread	0.3

Recommended Daily Intake

relates to calories in diet (0.096 μg per 240 calories), so is about 1.5 mg. *See* recommended daily intakes

Symptoms of Excess Intake

Oral: none reported
Injection: may cause hypersensitivity reactions very rarely

Functions

Acts as coenzyme in converting glucose into energy in muscles and nerves

Stability in Foods

Very unstable—*See* losses in food processing

Deficiency Symptoms

Easy fatigue
Muscle weakness
Loss of appetite
Nausea
Digestive upsets
Constipation
Irritability
Depression
Impaired memory
Lack of concentration
Tender calves
Tingling and burning in toes and soles

Deficiency Results in

Beriberi (rare in Europe and the West)

Vitamin B₁ cont.

Deficiency Caused by	Therapeutic Uses
High empty-calorie diets	Beriberi
Pregnancy	Improvement of mental
Breast-feeding	ability
Fever	Insect repellant
Surgery	Indigestion
Physical and mental	Improving heart
stress	functions
Alcohol	Alcoholism
Habitual antacid	Lumbago, sciatica,
preparations	trigeminal neuralgia,
	facial paralysis
	Optic neuritis (50-600
	mg daily)

B₂, a water-soluble member of the vitamin B complex. Has a strong yellow color, enough to cause strongly-colored urine, but is harmless. Known also as riboflavin(e), lactoflavin(e), and vitamin G, isolated from whey by Dr. R. Kuhn in 1933, after being recognized in yeast by Dr. O. Warburg in 1932.

Best Food Sources in mg per 100 g		Best Food Sources cont.	
		Eggs	0.47
Yeast extract	11.00	Wheat bran	0.36
Dried brewer's		Meats	0.22
yeast	4.30	Soy flour	0.31
Liver	2.50	Yogurt	0.26
Wheat germ	0.68	Milk	0.19
Cheese	0.35	Vegetables (green)	0.15
		Legumes	0.15

Vitamin B₂ cont.

Stability in Foods	Deficiency Caused by
Destroyed readily by light and in alkaline solution—*See* losses in food processing	Alcohol Tobacco Contraceptive pill
Therapeutic Uses	**Symptoms of Excess Intake**
Mouth ulcers Gastric and duodenal ulcers Eye ulceration	None have been reported except strong yellow color in urine, which is harmless. So safe it is used as a food colorant.

B₆, a water-soluble member of the vitamin B complex. Known as pyridoxine but also exists as pyridoxal and pyridoxamine—all equally active. Present in supplements as hydrochloride and phosphate.

Antidepression vitamin.

Isolated from liver by Professor Paul Gyorgy at the University of Pennsylvania in 1934.

Recommended Daily Intake	Stability in Foods
should be at least 1.7 mg. *See* recommended daily intakes	Generally stable except in heated milk—*See* losses in food processing

Vitamin B$_6$ cont.

Best Food Sources in mg per 100 g

Dried brewer's yeast	4.20
Wheat bran	1.38
Yeast extract	1.30
Wheat germ	0.92
Oat flakes	0.75
Pig liver	0.68
Soy flour	0.57
Bananas	0.51
Wheat grains	0.50
Nuts	0.50
Meats	0.45
Fatty fish	0.45
Brown rice	0.42
Potatoes	0.25
Vegetables	0.16
Eggs	0.11

Functions

Acts as the coenzyme form Pyridoxal-5-phosphate in amino acid metabolism and in all other functions.

Needed for formation of brain substances and nerve impulse transmitters

Blood formation

Energy production

Antidepressant

Antiallergy

Deficiency Symptoms

Splitting of lips
Inflamed tongue
Scaly skin on face
Inflamed nerve endings
Migraine
Mild depression
Irritability
Breast discomfort
Swollen abdomen
Puffy fingers
Puffy ankles

Deficiency Caused by

Contraceptive pill
Many drugs
   (e.g., isoniazid, hydrazine, penicillamine)
Alcohol
Smoking

Deficiency Results in

In infants:
Convulsions

In adults:
Depression
Skin disease
Anemia
Premenstrual tension
Kidney stones
Atherosclerosis

Vitamin B₆ cont.

Recommended Daily Intake

should be at least 2 mg.
See recommended daily intakes

Deficiency Symptoms

Bloodshot eyes
Feeling of grit under eyelids
Tired eyes, sensitive to light
Cracks and sores in corners of mouth
Inflamed tongue and lips
Scaling of skin around face
Hair loss
Trembling
Dizziness
Insomnia
Slow learning

Dependency States Requiring High Intakes May Include

Asthma
Urticaria
Mental retardation
Premenstrual tension
Convulsions

Functions

Acts as coenzymes flavin mononucleotide (FMN) and flavin dinucleotide (FDN) in converting protein, fats, and sugars into energy.
Needed to repair and maintain body tissues and mucous membranes.
Acts in conversion of tryptophan to nicotinic acid along with vitamin B₆.

Therapeutic Uses

Premenstrual tension
Depression induced by the contraceptive pill
Morning sickness
Travel sickness
Radiation sickness
Antidote to hydrazine
Infantile convulsions
Skin lesions of face
Anemia
Bronchial asthma
Skin allergies

Incompatible with

The drug levodopa

Vitamin B₆ cont.

Therapeutic Dosages	Symptoms of Excess Intake
Should NOT exceed 25 mg daily in treating nausea (morning sickness) of pregnancy Should NOT exceed 200 mg daily in all other uses	Noted only with minimum daily intakes of more than 200 mg taken for at least one year Unstable gait with numbness in the feet and hands Changes in the feeling in the lips and tongue

B₁₂, a water-soluble member of the vitamin B complex. Contains cobalt, hence known as cobalamin. Also known as antipernicious anemia vitamin; cyano/cobalamin; hydroxocobalamin; aquacobalamin; LLD factor; extrinsic factor; and animal protein factor. Deep red crystalline substance. Last true vitamin discovered. Isolated from the liver in 1948 by Dr. E. Lester Smith in the UK almost simultaneously with Dr. K. Folkers in the US. Now obtained by deep fermentation.

Best Food Sources in μg per 100 g			
Pig liver	25.0	*Best Food Sources cont.*	
Pig kidney	14.0	Eggs	2.0
Fatty fish	5.0	Cheese	1.5
Pork	3.0	Confined to foods of animal origin with possible exception of spirulina algae.	
Beef	2.0		
Lamb	2.0	**Storage**	
White fish	2.0	In liver and kidneys	

Functions

Acts as two coenzymes,
  methylcobalamin and
  5-deoxyadenosyl-
  cobalamin
Needed for synthesis of
  DNA (deoxyribo-
  nucleic acid), the basis
  of all body cells
Maintains healthy myelin
  sheath (nerve
  insulator)
Detoxifies cyanide in
  food and tobacco
  smoke

Absorption from Food and Oral Supplementation

Needs unique mechanism
  involving specific
  protein in stomach
  called intrinsic factor
  and calcium
Maximum of 8 μg
  absorbed by this
  mechanism. Only 1
  percent of oral dose
  absorbed by simple
  diffusion

Deficiency Results in

Pernicious anemia

Deficiency Symptoms

Smooth, sore tongue
Nerve degeneration
  causing tremors,
  psychosis, mental
  deterioration
Menstrual disorders
Hand pigmentation
  (black people only)
Typical symptoms of
  anemia

Deficiency Caused by

Nonabsorption due to
  lack of intrinsic factor
Sprue
Intestinal parasites
Veganism
Pregnancy
Old age
Alcohol
Heavy smoking

Therapeutic Uses

Pernicious anemia (must
  be given by intra-
  muscular injection)
Moodiness
Poor memory
Paranoia
Mental confusion
Tiredness
Appetite stimulant

Vitamin B$_{12}$ cont.

Recommended Daily Intake	**Symptoms of Excess Intake**
should be at least 3 μg. *See* recommended daily intake	None reported from oral use. Very rarely an allergic reaction from injections

B$_{12_b}$,   hydroxocobalamin. *see* B complex.

B$_{12_c}$,   nitritocobalamin. *see* B complex.

B complex,   a mixture of the B vitamins that tend to occur together in foods of animal, plant, and microorganism origin. The B complex consists of eight members: thiamin (B$_1$); riboflavin (B$_2$); nicotinic acid (B$_3$); pantothenic acid (B$_5$); pyridoxine (B$_6$); biotin; folic acid; and B$_{12}$. All of these are true vitamins. Some authorities include choline and inositol, which can, however, be synthesized by the body.

PABA, pangamic acid, orotic acid, and laetrile are part of the B complex in foods but are regarded as factors, not vitamins.

Backache,   when due to spinal disk injuries, can be relieved or prevented by vitamin C (100 mg three times daily, or possibly more, up to 2,000 mg daily).

Bacterial vitamin H,   *see* para-aminobenzoic acid.

Baker's yeast,   *Saccharomyces cerevisiae. Fresh, compressed variety* contains (in mg per 100 g): carotene (trace); thiamin (0.71); riboflavin (1.7); nicotinic acid (13.0); pyridoxine (0.6); folic acid (1.25); pantothenic acid (3.5); biotin (0.06); vitamin C (trace); and vitamin E (trace).

Dried variety contains (in mg per 100 g): carotene (trace); thiamin (2.33); riboflavin (4.0); nicotinic acid (43.0) pyridoxine (2.0); folic acid (4.0); pantothenic acid (11.0); biotin (0.2); vitamin C (trace); and vitamin E (trace).

A rich source of RNA and DNA, which together account for 12 percent of dried yeast.

Minerals

Fresh, compressed variety contains (in mg per 100 g): sodium (16); potassium (610); calcium (25); magnesium (59); phosphorus (390); iron (5.0); copper (1.6); and zinc (2.6). Also contains chromium and selenium.

Dried variety contains (in mg per 100 g): sodium (50); potassium (2,000); calcium (80); magnesium (230); phosphorus (1,290); iron (20.0); copper (5.0); and zinc (8.0). Also contains chromium and selenium. All contents are increased over three fold in the dried variety.

Bananas, the edible part only.

Vitamins

In the raw state, the carotene level is 200 μg per 100 g; vitamin E is 0.2 mg per 100 g. B vitamins present are (in mg per 100 g): thiamin (0.04); riboflavin (0.07); nicotinic acid (0.8); pyridoxine (0.51); and pantothenic acid (0.26). Folic acid level is 22 μg per 100 g; biotin is absent. A useful source of vitamin C at 10 mg per 100 g.

Minerals

Virtually sodium-free with a very good level of potassium. Other minerals are present but in low concentration. The edible part only contains (in mg per 100 g): sodium (1); potassium (350); calcium (7); magnesium (42); phosphorus (28); iron (0.4); copper (0.16); zinc (0.2); sulfur (13); and chloride (79).

Barbiturates, sedatives and tranquilizers. Enhance the excretion and metabolism of vitamin C levels and reduce the conversion of vitamin D to 25-hydroxyvitamin D.

Barium, chemical symbol Ba. Atomic wieght 137.3. Has no use in the metabolism of animals or humans, but in the form of its soluble salts is highly toxic. A fatal dose of barium chloride may be as low as 1 g. Symptoms of poisoning include: vomiting; colic; diarrhea; slow irregular pulse; high blood pressure; convulsive tremors; and muscular paralysis.

Has been used in female contraceptive devices but these were regarded as presenting a potential cervical cancer risk in susceptible individuals. Still used in the form of insoluble barium sulfate in "barium meals," where it shows up the gastrointestinal tract on x-rays for investigational purposes.

Basedow's disease, *see* hyperthyroidism.

Beans, *see* legumes.

Bean sprouts, canned varieties are devoid of vitamins A, D, E, and carotene. A poor source of B vitamins with levels of (in mg per 100 g): thiamin—0.02; riboflavin—0.03; nicotinic acid—0.5; and pyridoxine—0.03. No pantothenic acid detected. Traces only of folic acid (12 μg per 100 g) and biotin. When canned, provide only 1 mg vitamin C per 100 g; when fresh, vitamin C level is 30 mg.
Minerals
A useful source of iron and potassium, but sodium content is introduced during canning. Minerals present in canned variety are (in mg per 100 g): sodium (80); potas-

sium (36); calcium (13); magnesium (10); phosphorus (20); iron (1.0); copper (0.09); zinc (0.8); and chloride (120).

Bed sores,   decubitus ulcers or pressure sores. Their healing rate is increased with vitamin C (500 mg daily).

Beef extract,   the richest source of the B vitamins but devoid of carotene, vitamin E, and vitamin C. B vitamins present are (in mg per 100 g): thiamin (9.1); riboflavin (7.4); nicotinic acid (85); pyridoxine (0.53). Folic acid level is 1,040 μg per 100 g; vitamin B_{12} content is 8.3 μg per 100 g.

Minerals
   Very high sodium content because of salt addition, but potassium is also very high because of concentration of the extract from the original beef. Rich in iron, zinc, copper, and phosphorus with useful quantities of calcium and magnesium. Minerals present are (in mg per 100 g): sodium (4,800); potassium (1,200); calcium (40); magnesium (61); phosphorus (590); iron (14.0); copper (0.45); zinc (1.8); and chloride (6,800).

Beer,   beers and lagers of all kinds, whether bottled or draft, provide useful quantities of the B vitamins (apart from thiamin), including vitamin B_{12}, which has been produced by the fermenting microorganism. Fat-soluble vitamins are absent, though there is a trace of carotene in all types. B vitamins present are (in mg per 100 ml): thiamin (traces only); riboflavin (0.02-0.06); nicotinic acid (0.39-1.20); pyridoxine (0.012-0.042); and pantothenic acid (0.10). Folic acid level is 4-9 μg per 100 ml; biotin level is constant at 1 μg per 100 ml. Vitamin B_{12} is present in the range 0.11-0.37 mg per 100 ml. All beers and lagers are devoid of vitamin C.

Minerals

Can supply useful potassium and iron intakes depending upon the type, but is generally low in sodium and other minerals. In beers and lagers of all kinds, bottled or draft, minerals present are (in mg per 100 g): sodium (2-23); potassium (33-130); calcium (3-14); magnesium (3-20); phosphorus (3-40); iron (0.01-1.21); copper (0.01-0.08); zinc (0.01-0.04); and chloride (4-57).

Beriberi, a disease due specifically to lack of vitamin B_1. Characterized by loss of mental alertness, respiratory problems, and water retention leading to heart and circulation problems. Early symptoms are fatigue, loss of appetite, nausea, muscle weakness, and digestive upsets. Mental symptoms include depression, irritability, impairment of memory, and loss of powers of concentration. Therapy is 25 mg vitamin B_1 daily.

Beta-tocopherol, *See* E (vitamin).

Bile acids, the constituents of bile that are needed to emulsify fats in the digestive process. Produced from cholesterol by the action of enzyme-dependant vitamin C, so the conversion represents the main mechanism for reducing blood cholesterol levels.

Bioavailability, a measure of how much of a dietary mineral actually becomes available for utilization by the body. This depends upon: the form in which the mineral is presented in the food; other factors in the food; how easily it is absorbed and assimilated; the body status of that particular mineral; and ease of excretion. Examples of bioavailability of iron: 95 percent is available from steak and corned beef; 75 percent is available from bran cereal; 57 percent from white bread; and 10 percent from a boiled egg. The low figure for eggs is due to binding of iron by a specific protein in the food, which becomes coagulated and resistant to digestion.

Bioflavonoids,   originally called vitamin P. Known also as flavones and bioflavonoid complex. Always accompany vitamin C in foods. Water-soluble bioflavonoids include: rutin; hesperidin; quercetin; nobiletin; tangeritin; sinensetin; eriodictyol; heptamethoxy flavone; myricetin; and kaempferol.

Richest food sources are: citrus fruits (skins and pulps); apricots; cherries; grapes; green peppers; tomatoes; papaya; broccoli; cantaloupe; and buckwheat. The entire complex is present in lemons. Buckwheat is the richest in rutin. The central white core of citrus fruits is the richest source.

Stability is high, even in canned fruits and vegetables.

Functions with vitamin C in maintaining the integrity of blood vessels, particularly the capillaries; as anti-inflammatory agents; and as anti-infective agents.

Deficiency symptoms include small hemorrhages under the skin and easy bruising.

Toxicity symptoms have not been reported.

Therapeutic use has been found beneficial in: menstrual problems, particularly functional uterine bleeding; varicose veins; varicose ulcers; hemorrhoids; excessive bruising especially when associated with sports; thrombosis; nosebleeds; and bleeding gums. Two types of bioflavonoids with specific distinct actions are:

1. Methoxylated type, which occur almost exclusively in citrus fruits. Nobiletin possesses an anti-inflammatory action. Other methoxylated bioflavonoids prevent stickiness of platelets and hence thin the blood. Nobiletin and tangeretin act as detoxifying agents. Other methoxylated bioflavonoids possess anti-infective properties.

2. Hydroxylated bioflavonoids, such as quercetin, myricetin, and kaempferol, appear to prevent cataract formation and act as antioxidants to preserve foods. Rutin is specific in treating high blood pressure, arteriosclerosis, and hemorrhages under the skin.

Bios I, *see inositol.*

Bios II, *see biotin.*

Biotin, a water-soluble member of the vitamin B complex. Also known as vitamin H, bios II, and coenzyme R. Isolated from liver by Dr. Paul Gyorgy in 1941.
  Natural form is D-biotin.

Best Food Sources in µg per 100 g		Functions
Dried brewer's yeast	80	Acts as coenzyme in wide variety of body actions including:
Pig kidney	32	Energy production
Pig liver	27	Maintaining healthy:
Yeast extract	27	skin
Eggs	25	hair
Wheat grains	20	sweat glands
Wheat bran	14	nerves
Wheat germ	12	bone marrow
Whole wheat bread	6	sex glands
Corn	6	
Fish	5	
Meats	3	**Stability in Foods**
Rice	3	
Vegetables	1	Very stable. *See* losses in food processing

Biotin cont.

Recommended Daily Intake

Should be at least
  300 µg. *See* recom-
  mended daily intakes
Difficult to assess
  because of large-scale
  production by healthy
  intestinal bacteria

Symptoms of Excess Intake

None have been reported
10 mg given to babies
  with no ill effects

Deficiency Caused by

Antibiotics
Feeding newborn child
  with unfortified dried
  milk
Excessive intakes of
  raw egg whites
Stress

Deficiency Symptoms

In infants: Dry face
  and scalp
  Persistent diarrhea
In adults: Fatigue
  Depression
  Nausea
  Sleepiness
  Smooth, pale tongue
  Loss of appetite
  Muscular pains
  Loss of reflexes
  Hair loss

Therapeutic Uses

Seborrheic dermatitis
Leiner's disease
Alopecia
Scalp disease
Skin conditions
Possibly to prevent crib
  deaths (Sudden Infant
  Death Syndrome)

Birth defects, can sometimes be associated with vitamin deficiencies in the mother. Pantothenic acid deficiency can cause stillbirths, premature births, malformed babies, and mentally retarded babies. Riboflavin deficiency can cause congenital malformations, including cleft palate.

Folic acid deficiency has been implicated in neural tube defects leading to spina bifida.

Bismuth, chemical symbol Bi. Atomic weight 209. Not an essential mineral for animals or humans but widely used in the past in the treatment of syphilis and yaws. Its insoluble salts are still used as protective agents in the gastrointestinal tract and by application to the skin.

Acute toxic effects include: gastrointestinal disturbance; loss of appetite; headache; malaise; skin reactions; discoloration of mucous membranes; mild jaundice; and a blue line on the gums. Kidney changes may occur.

Chronic toxic effects include a nerve syndrome characterized by deterioration of mental ability, confusion, tremor, and impaired coordination. Noticed mainly in colostomy and ileostomy patients taking insoluble bismuth subgallate over prolonged periods.

Medical uses of bismuth include:

1. Treatment of syphilis by injection of the element or its salts.
2. Antacid action in treating indigestion.
3. An astringent action in treating diarrhea.
4. A protective action on mucous membranes and raw surfaces in those who have undergone colostomy or ileostomy.

Bismuth carbonate, provides 80-82.5 mg bismuth in each 100 mg. Dose is 0.6-2 g to a maximum daily dose of 15 g. Used internally as a mild antacid in treating dyspepsia and gastric and duodenal ulcers. Used externally in mild irritant skin conditions. For toxic effects, *see* bismuth.

Bismuth subgallate, provides 46-52 mg bismuth in each 100 mg. Dose is 0.6-2 g when used orally for its astringent properties in the treatment of diarrhea, dysentery, and ulcerative colitis. Administered by mouth to help control the odor and consistency of stools in those with colostomy or ileostomy.

Employed as a dusting powder for treating eczema and similar skin diseases. Incorporated into suppositories in the treatment of hemorrhoids. For toxic effects, *see* bismuth.

Blindness, night,   characterized by an inability to see in the dark. A specific result of vitamin A deficiency. Prevented and cured by vitamin A (2,500-7,500 IU daily).

Blood,   the vitamins required for healthy blood production include B_{12}, folic acid, E, C, and B_6.

Blood clot,   thrombosis. In the heart, coronary thrombosis. In the brain, cerebral thrombosis or stroke. Supplement with vitamin E (400-800 IU daily) and lecithin (15 g daily). Medical treatment includes vitamin K antagonists, e.g., warfarin.

Blood pressure,   is usually measured at two levels: the higher is the systolic, or maximum pressure of a heart contraction; the lower is the diastolic, or resting heart pressure. Hypertension is regarded as a diastolic pressure greater than 90 mm.

High blood pressure may respond to choline (up to 1,000 mg daily) or as lecithin, up to 15 g daily. Rutin (up to 600 mg daily) is reputed to help reduce high blood pressure.

Body content,   the minerals calculated to be present in a person weighing 155 lb (70 kg) are shown in Figure 4. These figures are only average and in no way refer to a "nor-

mal" value. Such a term is meaningless as healthy individuals may vary in their mineral content yet show no
abnormality. Mineral levels may be affected by: aging, due
to accumulation of toxic trace minerals in the body; past
and current medical history; sex; dietary trends; local environment, which can contribute varying quantities of
minerals from air, water, and food; the presence of other
minerals with an antagonistic effect against the desirable
ones; the time of day the body sample is taken (e.g., before
or after meals); and the analytical techniques used to
measure minerals.

Figure 4: Minerals present in a person weighing 155 lb (70 kg)

Metallic minerals	grams	Nonmetallic minerals	grams
Calcium	1,200	Oxygen	43,500
Potassium	250	Carbon	12,590
Sodium	70	Hydrogen	6,580
Magnesium	42	Nitrogen	1,815
Iron	6	Phosphorus	680
Zinc	2.3	Chlorine	115
Copper	0.072	Sulfur	100
Vanadium	0.025	Silicon	18
Tin	0.017	Fluorine	2.6
Manganese	0.012	Iodine	0.013
Molybdenum	0.008		
Chromium	0.002		
Nickel	0.002		
Cobalt	0.001		

Body odor, is due to: overactivity of the sweat glands;
hormonal changes in the female; metabolic upset, e.g.,
sweet smell (due to acetone) of the diabetic's skin, and
nitrogenous smells in persons suffering from kidney failure;
and excess dietary intake of garlic. Many cases respond to

skin application of powders containing zinc oxide or talc, which absorbs the substances that produce the body odor; some respond to topical application of other types of deodorants. Oral treatment that is most effective includes a combination of magnesium (400 mg), zinc (20 mg), vitamin B_6 (25 mg), and para-aminobenzoic acid (100 mg) daily. These nutrients appear to act as waste scavengers, removing substances that give off acrid odors in the body.

Boils, tender, inflamed areas of the skin containing pus at the site of infection. Pus consists of dead white blood cells, living and dead bacteria (usually *Staphylococcus aureus*), and fragments of dead tissue. Standard treatment is oral antibiotics. Studies showed that people with recurrent boils had low levels of blood zinc. When they were supplemented with 25-50 mg of zinc daily, blood zinc levels rose and healing of the boils accelerated. In addition, while blood zinc levels were maintained, new boils did not appear.

Bone, normal development and healthy maintenance need vitamin D and vitamin A at minimum daily intakes of 250 IU and 2,500 IU respectively.

Bone pain of cancer has been relieved with very high doses (up to 10 g daily) of vitamin C.

Bone phosphate, edible, a food additive that consists mainly of hydroxyapatite. Used as an anticaking agent and as a mineral supplement. Provides 39.9 mg calcium and 18.5 mg phosphorus per 100 mg. Acceptable daily intake is up to 70 mg phosphorus per kg body weight.

Bone meal, the main constituent is calcium hydroxyapatite, which provides 40 mg calcium per 100 mg plus 18.5 mg phosphorus. Other constituents are protein, fat, amino sugars, and traces of magnesium. Also available as amino acid-chelated bone meal, which provides 13.5 mg calcium per 100 mg, plus 7.5 mg phosphorus. The usual daily dose of either is up to 6 tablets (i.e., 400-500 mg calcium). Often used as an excipient or filler in tablet making.

Borax, also known as sodium borate; sodium tetraborate; sodium biborate; and sodium pyroborate. Provides 11.9 mg boron per 100 mg borax.

Boric acid, also known as boracic acid. Provides 17.5 mg boron per 100 mg boric acid.

Boron, chemical symbol B. Atomic weight 10.8. Occurs in nature as various compounds at an abundance of 10 mg per kg in the earth's crust.

Boron was shown in 1910 to be an essential element for plants. There is no evidence that it is needed by animals and humans. Human diets provide 2 mg per day, which is efficiently absorbed and excreted in the urine. Toxic symptoms appear at intakes of 100 mg or so. For this reason, the FAO/WHO authorities have now banned boron (as boric acid) as a food additive and preservative. Boron, in daily intakes of 5-20 mg, has been claimed to relieve the symptoms of arthritis, but the evidence is not very convincing.

Medicinal uses have included:

1. External application as a dusting powder or lotion (in the form of boric acid) to treat bacterial and fungal infections.

2. Treatment of mouth ulcers and eye infections, and as a nasal douche (in the form of a solution of borax).

Toxic effects of boric acid and borax include: a red rash with "weeping skin"; vomiting; blue-green colored diarrhea; depressed blood circulation; profound shock; coma; and convulsions.

Fatal dose in adults is 15-20 g; in infants 3-6 g. Repeated intakes of small amounts can lead to accumulative effects.

In children, toxicity can occur by the application of boron-containing dusting powders to broken areas of skin. For this reason, such dusting powders should not contain more than 5 percent boric acid or borax. Absorption from solutions applied to body cavities and mucous membranes can be significant, so such solutions are not recommended as douches for the vagina, bladder, wounds, and ulcers.

Bran, all types are rich in vitamins and minerals as shown in Figures 5 and 6.

Bread, usually has high sodium and chloride levels due to added salt in all varieties. White bread contains more calcium than whole grain because the mineral is added (*see* Figure 7), but white bread is inferior in vitamin content (*see* Figure 8).

Brewer's yeast, *Saccharomyces cerevisiae.* Dried variety contains (in mg per 100 g): carotene (trace); thiamin (15.6); riboflavin (4.28); nicotonic acid (37.9); pyridoxine (4.2); pantothenic acid (9.5); biotin (0.08); folic acid (2.4); and vitamin C (trace).

Rich source of RNA and DNA, which together account for 12 percent of dried yeast.

Minerals

Fairly low in sodium but an excellent provider of potassium, calcium, magnesium, manganese, iron, copper, and phosphorus. Supplies significant quantities of chromium and selenium. Dried variety contains (in mg per 100 g): sodium (121); potassium (1,700); calcium (210); magnesium (231); mangenese (0.53); iron (17.3); copper (3.32); and phosphorus (1,753).

Figure 5: Vitamin content of bran

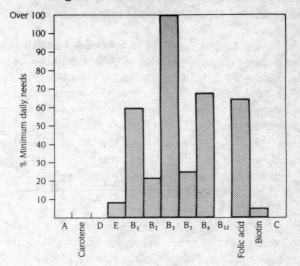

Figure 6: Mineral content of bran

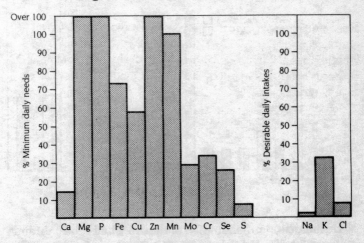

Figure 7: Vitamin content of bread

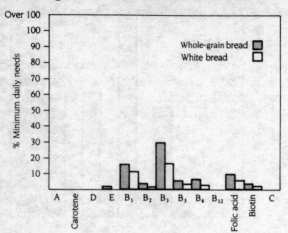

Figure 8: Mineral content of bread

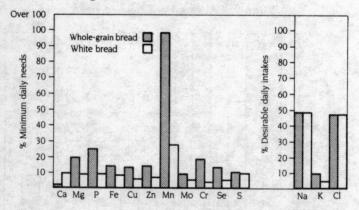

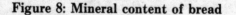

Bronchitis, inflammation of the bronchial tubes. Vitamin
A (7,500 IU daily) helps in therapy by stimulating the

mucous membrane of the respiratory tract to resist infection. Vitamin C (500-1,000 mg daily) increases resistance to bacterial and viral infections.

Bruises, hemorrhages under the skin due to capillary fragility. Color changes are related to the conversion of blood hemoglobin to bile pigments. Excessive bruising is prevented by adequate intakes of vitamin C plus bioflavonoids, particularly in those involved in body contact sports.

Bruxism, grinding of the teeth, often carried on during sleep, that can give rise to dental problems. Has been overcome by increasing the daily intake of calcium pantothenate (100 mg) and calcium (300 mg).

Burns, infection and pain of burned area of skin is reduced by a spray of 3 percent vitamin C solution (sterile). The healing rate is increased by massive doses (up to 10 g) of vitamin C orally. Complemented by simultaneous intake of vitamin E (400 IU twice daily) plus vitamin E cream or ointment (100 IU per g).

Butter, salted. A good source of fat-soluble vitamins, but negligible quantities of water-soluble vitamins are present. Provides (in μg per 100 g): vitamin A (750); carotene (470); vitamin D (0.76); and vitamin E (2,000).

Minerals

A high-sodium food because of salt added during production. Only traces of the other minerals are present. Minerals present in salted butter are (in mg per 100 g): sodium (870); potassium (15); calcium (15); magnesium (2); phosphorus (24); iron (0.2); copper (0.03); zinc (0.15); sulfur (9); and chloride (1,340).

C

C, a water-soluble vitamin. Known also as: L-ascorbic acid; antiscorbutic acid; hexuronic acid; cevitaminic acid; L-xyloascorbic acid; ascorbyl palmitate; and ascorbyl nicotinate. A white, crystalline powder. Isolated from fruits, paprika, and adrenal glands by Dr. Albert Szent-Gyorgyi in 1922 in Hungary. Shown in 1932 by Dr. Szent-Gyorgyi and Dr. W.A. Waugh and Dr. C. G. King (US) to cure scurvy.

Best Food Sources in mg per 100 g		Functions
Acerola cherry		Antioxidant
juice	3,390	Promotes iron absorption from food
Rose hip syrup	295	Maintains healthy
Black currants	200	collagen
Guavas	200	Provides resistance to
Parsley	150	infection
Kale	150	Controls blood
Horseradish	120	cholesterol levels
Broccoli tops	110	Makes folic acid active
Green peppers	100	Produces antistress
Brussels sprouts	90	hormones
Citrus fruits	50-80	Produces brain and
Watercress	60	nerve substances
Cabbage	60	Maintains healthy:
Mustard tops	50	bones
All other fruits and		teeth
vegetables	20-40	blood system
		sex organs
		As natural antihistamine

Vitamin C cont.

Deficiency Symptoms

Weakness
Lassitude
Muscle and joint pains
Irritability
Bleeding gums
Gingivitis
Loosening of teeth
Hemorrhages in:
  skin
  eyes
  nose

Therapeutic Uses

Scurvy
Iron-deficiency anemia
Bleeding under the skin
Respiratory diseases
Bleeding gums
Psychiatric states
Colds and influenza
Cancer
High blood cholesterol
  levels
Antihistamine
Alcoholism
Arthritis and leg cramps

Stability in Foods

Most unstable vitamin—
see losses in food
processing

More Needed Daily by

Those who take:
  aspirin
  contraceptive pill
  antibiotics
  barbiturates
  corticosteroids
  antiarthritic drugs
Those under stress
The elderly
Athletes
Alcohol drinkers
Anyone undergoing
  surgery
Those with infectious
  diseases
Anyone with accidental
  wounds
Anyone undergoing
  dental surgery
Diabetics
Those with gastric and
  duodenal ulcers

Recommended Daily Intake

Should be at least
60 mg. *See* recommended
daily intakes

Deficiency Disease

scurvy

Vitamin C cont.

Symptoms of Excess Intake	These are highly unlikely with daily doses below 3 g
Nausea	
Abdominal cramps	Generally regarded as a safe vitamin
Diarrhea	

Cadmium, chemical symbol Cd. Atomic weight 112.4. It is not an essential nutrient for humans and can be toxic at high intakes. Occurs in nature associated with zinc ores, so it is liberated when zinc is extracted. Earth's abundance is 0.1 to 0.2 mg per kg.

At birth, cadmium is absent from the body, but it is absorbed in very small amounts and accumulates over 50 years or so to a body content of 20 to 30 mg. More than half of this is found in the liver and kidneys. At a concentration of 22.4 mg per 100 g it can damage the kidneys. Within the tissues and organs, most cadmium is immobilized by complexing with a specific protein called metallothionein. This serves to detoxify cadmium and other toxic minerals by makng them unavailable to the tissues and organs. When metallothionein is deficient or saturated, toxic effects of cadmium appear. Excretion is very slow, at a level of only 0.01 percent of the body levels daily.

Sources of cadmium include: the atmosphere in the vicinity of industrial smelting and plating plants; fertilizers such as superphosphates, where 15-21 mg per kg may be present; drinking water, which can contribute 1.1 μg per liter (soft water provides more than hard water since galvanized pipes contain cadmium); vegetables grown on land irrigated by contaminated water or polluted by factory waste; tobacco smoke, up to 5 μg per day, from which cadmium is better absorbed than from food and drink; and dental amalgams.

Food sources of cadmium include: oysters (3-4 µg per g wet weight); liver and kidneys (1-2 µg per 100 g); fruits, vegetables, and nuts (0.04-0.08 µg per g); and soy beans (1 µg per g) that have been grown on soil heavily fertilized with salvage sludge. Muscle meats and milk are poor sources. Cadmium is lost by food refining and processing, as are the essential trace minerals.

Daily intakes of 55-70 µg per person have been proposed by WHO as tolerable. Calculated intakes have been reported as: 60-90 µg per day for young adult female New Zealanders; from 27-64 µg per day in children confined to institutions; 26 µg per day in daily food intakes of Americans; and from 50-150 µg per day among various other countries.

Competes with zinc, copper, and selenium in absorption and metabolism, probably by virtue of competition for some protein-binding sites.

Excess intake can cause anemia, probably by antagonizing copper and iron functions in blood formation; high blood pressure, probably through kidney damage; injurious effects on the reproductive organs in animals; Itai-itai disease (*see* Itai-itai); and atherosclerosis. Protection against excessive accumulation of cadmium is possible by adequate intake of zinc, copper, and selenium in the diet. Vitamin C at daily dose levels of 500-1,000 mg protects against cadmium poisoning and helps rid the body of the mineral.

Acute toxicity effects after eating cadmium include: nausea; vomiting; abdominal cramps; shock; and gastric and intestinal bleeding. After inhalation, the effects are: eye irritation; headache; vertigo; cough; constriction of the chest; weakness in the legs; difficulty in breathing; and pneumonia.

Chronic toxic effects include: yellow pigmentation of the teeth; soreness of the nostrils (cadmium sniffles); loss of smell; emphysema; pain in the back and limbs; bone changes leading to disability; and loss of protein in the urine.

Medicinal forms of cadmium include:

1. Cadmium sulfide, used in the control of seborrheic dermatitis and dandruff, usually in the form of shampoos. It may cause photosensitization.
2. Cadmium salts, used as antihelminthics (to destroy parasitic worms in swine and poultry).

Calciferol, *see* D (vitamin).

Calcitonin, a peptide (chain of amino acids) hormone produced by specific cells of the thyroid gland. Also known as thyrocalcitonin. It is secreted in response to high blood calcium levels and its action is to reduce blood calcium by inhibiting the rate of calcium release from the bone. Used medically in the treatment of high blood calcium levels and in Paget's disease.

Calcium, chemical symbol Ca. Atomic weight 40.08. A metallic macro-element present in the skeleton and teeth (1,100 g) with the remainder (10 g) in the nerves, muscles, and blood. Calcium in the blood is essential in the process of blood clotting. That in the nerves and in the muscles (including the heart) is necessary for nerve impulse transmission and muscular function.

Recommended Daily Intake	Best Food Sources in mg per 100 g (max.)	
Should be between 500 and 1,000 mg daily. *See* recommended daily intakes	Hard cheeses	1,200
	Soft cheeses	725
	Canned fish	400

Calcium cont.

Best Food Sources cont.

Nuts	250
Legumes	150
White flour (fortified)	140
Cow's milk	120
Root vegetables	80
Eggs	60
Cereals	60
Fruits	60
Wholegrain flour	40
Fish (fresh)	32
Human milk	35

Absorption from Food

Between 20 and 30 percent of that eaten. Higher figure applies when intakes are low.
Absorption more efficient in the presence of:
  vitamin D
  proteins
  lactose (milk sugar)
  stomach acid
  magnesium
Absorption inhibited by:
  phytic acid
  dietary fiber
  phosphate
  saturated fats
  rhubarb (contains oxalic acid)

Functions

Builds and maintains healthy bones and teeth
Controls excitability of nerves and muscles
Controls conduction of nerve impulses
Controls contraction of heart and other muscles
Assists in process of blood clotting
Controls blood cholesterol levels
Assists in absorption of vitamin B_{12}

Calcium Regulation

Under control of:
  vitamin D and hormones
  Calcitonin
  parathyroid
  estrogens (female sex hormones)
  thyroid hormone
  (*see also* D (vitamin), calcitonin, and parathyroid)
Excessive losses during and after menopause

Calcium cont.

Daily Losses

Urine—up to 350 mg;
higher in summer and
after menopause
Feces—up to 400 mg, of
which 130 mg is from
body and 270 mg is
undissolved from food
Sweat—only 15 mg
normally, but up to
100 mg per hour with
heavy work or exercise

Therapeutic Uses

Rickets
Osteomalacia
Tetany
Osteoporosis
Celiac disease
Allergy conditions
As detoxifying agent in
lead, mercury, alumi-
num, and cadmium
poisoning
Depression, anxiety,
panic attacks,
insomnia, overactivity
Arthritis, muscle and
joint pains
Pregnancy
Breast-feeding

Symptoms of Excess Intake

Highly unlikely under
normal conditions, as
body will reject and
excrete any calcium
that is above its needs.
Probable only if vitamin
D intake is also high
(*see* D (vitamin))
If prolonged, high cal-
cium and vitamin D
taken together can
cause deposition of
calcium in kidneys,
heart, and other soft
tissues.

Deficiency Symptoms

In children: Rickets,
characterized by:
excessive sweating of
the head
poor ability to sleep
constant head
movements
slowness in sitting,
crawling, walking
bow legs, knock knees,
and pigeon breast
In adults: Osteomalacia,
causing:

Calcium cont.

Deficiency Symptoms cont.

bone pain
muscle weakness
delayed healing of
    fractures
(Both above conditions
    are similar to vitamin
    D deficiency)
Tetany—twitches
    and spasms

Deficiency Caused by

Low dietary intake
Lack of vitamin D
Increased intake of un-
    cooked bran, phosphates
    animal fats, oxalic acid
    (in rhubarb, etc.)
Contraceptive pill
Corticosteroid drugs
Malabsorption due to:
    lack of stomach acid
    celiac disease
    lactose intolerance
    diuretic drugs
Pregnancy
Breast-feeding

Calcium Supplements in mg per 100 mg

Amino acid-chelated cal-
cium (18); bone meal (40);
calcium acetate (25); calcium ascorbate (10.3);
calcium carbonate (40);
calcium chloride (27.2);
calcium glubionate (6.6);
calcium gluceptate (8.2);
calcium gluconate (8.9);
calcium glycerophosphate
(19.1); calcium phosphate
(38.7); calcium lactate (13);
calcium levulinate (13.1);
calcium orotate (20.6);
calcium sodium lactate
(7.8); calcium tetrahydrogen
phosphate (15.9); dibasic
calcium phosphate (29.5);
dolomite (21.7); and tribasic
calcium phosphate (38.8).
    Under present legisla-
tion, white flour may have
calcium carbonate (chalk)
or calcium sulfate added
to it as a source of calcium.

Calcium antagonists, a group of drugs that appear to
function by preventing or slowing the flow of calcium into
muscle cells. Also known as calcium blockers. Muscle cells
need calcium to activate contraction of heart and artery

muscles. The regulation of calcium movement into heart muscle cells is thus critical to heart muscle tone, resistance, and blood pressure. By blocking the flow of calcium by an antagonistic action, these drugs are valuable in treating angina pectoris, heart failure, high blood pressure, weak heart muscle, fast heartbeat, and coronary artery spasm. Adverse effects of calcium antagonists include transient headache, flushing, lethargy, dizziness, allergic reactions, low blood pressure, palpitations, and occasionally precipitation of anginal pain.

Calcium pantothenate,   calcium salt of pantothenic acid.

Cancer,   any malignant tumor that arises from the abnormal and uncontrolled division of cells that then invade and destroy the surrounding tissues. Malignant growths can be treated with high doses of vitamins in addition to conventional therapy.

Bladder: Sufficient vitamin C is needed to saturate the urinary system to protect against and treat cancer of the bladder. 500 mg three times daily is effective. Inositol (1,000 mg daily) also has inhibiting effect.

Breast: Clinical response is obtained with 200 IU vitamin E three times daily. Simultaneous intake of up to 10 g daily vitamin C may complement vitamin E therapy. The dose of C is arrived at by increasing intake by 1 g each day until diarrhea occurs. 1 g per day less than this is the maximum tolerated dose up to maximum of 10 g.

Colon: Use vitamin C with the same regimen as in treating breast cancer.

Lung: Prevention (particularly tobacco smokers) and treatment with beta-carotene (4.5 mg three times daily).

Skin: Preliminary reports suggest 0.05 percent retinoic acid applied directly to affected skin areas has a beneficial effect. Other retinoids may be more effective.

Other cancers: Vitamin C therapy as outlined for breast cancer may be beneficial.

Laetrile is claimed to be beneficial for all cancers but professional treatment is essential.

Minerals

It is important that the diet of anyone suffering from cancer is adequate in all the essential minerals as part of the general approach to nutritional control of the condition. However, one trace mineral of particular importance in the prevention and perhaps the treatment of cancer is selenium. Epidemiological evidence suggests that a population living in a low-selenium area has a higher cancer incidence than a comparable population living in a high-selenium area. For example, in the United States, where selenium intakes average 50-100 μg per person per day, the cancer rate is higher than in Bulgaria where the intake is about 250 μg per person per day. Within the same country, those with higher blood selenium levels have a lower incidence of cancer than those with lower blood selenium levels. Animal experiments have proved that some cancers can actually be cured with selenium supplementation. Selenium appears to function against cancer by:

1. Stimulating the immune system that protects against cancer.
2. Toughening the cell membrane and making it less prone to attack by cancer-producing antigens.

The quantity of selenium to act as a preventive is at least 200 μg per day; for treatment, more may be necessary to increase blood levels of selenium, perhaps up to 500 μg per day. Daily intakes of 2,000 μg have been taken under medical supervision in the treatment of cancer without any detectable damage to the liver, or other side effects.

Carnitine, a constituent of muscles and liver. Synthesis in the body is dependent on vitamin C. Functions as a transporter of fatty acids within body cells prior to using the acids for energy production.

Carotenemia, high blood levels of carotene that may cause yellow coloration of the skin. Completely harmless and removed by reducing intake of carotenes. The eyeballs remain white, which distinguishes carotenemia from jaundice.

Carotenoids, colored pigments widely distributed in animals and plants. More than 100 have been identified in nature. Includes the carotenes designated alpha-, beta-, and gamma-carotene that can give rise to vitamin A. Cryptoxanthin and beta-zeacarotene are also vitamin A precursors. Conversion takes place in the intestines and liver.

Richest food sources are (in μg per 100 g): carrots (12,000); parsley (7,000); spinach (6,000); turnip tops (6,000); spring greens (4,000); sweet potatoes (4,000); watercress (3,000); broccoli (2,500); cantaloupes (2,000); endives (2,000); ox liver (1,540); pumpkins (1,500); apricots (1,500); lettuce (1,000); prunes (1,000); tomatoes (600); spring cabbage (500); peaches (500); asparagus (500); butter (470); cheese (210); cream (125); and cow's milk (22).

Relationship between carotenes and vitamin A is as follows:

1 retinol equivalent = 1 microgram retinol
                             = 6 micrograms beta-carotene
                             = 12 micrograms other carotene precursors
                             = 3.33 IU vitamin A activity from retinol
                             = 10 IU vitamin A activity from beta-carotene

Beta-carotene is the most potent precursor of vitamin A.

Destroyed by high temperatures, oxygen, and light, particularly with traces of iron and copper. Losses of 40 percent in boiling water (60 mins); 70 percent in frying (15 mins); 20 percent in freezing, canning, and cooking; 20 percent in controlled drying of fruits and vegetables; and virtually complete destruction in uncontrolled drying (in the sun).

Functions of carotenes are as precursors of vitamin A. No other specific function is known.

Deficiency is not known to cause any specific disease.

Deficiency symptoms are not known.

Recommended dietary intakes of vitamin A can be obtained from carotenes alone. Normal diets supply 50 percent of vitamin A needs as the vitamin and 50 percent as carotenes.

Toxicity has not been reported for carotenes. The main symptom of excess intake is a yellowing of skin that is reversible and harmless.

Therapy with beta-carotene is claimed to be beneficial in lung cancer in animal tests. It appears to be protective against lung cancer induced by tobacco smoking.

Cataracts, opacity of the eye lens. Can be induced by deficiency of vitamins B_2 and C and the mineral calcium. May be prevented by vitamin B_2 (10 mg daily), vitamin C (500 mg daily), and calcium (500 mg daily).

Cathartics, purgatives and laxatives. Prevent the absorption of vitamin K and riboflavin.

Cephalosporins, antibiotics. Prevent the absorption of vitamins K, B_{12}, and folic acid.

Cheese, supplies most vitamins and minerals but

especially rich in fat-soluble vitamins and calcium (*see* Figures 9 and 10).

Figure 9: Vitamin content of cheeses

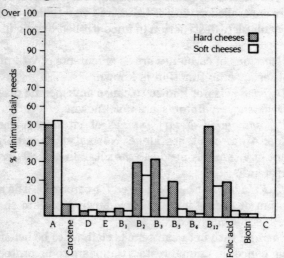

Figure 10: Mineral content of cheeses

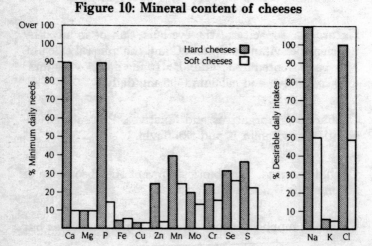

Hard cheeses comprise Cheddar, Danish Blue, Stilton, Camembert, and Edam. Soft cheeses are the cottage and cream varieties.

Chelation,   is the process whereby a mineral is incorporated into a ring structure by the chelating agent. From the Greek *chelos,* meaning claw. The process is essentially a transformation of an inorganic to an organically bound mineral. The resulting mineral chelate has a stability determined by the chelating group. There are three levels of stability:

1. Strong chelates, such as those formed by the chelating agents ethylenediaminetetraacetic acid (EDTA) and D-penicillamine, which are used in medicine to remove unwanted toxic minerals from the body. Once the chelate is formed, it is strong enough to pass through the body unchanged and hence gets excreted.
2. Weak chelates, such as mineral ascorbates, citrates, lactates, and gluconates formed from the mineral and sugar-type residues, have a stability comparable to mineral salts and are hence easily dissociated.
3. Intermediate-strength chelates can be either amino acid chelates or orotates. These are strong enough to be absorbed intact but weak enough for the mineral to be transferred to other groups within the body by normal metabolic processes. Amino acid chelates are true biological chelates since this is how the body absorbs certain minerals, stores them, transports them, and utilizes them. Orotates are synthetic derivatives of the mineral with orotic acid and there is little evidence of their functioning as such within the body.

Chelated minerals that occur naturally include: iron in hemoglobin; iron in hemosiderin; iron in ferritin; magnesium in chlorophyll; zinc in insulin; manganese in transmanganin in the blood; copper in hemocyanin (found in the blood of insects, crabs, and octopi); calcium in milk; chromium in yeast; selenium in yeast; and cobalt in vitamin B_{12}.

Chick antidermatitis factor,   *see* pantothenic acid.

Chicken,   *see* meats.

Chilblains,   congestion and swelling of the skin due to cold, accompanied by severe itching or burning. Can be treated orally with nicotinic acid (25 mg) and acetomenaphthone (10 mg), complemented by creams containing methylnicotinate (1 percent) plus other nonvitamin ingredients.

Children,   vitamin needs are related to weight, but requirements for growth must also be taken into account. Children are likely to have faddish and fickle appetites, and have a taste for foods of high caloric but low vitamin content. Good diet is most important to health but may benefit from low-level supplementation of vitamins and minerals.

For recommended dietary intakes *see* Figure 11.

Chinese-restaurant syndrome,   also known as the Ho Man Kwok syndrome. Symptoms start 15 minutes after eating Chinese food and consist of a numbness at the back of the neck that gradually radiates to both arms and to the back. There is a general weakness and palpitation of the heart. It has been suggested that the monosodium glutamate that occurs naturally in soy sauce may provide a local high concentration of sodium that causes the unpleasant effects. Also possible that the high glutamic acid (an amino acid) content may contribute to the reaction.

Chloramphenicol, an antibiotic. Prevents the formation of vitamin K by intestinal bacteria.

Chlorbutol, an antinausea agent. Enhances the excretion and metabolism of vitamin C.

Chloride, chemical symbol Cl. Atomic weight 35.5. Abundance in igneous rock is 0.031 percent by weight; in sea water 1.9 percent by weight, primarily as sodium chloride. An essential mineral form of chlorine in plants, animals, and humans.

Chloride is usually associated with sodium, both in food and in body fluids; high sodium levels are paralleled by high chloride levels and vice versa. In body fluids, chloride is negatively charged (anion) and it neutralizes the positively charged sodium and potassium (cations). Body content of chloride is about 115 g. This amount is kept constant by excretion of excess chloride in urine, sweat, and the gastrointestinal tract. Most people are in positive chloride balance since adequate diets provide more than enough. In parallel with sodium, excessive losses can be caused by heavy sweating and diarrhea. In addition, chloride in the form of hydrochloric acid may be lost to a significant degree in persistent vomiting. Normal blood plasma levels of chloride lie between 348 and 376 mg per 100 ml.

Functions of chloride are:
1. To act as the main anion to sodium and potassium cations in the maintenance of body water levels and neutrality.
2. To provide chloride for the production of hydrochloric acid by the stomach.

Food sources of chloride parallel those of sodium. Foods rich in sodium are rich in chloride; poor sources of

Figure 11: Recommended dietary intakes for children

COUNTRY	AGE (years)	SEX	VIT A µg	VIT D µg	VIT E mg	VIT B₁ mg	VIT B₂ mg	NIC ACID mg	VIT B₆ mg	FOLIC ACID µg	VIT B₁₂ µg	VIT C mg
AUSTRALIA	0-0.5	Both	–	–	–	–	–	–	0.25	–	–	–
	1-2	Both	250	10	–	0.5	0.7	9	0.6	100	0.9	30
	13-14	Both	725	–	–	1.0	1.3	17	1.5	200	2.0	40
	16-17	Both	750	–	–	1.2	1.5	20	2.0	200	2.0	50
NEW ZEALAND	0-0.5	Both	300	7.5	5	0.2	0.4	5	0.4	50	0.3	20
	1-2	Both	300	10	5	0.6	0.7	8	0.6	100	0.3	25
	13-14	Both	725	10	10	0.9	1.4	16	1.6	200	3.0	45
	16-17	Both	750	10	13.5	1.2	1.7	19	2.0	200	3.0	60
US	0-0.5	Both	420	10	3	0.3	0.6	6	0.3	30	0.5	35
	0.5-1.0	Both	400	10	4	0.5	0.4	8	0.6	45	1.5	35
	1-3	Both	400	10	5	0.7	0.8	9	0.9	100	2.0	45
	4-6	Both	500	10	6	0.9	1.0	11	1.3	200	2.5	45
	7-10	Both	700	10	7	1.2	1.4	16	1.6	300	3.0	45
	11-14	M	1,000	10	8	1.4	1.6	18	1.8	400	3.0	50
		F	800	10	8	1.1	1.3	15	1.8	400	3.0	50
	15-18	M	1,000	10	10	1.4	1.7	18	2.0	400	3.0	60
		F	800	10	8	1.1	1.3	14	2.0	400	3.0	60
FAO/WHO	0-1.0	Both	300	10	–	0.3	0.5	5.4	–	60	0.3	20
	1-3	Both	250	10	–	0.5	0.8	9.0	–	100	0.9	20
	4-6	Both	300	10	–	0.7	1.1	12.1	–	100	1.5	20
	7-9	Both	400	2.5	–	0.9	1.3	14.5	–	100	1.5	20
	10-12	M	575	2.5	–	1.0	1.6	17.2	–	100	2.0	20
		F	575	2.5	–	0.9	1.4	15.5	–	100	2.0	20
	13-15	M	725	2.5	–	1.2	1.7	19.1	–	200	2.0	30
		F	725	2.5	–	1.0	1.5	16.4	–	200	2.0	30
	16-19	M	750	2.5	–	1.2	1.8	20.3	–	200	2.0	30
		F	750	2.5	–	0.9	1.4	15.2	–	200	2.0	30

	Age	Sex										
UK	0-1	M	450	7.5	–	0.3	0.4	5	–	–**	–	20
		F	450	7.5	–	0.3	0.4	5	–	–**	–	20
	1	M	300	10	–	0.5	0.6	7	–	–**	–	20
		F	300	10	–	0.4	0.6	7	–	–**	–	20
	2	M	300	10	–	0.6	0.7	8	–	–**	–	20
		F	300	10	–	0.5	0.7	8	–	–**	–	20
	3-4	M	300	10	–	0.6	0.8	9	–	–**	–	20
		F	300	10	–	0.6	0.8	9	–	–**	–	20
	5-6	M	300	10*	–	0.7	0.9	10	–	–**	–	20
		F	300	10	–	0.7	0.9	10	–	–**	–	20
	7-8	M	400	10	–	0.8	1.0	11	–	–**	–	20
		F	400	10	–	0.8	1.0	11	–	–**	–	20
	9-11	M	575	10	–	0.9	1.2	14	–	–**	–	25
		F	575	10	–	0.8	1.2	14	–	–**	–	25
	12-14	M	725	10	–	1.1	1.4	16	–	–**	–	25
		F	725	10	–	1.1	1.4	16	–	–**	–	25
	15-17	M	750	10	–	1.2	1.7	19	–	–**	–	30
		F	750	10	–	0.9	1.7	19	–	–**	–	30
CANADA	0-0.5	Both	400	10	3	0.3	0.4	5	0.3	40	0.3	20
	0.5-1.0	Both	400	10	3	0.5	0.6	6	0.4	60	0.3	20
	1-3	Both	400	10	4	0.7	0.8	9	0.8	100	0.4	20
	4-6	Both	500	5	5	0.9	1.1	12	1.3	100	1.5	20
	7-9	M	700	2.5	6	1.1	1.3	14	1.6	100	1.5	30
		F	700	2.5	6	1.0	1.2	13	1.4	100	1.5	30
	10-12	M	800	2.5	7	1.2	1.5	17	1.8	100	3.0	30
		F	800	2.5	7	1.1	1.4	15	1.5	100	3.0	30
	13-15	M	1,000	2.5	9	1.4	1.7	19	2.0	200	3.0	30
		F	800	2.5	7	1.1	1.4	15	1.5	200	3.0	30
	16-18	M	1,000	2.5	10	1.6	2.0	21	2.0	200	3.0	30
		F	800	2.5	6	1.1	1.3	14	1.5	200	3.0	30

*Supplements of 10 µg daily recommended only during winter months for children of more than 5 years of age.
**Intakes not yet recommended, but in adults are 300 µg.

sodium, like fruits, vegetables, nuts, and whole grains, are also poor providers of chloride. *See* sodium and the entries for individual food for contents.

Deficiency of chloride in body fluids is highly unlikely, but may parallel excessive sodium losses. No symptoms can be attributed specifically to lack of chloride. The only possible local deficiency of body chloride is in the condition of achlorhydria, where the stomach cells fail to produce hydrochloric acid. This is due to a breakdown in the production mechanism, not to a lack of chloride.

Supplementary forms of chloride include: sodium chloride (100 mg provides 60.7 mg chloride); potassium chloride (100 mg provides 47.6 mg chloride). Hydrochloric acid may be taken as betaine hydrochloride, glutamic acid hydrochloride, or dilute hydrochloric acid. *See* hydrochloric acid.

Increased blood plasma levels of chloride are seen in anemia, heart disease, kidney disease, and pregnancy (eclampsia).

Decreased blood plasma levels of chloride are seen in diabetes, fevers, and pneumonia.

Urinary excretion of chloride is increased in a diet rich in salt, in rickets, and in liver cirrhosis. It is decreased in chronic kidney disease, early stages of pneumonia, cancer, and gastritis.

Excessive dietary levels of chloride are likely only with increased salt and potassium chloride intakes. The toxic effects of both of these are related, respectively, to the sodium and potassium moieties (*see* sodium; potassium). No toxic effects have been attributed to chloride, but it has been suggested recently that the high blood pressure-inducing effect of excessive salt intakes, which may be mediated through the hormones renin and aldosterone, could be a function of high chloride rather than high sodium in the diet.

Chlorine dioxide, a food additive used as a bleaching and improving agent for flour.

Chocolate, hot, a useful source of some vitamins. Figures are for the dry form. Vitamin E content is 0.9 mg per 100 g. B vitamins present are (in mg per 100 g): thiamin (0.06); riboflavin (0.04); nicotinic acid (1.1); and pyridoxine (0.02). Folic acid level is $10\mu g$ per 100 g. Devoid of vitamin C.

Minerals
High sodium, potassium, magnesium, phosphorus, and iron levels. A good source of copper and zinc. The dried form contains (in mg per 100 g): sodium (250); potassium (410); calcium (33); magnesium (150); phosphorus (190); iron (2.4); copper (1.1); zinc (1.9); and chloride (130).

Cholecalciferol, *see* D_2 (vitamin).

Cholesterol, a fatty substance with three essential functions in the body: as a constituent of cell membranes, particularly the myelin sheath that insulates nerves; as a precursor of bile acids; and as a precursor of steroid hormones (sex, antistress, water balance, and metabolic). The actual production of steroid hormones needs vitamin C and pantothenic acid.

Cholesterol exists in blood and organs as HDL-cholesterol (high-density lipoprotein), LDL-cholesterol (low-density lipoprotein), and VLDL-cholesterol (very low density lipoprotein). A high ratio of HDL to LDL and VLDL is desirable to protect against atherosclerosis, arteriosclerosis, and coronary heart disease. HDL is increased by taking PUFA instead of animal fats and by taking 600 IU of vitamin E daily.

High blood cholesterol levels can be reduced by taking 500 mg vitamin C daily or by taking 3 g nicotinic acid daily.

Cholestyramine, an anticholesterol agent. Prevents the absorption of vitamins A, D, E, K, and B_{12}.

Choline, a water-soluble member of the vitamin B complex. Known also as amanitine, lipotropic factor. Not a true vitamin as it is synthesized in the liver in limited quantities. An active constituent of lecithin. Present in supplements as choline bitartrate, choline chloride, phosphatidyl-choline, and lecithin. A colorless, crystalline substance.

Best Food Sources in mg per 100 g		Best Food Sources cont.	
Lecithin granules	3,430	Whole wheat bread	80
Desiccated liver	2,170	Green leafy vegetables	80
Beef heart	1,720	Other fruits	44
Egg yolk	1,700	Root vegetables	40
Lecithin oil	800	Milk	30
Liver	650		
Beef steak	600	**Functions**	
Wheat germ	505	As fat-stabilizing agent	
Dried brewer's yeast	300	As precursor of:	
Cereals	240	betaine, needed in metabolism	
Nuts	220	acetylcholine, a nerve substance	
Legumes	120	As component of lecithin	
Citrus fruits	85		

Choline cont.

Stability in Foods	Absorption from Foods

Stability in Foods

Very stable

Deficiency Symptoms

Nothing specific, but
lack can lead to:
  fatty liver
  nerve degeneration
  senile dementia
  high blood pressure
  reduced resistance to
   infection
  atherosclerosis
  thrombosis
  stroke
  high blood cholesterol

Therapeutic Uses

Angina
Atherosclerosis
Thrombosis
Stroke
High blood pressure
Alzheimer's disease
Senile dementia

Absorption from Foods

Absorbed better as
lecithin than as choline

Increased Intakes

Needed by:
  alcoholics
  diabetics
  those with deficiency
   symptoms

**Recommended Daily
Intake**

Difficult to assess
because of body synthesis.
Probably between 500 and
1,000 mg

**Symptoms of Excess
Intake**

None reported apart
from occasional mild
nausea

Chromium, chemical symbol Cr. Atomic weight 52.0.
Exists in many forms but trivalent chromium is the only
form that can be used by the body. An essential trace element for animals and humans.

Chromium cont.

Best Food Sources in μg per 100 g		Functions
Egg yolk	183	Acts as the glucose tolerance factor (GTF)—no other functions known. GTF stimulates insulin activity directly by binding to both insulin itself and specific insulin receptors. Chromium alone does not do this.
Molasses	121	
Dried brewer's yeast	117	
Beef	57	
Hard cheese	56	
Liver	55	
Fruit juices	47	
Whole-grain bread	42	GTF therefore:
Bran	38	controls blood glucose by promoting uptake by muscles and organs
Alcoholic beverages	30	
Cereals	30	
Honey	29	stimulates burning of glucose for energy
Wheat germ	23	
Vegetables	21	controls blood cholesterol levels
Fruit	10	

Best Food Sources in μg per 100 g

Egg yolk	183
Molasses	121
Dried brewer's yeast	117
Beef	57
Hard cheese	56
Liver	55
Fruit juices	47
Whole-grain bread	42
Bran	38
Alcoholic beverages	30
Cereals	30
Honey	29
Wheat germ	23
Vegetables	21
Fruit	10

Poor Food Sources

White flour
Shellfish
Fish
Poultry
Egg white
Nonfat milk
Food refining and processing remove most of the chromium from original foodstuffs. Hence highly refined diets will also lead to deficiency

Functions

Acts as the glucose tolerance factor (GTF)—no other functions known. GTF stimulates insulin activity directly by binding to both insulin itself and specific insulin receptors. Chromium alone does not do this.

GTF therefore:
controls blood glucose by promoting uptake by muscles and organs
stimulates burning of glucose for energy
controls blood cholesterol levels
reduces fat levels in blood
increases HDL cholesterol
reduces arteriosclerosis in experiments with rats
stimulates protein synthesis
stimulates production of essential nerve substances
increases resistance to infection
suppresses hunger symptoms through brain "satiety center"

Chromium cont.

Deficiency Results in

Causes condition resembl-
ing diabetes in experi-
ments with rats
Impairs glucose uptake by
muscles in malnourished
children
Nervous conditions
Increased blood choles-
terol levels
Formation of arterio-
sclerotic plaques
Increased blood fat levels
May be a factor in heart
disease
Possibly related to some
human diabetes

Deficiency Caused by

Diets high in refined and
processed foods
Excessive losses from the
body in some diseases
Prolonged slimming
regimens
Pregnancy
Severe malnutrition
Prolonged intravenous
feeding
Alcoholism

Deficiency Symptoms

Similar to those of
hypoglycemia, and are:
  irritability
  frustration
  intolerance
  mental confusion
  weakness
  depression
  learning disabilities
Also:
  alcohol intolerance
  nervousness
Some symptoms are simi-
lar to early stages of
diabetes:
  frequent passing of urine
  thirst
  hunger
  weight loss
  itching

Therapeutic Uses

Successful in some child
and adult diabetes
Diabetes of pregnancy
Maturity-onset diabetes
Reducing high blood
cholesterol
Some cases of
hypoglycemia (low blood
sugar)

Chromium cont.

Body Content

Adult content is between 5.2 and 10.4 mg, but there is wide geographical variation, e.g.:

Europe and North
America   6.00 mg
Africa   7.45 mg
Middle East   11.8 mg
Far East   12.5 mg

Incidence of diabetes and heart disease decreases with increasing chromium levels

Levels decline with age

Of a content of 5 mg, 2 mg is present in skin; 1.2 mg in bone; 0.9 mg in muscle, and 0.3 mg in fat.

Symptoms of Excess Intake

None have been reported. Low toxicity is the result of very poor absorption.

Hexavalent chromium is more toxic, but this is never used in supplements or found in foods

Chromium Supplements in μg per 100 μg

Chromium trichloride or chromic chloride (32.8); chromium acetate (22.7); and amino acid-chelated chromium (2)

Yeast is an excellent supplement, even more efficient because it contains chromium as GTF. GTF is 50 times more effective than other forms of chromium and is 20 times more readily absorbed. GTF from yeast is 10 times more effective than chromium in foods such as liver, wheat germ, and seafoods.

Recommended Daily Intake

None available, but the US Food and Nutrition Board suggests a safe and adequate range of intake is 50-200 mg chromium daily, depending upon age

Chromium cont.

Body Turnover	Body Turnover cont.
Absorption from food is very poor and is between 3 and 10 percent. Only 1 percent of added chromium (as salts) is absorbed	When incorporated into yeast, chromium absorption increases to between 10 and 25 percent Excretion is in the feces and urine, where up to 10 μg can be lost daily

Cigarette smoking,   four main poisons are: acetaldehyde; cancer-producing substances (carcinogens); carbon monoxide; and nicotine.

Toxic effects of acetaldehyde, carbon monoxide, and nicotine are neutralized by vitamin B_1, vitamin C, and cysteine. Beta-carotene protects against carcinogens.

Heavy smoking can inactivate vitamin B_{12}, inducing pernicious anemia and eventually blindness. Treat with injections of hydroxocobalamin.

Cirrhosis,   a chronic progressive disease of the liver characterized by destruction of liver cells and overgrowth of connective tissue. Complementary vitamin treatment includes high doses of vitamin B complex plus fat-soluble vitamins A, D, E, and K to overcome excessive loss due to disease. Choline (up to 3,000 mg daily) may be needed to prevent fatty infiltration.

Citrovorum factor,   *see* folinic acid.

Claudication, intermittent,   pains in the calves induced by walking and due to narrowing of the leg blood vessels. Treated with vitamin E (400-600 IU daily).

Cobalamin,   *see* B$_{12}$ (vitamin).

Cobalt,   chemical symbol Co. Atomic weight 58.9. Widely
distributed in nature. Abundance in the earth's crust is
0.001-0.002 percent. Occurs as cobaltite, linnaeite, smaltite,
and erythrite. Essential trace mineral only as a constituent
of vitamin B$_{12}$. Ruminants have a requirement only for
cobalt, as the microorganisms in their rumens can incor-
porate the mineral into vitamin B$_{12}$. Other animals and
humans cannot do so, and a dietary source of the vitamin
is essential for health. Vitamin B$_{12}$ can only be synthesized
by microorganisms.

Body content of cobalt averages 1.1 mg. 43 percent of
this is stored throughout the muscle tissues; 14 percent
is in the bone; the remainder is distributed throughout the
other tissues, mainly in the liver and kidneys. Blood levels
vary over a wide range—from 0.007-0.036 μg cobalt per 100
ml whole blood in one study to 0.17-1.5 μg cobalt in
another. Most of the cobalt of blood is found in the red
blood cells rather than in the plasma.

Dietary intakes of cobalt depend upon the amount of
mineral in the soil and hence in the plants and animals that
thrive on that soil. Children in the US were found to have
diets containing 0.25-0.69 mg cobalt per kg food. In the
diets of adults, intakes were 0.30-1.77 mg cobalt per day.
Much lower levels are found in the diets of most Japanese
who eat only 0.01 mg daily. WHO sources recommend a
minimum daily intake of 1 μg cobalt to be absorbed.

Food sources rich in cobalt include fresh, green leafy
vegetables and some fish; poor sources are cereal and dairy
products. Typical values are (in μg per 100 g): vegetables—
20-60; scallops—225; cod—120; liver—15; kidney—25;
muscle meats—12; and dairy products—1-3. Some of the
cobalt in meat, fish, and dairy products is present in their
vitamin B$_{12}$ content and the rest is the mineral in some

other form. In vegetables and cereals, all the cobalt is in the other forms.

Functions of cobalt reside only in its presence in vitamin B_{12}. Many of the vitamin's functions are mediated through the cobalt portion of the molecule and they include: synthesis of DNA; production of red blood cells; synthesis of methionine; synthesis of choline; and synthesis of creatine. All of these involve transfer of active methyl groups from folic acid (B vitamin) to cobalt, and hence to a receptor substance. Other functions include the maintenance of myelin, the fatty sheath that insulates nerves, and the detoxification of cyanide introduced through food and tobacco smoke.

Deficiency of mineral cobalt is unknown, but deficiency of vitamin B_{12} causes pernicious anemia. This anemia cannot be treated with cobalt; it responds only to injections of the vitamin.

Therapy with cobalt has been used in the past to try and stimulate the bone marrow to produce more red and white blood cells, but there is no convincing evidence that it helps. It has also been used to reduce high blood pressure because of its action in causing dilation of blood vessels, but quantities of 50 mg oral cobalt chloride daily were required for periods up to 65 days.

Therapeutic forms include: cobaltous carbonate; cobaltous chloride; and cobaltous nitrate. These are usually added to animal feeds.

Food additives containing cobalt are no longer used. Once it was added during beer-brewing to improve the quality of the "head" of the glass. This practice led to toxic effects (see below) and the practice is no longer carried out.

Toxic effects of cobalt are highly unlikely with intakes from a normal diet. When used therapeutically in doses of 29.5 mg daily, side effects included goiter, hypothyroidism, and heart failure. Intakes of up to 17.7 mg daily by heavy beer drinkers who drank up to 12 liters of beer (cobalt content about 1.5 mg per liter) caused heart disease and death. Protein intake in these people was low; high-protein dietary levels are believed to protect against cobalt toxicity. Other toxic effects of cobalt noted in animals and humans include overproduction of the red cell, (polycythemia vera). In animals, high intakes (4-10 mg cobalt per kg body weight) can cause anemia, loss of appetite, and low body weight.

Cobaltous carbonate, provides 25.9 mg cobalt in 100 mg carbonate (as hexahydrate). A nutritional factor used in cobalt or vitamin B_{12} deficiency in ruminants.

Cobaltous chloride, provides 24.7 mg cobalt in 100 mg chloride (as hexahydrate). A nutritional factor used in cobalt or vitamin B_{12} deficiency in ruminants. Large amounts may lead to death in children. Toxic effects include skin flushing; chest pains; dermatitis; tinnitus (ringing in the ears); nausea; vomiting; nerve deafness; myxedemia; and heart faliure.

Cobaltous nitrate, provides 20.0 mg cobalt in 100 mg nitrate (as hexahydrate). A nutritional factor used in cobalt or vitamin B_{12} deficiency in ruminants. Has been used as a dietary supplement of cobalt in humans.

Cocoa, the powder supplies carotene, vitamin E, and some B vitamins, but is devoid of vitamin C. Carotene level is 40 μg per 100 g. Vitamin E content is 3.2 mg per 100 g. B vitamins present are (in mg per 100 g): thiamin (0.16); riboflavin (0.06); nicotinic acid (7.3); and pyridoxine (0.07). Folic acid level is 38 μg per 100 g.

Minerals

A rich source of sodium but even richer in potassium. An excellent provider of all minerals. The powder supplies (in mg per 100 g): sodium (950); potassium (1,500); calcium (130); magnesium (520); phosphorus (660); iron (10.5); copper (3.9); zinc (6.9); and chloride (460).

Coconut, supplies less vitamin E and fewer B vitamins than other nuts, but does contain some vitamin C. Desiccated coconut is richer in most vitamins than the fresh edible part. Vitamin E content of the edible part is 1.0 mg per 100 g; the desiccated variety is devoid of vitamin E. B vitamins present in fresh and desiccated coconut, respectively, are (in mg per 100 g): thiamine (0.03 and 0.06); riboflavin (0.02 and 0.04); nicotinic acid (1.0 and 1.8); pyridoxine (0.04 and 0.09); and pantothenic acid (0.20 and 0.31). Folic acid levels are 26 and 54 μg per 100 g for fresh and desiccated coconut, respectively. Vitamin C content of fresh coconut is 2 mg per 100 g, but there is none in the desiccated variety.

Coconut milk supplies traces of most of the vitamins that are in the flesh. Only traces of vitamin E are present. B vitamins present are (in mg per 100 g): thiamin and riboflavin (traces only); nicotinic acid (0.2); pyridoxine (0.03); and pantothenic acid (0.05). No folic acid or biotin have been detected. Vitamin C level is 2 mg per 100 g.

Minerals

Regarded as a good provider of potassium, magnesium, phosphorus, iron, copper, and zinc. A low-sodium food, the desiccated variety is richer in all minerals than the fresh nut. Mineral contents for fresh and desiccated coconut, respectively, are (in mg per 100 g): sodium (17 and 28); potassium (440 and 750); calcium (13 and 22); magnesium (52 and 90); phosphorus (94 and 160); iron (2.1 and 3.6); copper (0.32 and 0.55); zinc (0.5 (desiccated not measured));

sulfur (44 and 76); and chloride (110 and 220). The milk provides more calcium but less of other minerals.

Cod-liver oil,   a rich source of fat-soluble vitamins but completely devoid of the water-soluble variety. Provides (in mg per 100 g): vitamin A (18.0); vitamin D (0.21); and vitamin E (20.0).

Also contains polyunsaturated fatty acids known as eicosapentaenoic acid (EPA) (9.0 percent) and docosahexaenoic acid (DHA) (8.0 percent), which have essential roles in body metabolism. Total polyunsaturated fatty acids present are 23 g per 100 g oil.

Minerals

Contains the following minerals, in trace amounts only: sodium; potassium; calcium; magnesium; phosphorus; iron; copper; zinc; sulfur; and chloride.

Coffee,   all types are devoid of carotene and vitamin E. A rich source of nicotinic acid.

Ground, roasted coffee supplies (in mg per 100 g): riboflavin (0.20) and nicotinic acid (10.0). The quantity of nicotinic acid increases during the roasting process because it is liberated from a bound form. Dark-roasted varieties may contain 30 to 40 mg nicotinic acid per 100 g. No other vitamins have been measured.

Infused, ground coffee supplies much lower quantities (in mg per 100 g): riboflavin (0.01) and nicotinic acid (0.7).

Instant coffee (in dried form) is a very rich source of nicotinic acid at between 24.9 and 41.5 mg per 100 g. Riboflavin content is 0.11 mg per 100 g. Also contains (in mg per 100 g): pyridoxine (0.03) and pantothenic acid (0.4).

Decaffeinated coffee (in dried form) provides vitamin levels similar to ground, roasted varieties. Instant decaffeinated coffee has vitamin levels similar to instant coffee.

Minerals

Fairly low in sodium but very rich in potassium, calcium, magnesium, phosphorus, iron, copper, and sulfur. As a drink, all concentrations are reduced. The instant variety is richer in all minerals than ground coffee because it is concentrated.

Ground, roasted coffee (in mg per 100 g): sodium (74); potassium (2,020); calcium (130); magnesium (240); phosphorus (160); iron (4.1); copper (0.82); sulfur (110); and chloride (24).

Infused, ground coffee (in mg per 100 g): sodium (trace); potassium (66); calcium (2); magnesium (6); phosphorus (2); iron (trace); copper (trace); and chloride (trace).

Instant coffee (in mg per 100 g): sodium (41); potassium (4,000); calcium (160); magnesium (390); phosphorus (350); iron (4.4); copper (0.05); zinc (0.5); and chloride (50).

Colchicine, used to treat gout. Prevents the absorption of vitamins A and B_{12}.

Cold, a viral infection of the upper respiratory tract. Also known as coryza, rhinitis, and head cold.

Increase vitamin A intake during the period of illness. Treat with vitamin C at an intake of 1 g every four hours until relief is obtained, then gradually reduce over one week to 1 g per day; then take a 500 mg maintenance dose.

Minerals

Symptoms have been relieved by sucking lozenges containing 23 mg zinc as a zinc gluconate, every two hours while awake. In this trial, 20 percent of those who had had colds for less than three days lost their cold symptoms within 24 hours; those who sucked a placebo lozenge did not lose their symptoms. After a week, 86 percent of those who had taken zinc recovered; 50 percent of those taking placebo lozenges still had symptoms. Zinc tablets that are swallowed do not have any beneficial effect in relieving cold symptoms, so it is possible that the mineral has a direct action on the cold viruses in the mouth, nose, and throat, which stops their multiplication.

Cold sores, caused by a herpes virus. They begin as small, tender lumps on the lips, tongue, roof of the mouth, gums, or cheek, usually preceded by a tingling or itching sensation. The lumps usually develop into painful ulcerations that form a scab in about a week. Healing takes between ten days and three weeks. Cold sores may be prevented or treated with supplementary zinc. Studies indicate that 25-50 mg of elemental zinc daily is needed for therapy. Complementary vitamin C (500 mg daily) may also help. Zinc creams applied directly to a developed cold sore have been claimed to accelerate healing. The mineral apparently blocks reproduction of the virus, allowing natural healing to proceed. *See* cold.

Colitis, a chronic, inflammatory, and ulcerative disease of the colon. Drug treatment should be supplemented with a high-potency multivitamin preparation plus extra vitamin C and B_6 when on corticosteroids.

Collagen, the main protein of the connective tissues (skin, joints, and vital organs) throughout body. The starting material for the production of gelatin. The rate of wound healing depends upon the rate of production of collagen, itself dependent upon vitamin C.

Vitamin C (500 to 1,000 mg daily) is often given routinely to patients undergoing surgery and recovering from accidental injury, to accelerate the healing process.

Colon cancer, *see* cancer.

Constipation, persistent cases may respond to vitamin
B₁ (10 mg daily). Complete vitamin B complex is sometimes used to stimulate intestinal bacterial growth to
relieve constipation, particularly after antibiotic treatment.

Contraceptives, *barrier types,* such as condoms or dia-
phragms, with or without contraceptive creams or jellies,
have no known effect on vitamin or mineral requirements.

Intrauterine device (IUD). Excessive bleeding controlled by bioflavonoids (1,000 mg daily) or vitamin E (100
IU every other day). *See* Intrauterine devices.

Oral. Consist of synthetic estrogens and progestogens
that can increase requirements for certain vitamins. Supplementary vitamin B_6 (25-50 mg), vitamin B_{12} (5 µg), folic
acid (200 µg), vitamin E (100 IU), and vitamin C (100 mg)
are needed daily.

Convalescence, the stage after an illness often characterized by mild deficiency of vitamins, induced by low food
intake and by medications. Supplement with a general
multivitamin preparation plus extra vitamin C (500-1,000
mg) in illnesses due to infection, and in the postoperative
period.

Copper, chemical symbol Cu, from the latin word
cuprum. Atomic weight 63.5. An essential trace element
for humans, animals, and many plants.

Recommended Daily Intake	Therapeutic Uses
Should be at least 2 mg daily, which is met by most diets	Treating deficiency Anemia (rare) Rheumatoid arthritis

Copper cont.

Best Food Sources in mg per 100 g

Liver	8.0
Shell fish	7.6
Dried brewer's yeast	3.3
Olives	1.6
Nuts	1.4
Legumes	0.8
Cereals	0.7
Meat, fish, and poultry	0.3
Whole-grain bread	0.3
Dried fruits	0.3

Excretion

Copper stored in the liver is normally incorporated into bile from where it is secreted into the intestine, and hence excreted into the feces

Nonfood Sources

Processing and storage of food

Pesticides and fungicides left behind in the food

Copper containers

Copper pipes that carry water

Copper kettles

Functions

Acts as co-factor for many enzymes, including:
  natural coloring pigments that form in skin and hair
  those needed for skin healing
  those that protect against toxic agents
  those concerned with nerve impulses in the brain
  Blood formation, when it aids iron absorption and incorporation into hemoglobin
  In formation of healthy bones
  In developing resistance to infection

Medicinal Sources

Expectorant cough mixtures

Cough suppressant preparations

Decongestant preparations

Antialgae solutions in swimming pools

Copper cont.

Body Content

Adult content is between 75 and 150 mg. Half of this is contained in the skeleton and muscles. A further 10 percent is in the liver, with significant amounts in the brain, kidney, and heart. As an adult ages, copper decreases in the liver and that in the brain increases to the same concentration, but the significance of this is not known.

The livers of infants have copper concentrations ten times greater than those of adults. This acts as a store, since milk is not a rich source of the trace mineral.

Deficiency Symptoms

In infants: Failure to thrive
   Pale skin
   Diarrhea
   Depigmentation of hair and skin
   Prominent dilated veins in skin
In adults: Anemia

Deficiency Symptoms cont.

Water retention
Irritability
Brittle bones
Hair depigmentation
Poor hair texture
Loss of sense of taste

Deficiency Noted In

Malnourished children
Malabsorption problems
Infantile anemia
Premature babies
Children with Menkes' syndrome (unable to absorb copper)
Those living on highly refined diets
Anyone with prolonged diarrhea
Those taking excessive amounts of zinc, cadmium, fluoride, or molybdenum
Those on high phytic acid diets (*see* phytic acid)

Copper Supplements in mg per 100 mg

Copper amino acid chelate (2); copper gluconate (14); and copper sulfate (25.4).

Copper cont.

Symptoms of Excess Intake	*Symptoms of Excess cont.*
Although toxicity of copper is generally low, acute high-concentration poisoning can occur, giving rise to: nausea; vomiting; abdominal pain; diarrhea; diffuse muscle pains; and abnormal mental states leading to coma and	death. An inability to rid the body of copper can also occur in two hereditary diseases: Wilson's disease, and Indian childhood cirrhosis. Both need medical treatment to dispose of the excess copper.

Copper bangles, a traditional preventive and curative therapy for arthritis when worn on the wrist or ankle. It is generally believed that copper dissolves in the acid secretion of skin and is then absorbed in a form that can be utilized in the body. Blood levels of copper in arthritis are usually high, but the mineral is in a nonutilizable form. Confirmation that this hypothesis is true has come from studies indicating that fat-soluble copper salicylate (aspirin) complexes are absorbed through the skin. They are strikingly effective in reducing the inflammation of artificially induced arthritis in animals, and of the clinical condition in humans.

Corticosteroids, hormones produced by the adrenal glands from cholesterol. These, plus synthetic analogs (called steroid drugs), are used extensively in medicine at relatively high levels. They adversely affect certain vitamins and increase the requirements for vitamins B_6, C, and probably D. Needs are B_6 (25-50 daily in both sexes), C (500-1,000 mg daily), and D (400 IU daily). Zinc (15 mg daily) is also needed.

Cortisol, a natural corticosteroid. *See* corticosteroids.

Cortisone, a natural corticosteroid. *See* corticosteroids.

Coryza, a head cold. *See* cold.

Co-trimoxazole, an antibacterial agent. Impairs folic acid utilization.

Cramps, leg, when induced by exercise, is called intermittent claudication. Nocturnal (nighttime) cramps are treated with vitamin E (200 IU daytime, 200 IU before sleep) plus vitamin C (500 mg daily). Cramps due to restless leg syndrome are treated with vitamin E (400 IU daily).

Cream, shows seasonal variations in fat-soluble vitamins. Water-soluble constant levels are (in mg per 100 g): thiamin 0.03; riboflavin 0.12; nicotinic acid 0.64; pyridoxine 0.03; folic acid 0.004; pantothenic acid 0.30; biotin 0.0014; vitamin C 1.2; vitamin B_{12} 0.2 μg.

Light cream provides (per 100 g): vitamin A (0.14-0.2 mg); carotene (0.07-0.125 mg); vitamin E (0.4-0.5 mg); and vitamin D (0.08-0.16 μg).

Heavy cream contains approximately twice as many fat-soluble vitamins as light cream.

Minerals

A low-sodium food supplying good quantities of calcium, phosphorus, and potassium, with useful amounts of the trace minerals.

Light cream provides (in mg per 100 g): sodium (42); potassium (120); calcium (79); magnesium (6); phosphorus (44); iron (0.31); copper (0.20); zinc (0.26); and chloride (72).

Heavy cream provides (in mg per 100 g): sodium (27); potassium (79); calcium (50); magnesium (4); phosphorus (21); iron (0.20); copper (0.13); zinc (0.17); and chloride (46).

Whipping cream provides (in mg per 100 g): sodium (34); potassium (100); calcium (63); magnesium (5); phosphorus (27); iron (0.25); copper (0.16); zinc (0.21); and chloride (58).

Cretinism, a syndrome of dwarfism, mental retardation, and coarseness of the skin due to lack of thyroid hormone from birth. Also known as congenital hypothyroidism and juvenile hypothyroidism. May affect as many as 20 percent of the population in isolated areas of Nepal, the Andes, Zaire, and New Guinea. An iodine deficiency during fetal or early life may lead to cretinism, and cretins are often associated with particular areas where iodine is deficient in the soil and water supply.

Infants afflicted have a characteristic look: the tongue is enlarged, the lips are thickened, and the mouth hangs open and drooling. The face is usually broad and the nose flat. The feet and hands are puffy and the hands are spade shaped. They are dull and apathetic, have low body temperature, and suffer from constipation and other gastrointestinal complaints. Cretins may be large at birth but as they age, they have defective development and often remain as dwarfs when adult. Mentally, they range from mildly backward to severely retarded. If diagnosed early enough, iodine or thyroid hormone treatment reverses the condition. In most communities, the condition is soon recognized. Only in the more remote areas is it prevalent.

As well as lack of iodine in prenatal or early life, other causes of cretinism are: iodide transport defect; failure to convert iodides to the hormones; defective synthesis of thyroglobulin; absent or undeveloped thyroid; failure to respond to thyroid hormones at the cellular level; and failure of the gland to respond to thyroid-stimulating hormone (TSH). In all causes, the only treatment is to give oral thyroid hormone, usually thyroxine.

Crohn's disease, a generalized inflammatory disease of the small intestine and lower intestinal tract. Also known as regional enteritis. Drug treatment is complemented by high-potency multivitamin supplementation. Extra vitamin C and B_6 is also recommended when on corticosteroids.

Cyanocobalamin, *see* B_{12} (vitamin).

Cycloserine, an antibiotic. Reduces the availability of folic acid.

Cystic fibrosis, an inherited disease usually starting in infancy and typified by chronic infection of the respiratory system, pancreatic insufficiency, and susceptibility to heat. Infection needs increased vitamin C intake (up to 1,000 mg daily); pancreatic insufficiency leads to fat malabsorption so increased intakes of vitamin A (7,500 IU), vitamin D (400 IU), and vitamin E (250 IU) are needed daily.

Cysts, cystic disease of the breast, a benign condition, is the most common disease of the female breast, occuring in about 5 percent of middle-aged women. Pain or premenstrual breast discomfort is a frequent symptom and cysts may be tender, but more often the condition has no symptoms. Discovery is usually by palpation.

Once malignancy has been discounted, treatment, apart from surgery, may be two-fold:

1. Vitamin E, 600 IU daily for eight weeks should give clinical response;
2. Oil of evening primrose, 3,000 mg daily divided into three doses.

D

D, a fat-soluble vitamin. Occurs naturally as chole-calciferol (D_3), which is found only in foods of animal origin, and as ergocalciferol (D_2), which is produced by the action of light on yeast. Isolated in 1930 from cod-liver oil by Dr. E. Mallanby. Known as the sunshine vitamin.

1 microgram vitamin D = 40 international units (IU).

Best Food Source in µg per 100 g

Cod-liver oil	210.00
Kippers	210.00
Mackerel	17.50
Canned salmon	12.50
Sardines	7.50
Tuna	5.80
Eggs	1.75
Milk	0.03

Nonfood Source

Substantial amounts are produced in the skin by the action of sunlight
Three hours of summer sun on the face produces 10 µg vitamin D. Winter light produces 1 µg. Whole body exposure needs less time

Functions

Only as 1.25-dihydroxy-vitamin D, which is produced by the liver and kidneys from dietary or skin vitamin D. The active form, 1.25-dihydroxy D, promotes absorption of calcium and phosphate from food. Causes release of calcium from the bone.

Deficiency Caused by

Lack of meat, poultry, fish, and dairy products in diet
Lack of exposure to sunshine
When sun exposure is sufficient, dietary sources are not required

Vitamin D cont.

Deficiency Results In

In children:
  Rickets
In adults:
  Osteomalacia
In both: Softening of the
  bones due to lack of
  calcium phosphate

Deficiency Symptoms

In children: Unnatural
  limb posture
  Excessive sweating of
    head
  Delayed ability to stand
  Knock-knees or bowlegs
In adults: Bone pain
  Muscular weakness
  Muscular spasms
  Brittle, easily broken
    bones

Therapeutic Uses

Rickets
Osteomalacia
Osteoporosis
Rheumatoid arthritis

Recommended Daily Intake

Should be at least 10 μg
  (400 IU). *See* recom-
  mended daily intakes.
Supplement should not
  exceed 10 μg daily

Symptoms of Excess Intake

The most toxic of the
vitamins:
  Loss of appetite
  Nausea
  Vomiting
  Constant thirst
  Head pains
In children: Thinness
  Irritability
  Depression

Stability in Foods

Very stable. *See* losses in
food processing

Deafness, may be due to otosclerosis, a disease where
the bones of the middle ear become fused and unable to
vibrate and transmit sound. Common in the elderly, where
it may be related to long-term vitamin A deficiency. Can-

not be cured by vitamin therapy but adequate intakes throughout life may prevent it.

Decubitus ulcer, *see* bedsores.

Deficiency, a lack of sufficient vitamin intake. For example, four stages of vitamin deficiency identified in volunteers deprived of B₁ were:

1. No obvious changes in first 5-10 days, but vitamin stores depleted.
2. Altered cell metabolism after 10-60 days.
3. Clinical defects after 30-180 days, with nonspecific symptoms like weight loss, appetite loss, malaise, insomnia, increased irritability.
4. Anatomical defects from 180 days on, leading to specific signs of gross deficiency that if untreated may have led to death.

Can be caused by: poor nutrition; poor cooking methods; overprocessing and overrefining of foods; habits like smoking tobacco and drinking alcohol; stress; medications; contraceptive pill; malabsorption; and inefficient utilization.

Deficiency causes, many factors can give rise to mild vitamin deficiency and most individuals are prone to the influence of one or more.

Apathy: Often a characteristic of people living alone, particularly those who have lost a spouse and those who no longer have a family to look after. There is little incentive to prepare adequate meals. Meals are often monotonous and less and less nourishing. Impaired digestion may be associated with the apathy and this further lowers the nutritional status. Often seen in the elderly, in middle-aged people living alone in a one-room apartment with poor cooking facilities, or in teenagers and students living alone for the first time.

Dental problems: Poor dentition due to loss of teeth or dental decay can make eating uncomfortable, leading to aversion to foods such as salads, meat, and vegetables. An unbalanced diet results, which can lead to poor nutrition, particularly in the elderly.

Excessive losses: Water-soluble vitamins tend to be excreted in the urine and sweat. Physical exertion can thus lead to excessive excretion of vitamins. Hot climates may have a similar effect.

Food fads: Often lead to deficiencies in the young when foods of high-caloric intake but low vitamin content, e.g., soft drinks, potato chips, candy, and cookies, are popular and make up the main part of the diet. Old people, too, are not immune to similar nutritional fads. Food fads of pregnancy are well known and very variable, but it has been suggested that they may be satisfying a demand for specific nutrients.

Food taboos: Often religious in origin, but may also stem from public health ideas, e.g., avoiding meat prone to parasitic infection. Complete avoidance of food as in fasting may be beneficial as an occasional habit, but extensive fasting can be harmful. Water-soluble vitamins may be depleted and body protein is known to be broken down as well as body fat.

Specific foods that are nutritionally sound may be avoided because of unfounded superstitious beliefs that they do harm. Many such beliefs exist in Africa. In Bolivia, any food containing animal blood is believed to make children mute; in Pakistan, buffalo milk is believed to make a person physically strong but mentally dull. Most affected are pregnant women who often suffer nutritionally from such beliefs during a period when their diet should be sound.

Individual requirements: Minimum daily requirements for vitamins are based on average intakes of a population or are an extension of animal studies applied to humans. Experiments indicate that individual animals of the same species can vary in their vitamin requirements as much as five-fold. It is likely that humans vary also, so that two people on a similar diet can show a wide variation in blood levels of vitamins, which may also reflect requirements.

Infections: Are more likely in those suffering from malnutrition, particularly among children. Infections can also aggravate malnutrition (e.g., by reducing the appetite) and in turn malnutrition weakens resistance to infection. The infections most likely to occur in malnourished children are bacterial (e.g., tuberculosis), viral (measles, which can be a killing disease in malnutrition), and parasitic. Deficiencies of vitamins A and C are most likely to predispose to infections. Keratomalacia, the end stage of vitamin A deficiency resulting in blindness, is often aggravated by a concurrent infection in children. Vitamin deficiency may lower resistance to infection by: reduced antibody formation; reduced activity of bacterial- and viral-engulfing white blood cells (phagocytes); decreased levels of protective enzymes (e.g., lysozyme in tears); and reduced integrity of the skin and mucous membranes (the wet surfaces of the body).

Infections can precipitate gross deficiencies of vitamins in those on a poor diet and even mild deficiencies in those on an adequate diet. For example, children with meningococcal meningitis, diarrhea, tuberculosis, measles, and other acute infections can develop vitamin A deficiency severe enough to cause them to develop keratomalacia and eventually blindness. Fever can cause symptoms of scurvy, due to vitamin C deficiency, in children even when there are apparently adequate intakes of the vitamin. Gross signs of thiamin deficiency can be precipitated in borderline cases following infections; diarrhea and beriberi result.

Lactation: Little is know about precise vitamin requirements in the woman who is breast-feeding her child, and ignorance is reflected in the varying figures suggested by different authorities. All agree, however, that increased vitamin intakes during this period are desirable.

Suggested vitamin intakes are given in Figure 12.

Figure 12: Suggested vitamin intakes during lactation

	Australia	Canada	New Zealand	UK	US	WHO/ FAO
Vitamin A μg	1,200	1,400	1,200	750	1,200	1,200
Vitamin D μg	10	5.0	10	10	10	10
Vitamin E mg	—	8.0	13.5	—	11	—
Vitamin C mg	60	60	60	60	100	60
Thiamin mg	1.3	1.5	1.3	1.1	1.6	1.1
Riboflavin mg	1.7	1.7	2.5	1.8	1.7	1.7
Nicotinic acid mg	22	25	21	21	18	18.2
Pyridoxine mg	3.5	2.6	2.5	—	2.5	—
Folic acid μg	300	250	400	300	500	500
Vitamin B_{12} μg	2.5	3.5	4.0	2	4.0	4.5

Malabsorption: Usually affects the fat-soluble vitamins, but pernicious anemia is due solely to an inability to absorb the water-soluble vitamin B_{12}.

Diseases, such as sprue, idiopathic steatorrhoa, pancreatic diseases, lack of bile production, etc., can cause generalized malabsorption of fats, which include the fat-soluble vitamins and thus can give rise to deficiency. Lack of intrinsic factor, needed to complex with vitamin B_{12} as a prerequisite for absorption, prevents the assimilation of the vitamin.

Malabsorption problems are medical conditions that are the province of the medical doctor and unsuitable for self-treatment.

Medications: The most common vitamin deficiency is that of B complex during antibiotic therapy. It is essential to supplement with the whole of the vitamin B complex for any ●tibiotic taken for more than three days. Pyridoxine is particularly vulnerable during drug therapy, but especially with corticosteroids, oral contraceptives, isoniazid, and penicillamine. *See* the entries for the individual drugs.

Other food nutrients: May affect the needs for certain vitamins. For example, high-polyunsaturated fatty acid intake (as in vegetable oils) requires high vitamin E levels to accompany it; thiamin intake is increased when high carbohydrate levels are part of the diet; and high protein intake requires more pyridoxine to be taken at the same time, as well as extra riboflavin. Less riboflavin is retained when protein intake is low.

Leucine is an amino acid that in high concentration requires extra nicotinic acid. Millet is a food with high-leucine content that is a significant part of the diet in India, but nicotinic acid intake does not always parallel that of the grain and deficiency of the vitamin can be induced.

Avidin is a protein unique to raw egg white that combines with and inactivates biotin. Cooking the egg white destroys avidin and thus prevents the inactivation of the vitamin.

Some raw fish contain the enzyme thiaminase, which destroys thiamin. Where raw fish is part of the staple diet, as in the Far East, thiamin deficiency can be induced. Some bacteria, e.g., *Bacillus thiaminolyticus*, can break down thiamin. Some 3 percent of Japanese are afflicted with this infective organism and show signs of mild thiamin deficiency.

Other vitamins: Excessive intakes of one vitamin may induce deficiency of another. Occurs mainly in animal experimentation, but one established case in humans is where an excess of folic acid can cause a deficiency of vitamin B_{12}. In lambs with a just-adequate intake of vitamin D, rickets can be induced by feeding high levels of carotene.

A deficiency of one vitamin can also induce a deficiency of another, e.g., vitamin C is needed to convert folic acid to its active form, folinic acid. In the absence of vitamin C, folic acid cannot be activated and anemia results. High intakes of folic acid in humans can mask a deficiency of vitamin B_{12}. Lack of folic acid gives rise to an anemia similar to that caused by lack of vitamin B_{12}. However, vitamin B_{12} deficiency also causes nerve degeneration in the spinal column. If only the anemia is being monitored, treatment of B_{12} deficiency with folic acid may appear to cure the anemia. The nerve degeneration is not affected and progresses until it becomes irreversible. Hence the importance of diagnosing whether anemia is due to folic acid or vitamin B_{12} deficiency, because the two vitamins function together in the production of normal red blood cells.

Parasitic infections: Specifically produce vitamin B_{12} deficiency. The parasite responsible is fish tapeworm, which utilizes dietary vitamin B_{12}, making it unavailable for absorption.

Physical activity: Increases the need for certain vitamins, particularly those concerned with stress (the vitamin B complex), energy requirements (thiamin), and muscle action (vitamins C and E). If increased levels are not supplied, mild deficiency can result. Recommended dietary intakes for men (20 to 26 years) in three different countries are given in Figure 13. *See also* athletes.

Poor diet: A poor selection of foods coupled with bad cooking methods, overprocessing, and overrefining can give rise to deficiency of vitamins. *See* losses in food processing.

Poor digestion: Can be caused by: defective mastica-

Figure 13: Recommended vitamin requirements for men aged 20-26 years

		UK	West Germany	USSR
Thiamin mg	Sedentary	1.0	1.7	1.8
	Moderately active	1.2	2.2	2.0
	Active	1.3	2.5	2.5
	Very active	1.3	2.9	3.0
Riboflavin mg	Sedentary	1.6	1.8	2.0
	Moderately active	1.6	1.8	2.5
	Active	1.6	1.8	3.0
	Very active	1.6	1.8	3.5
Nicotinic acid mg	Sedentary	8	14	12
	Moderately active	8	16	15
	Active	8	18	20
	Very active	8	20	25
Vitamin C mg	Sedentary	30	75	60
	Moderately active	30	75	70
	Active	30	75	100
	Very active	30	75	120

tion of the food in the mouth; reduction of volume and acidity of gastric secretions; reduction of digestive enzymes in pancreatic, liver, and intestinal secretions; and reduction of bile secretion. Vitamins are liberated as food is digested, so when this is inefficient, they do not become available for absorption.

Pregnancy: Many studies indicate marked reductions in blood levels of vitamin A, nicotinic acid, pyridoxine, vitamin B_{12}, folic acid, and vitamin C in pregnant women.

Most comprehensive studies were on pyridoxine and it has been concluded that pregnant women need 10 mg of the vitamin daily to maintain normal metabolic functions, compared with only 2 mg for nonpregnant women.

Folic acid is the most common deficiency. Recommended intakes during pregnancy are given in Figure 14.

Figure 14: Recommended vitamin requirements during pregnancy

	Australia	Canada	New Zealand	UK	US	WHO/ FAO
Vitamin A μg	750	900	750	750	1,000	750
Vitamin D μg	10	5.0	10	10	10	10
Vitamin E mg	—	7.0	13.5	—	10	—
Vitamin C mg	60	50	60	60	80	60
Thiamin mg	1.2	1.2	1.2	1.0	1.4	1.0
Riboflavin mg	1.5	1.5	2.5	1.6	1.5	1.5
Nicotinic acid mg	19	15	18	18	15	16.8
Pyridoxine mg	2.6	2.0	2.5	—	2.6	—
Folic acid μg	400	250	500	300	800	600
Vitamin B_{12} μg	3.0	4.0	4.0	2	4.0	5.0

Rapid growth: The growing child needs vitamins for the growth process as well as for normal metabolism. Most studies have been carried out in animals, when it was established that optimum levels of vitamins rather than adequate intakes were required to ensure maximum growth. However, most authorities agree that the need in children is relatively higher than that in adults when worked out on a body-weight or food-intake basis.

Slimming diets: When undertaken without professional advice reduced food and caloric intake may not supply the minimum requirements for vitamins. These, apart perhaps from thiamin, are required for health irrespective of calories in the diet. A reduction of calories from 2,500 to 1,000 per day, which most slimming diets supply, is therefore also likely to reduce the vitamin intake by a similar factor. If 2,500 calories are supplying barely the minimum needs for vitamins, deficiency must result if calories are reduced to 1,000. All slimming regimes should include a good general multivitamin-multimineral preparation daily as insurance against deficiency. This may also prevent the tiredness often associated with slimming diets.

Stress: Any stressful situation increases the requirements for some vitamins, notably the B group, C, and E. If increased amounts are not taken in the diet, mild deficiency may result. Quantities required may be two, three, or even five times the normal intakes. *See also* stress; athletes.

Deficiency groups,   it is now recognized by some authorities that certain segments of the population may be at risk of being deficient in vitamins and minerals and would benefit from supplementation. In most cases, a general, multivitamin-multimineral preparation supplying the minimum daily requirements is sufficient when taken regularly. For the reasons for lowered intake in these groups, *see* deficiency causes.

Groups at risk of deficiency are:

1. Pregnant women. *See* deficiency causes: Pregancy.
2. Nursing women. *See* deficiency causes: Lactation.
3. Women of childbearing age who may need supplementary iron. Simultaneous supplementation with vitamin C will ensure efficient absorption of the mineral, in the proportion 100 mg vitamin to 10 mg iron.
4. Those who embark on a weight-reducing diet without professional advice. *See* deficiency causes: Slimming diets.
5. Those who eat nutritionally inadequate snacks or foods that may have been overcooked or kept for long periods, thus losing most of their content of labile vitamins. *See* deficiency causes: Poor diet.
6. Children and adolescents in winter, and housebound adults who may not get sufficient vitamin D from sunlight falling on the skin. In the absence of sufficient dietary vitamin D, that produced in the skin becomes the main source of supply of the vitamin.

7. Children and adolescents who, because of fads, do not have a properly balanced diet. *See* deficiency causes: Food fads.

8. Those convalescing from an illness who have ground to make up in their nutrition. Deficiency of vitamins in convalescents is caused by: low intake of food during illness; effect of medications and infection, if it is present. *See* deficiency causes: Infections; Medications.

9. The elderly and others who, through various disabilities or apathy, fail to prepare balanced meals. *See* deficiency casues: Apathy; Dental problems; Poor digestion.

10. Those who live alone and often do not take the trouble to prepare fresh or adequate meals.

11. Athletes in training and those in physically active occupations. *See* athletes; deficiency causes: Physical activity.

Deficiency symptoms, specific symptoms and signs exist for most of the vitamin deficiencies, particularly when the vitamin level is seriously reduced. At this stage a medical practitioner should be consulted. However, mild abnormalities that could be associated with a less serious deficiency of a vitamin are now being recognized in certain segments of the population. In this respect, certain areas of the body provide useful information and, with proper interpretation, usually coupled with physical examination and medical history, can indicate poor nutrition. The more obvious areas are the skin, the mouth, and the eyes, but some symptoms of the gastrointestinal tract and the nerves can become apparent in the individual affected. Changes in the blood, the blood vessels, the heart, the bones, and the reproductive system associated with vitamin deficiency require more sophisticated diagnostic techniques that are best left to the medical practitioner.

The skin

Much of what is known about the effects of vitamin deficiencies has come from animal studies and these do not always translate to humans, but skin problems often respond to vitamin A.

Vitamin A: Hard, stippled skin, known as toad skin, has been attributed to vitamin deficiency, but it may also be attributed in part to polyunsaturated fatty acid deficiency. Small, raised lesions that are hard and deeply pigmented have been attributed to vitamin A deficiency. Many minor skin irritations and those like eczema, acne, and psoriasis often respond to vitamin A treatment, both topical and oral, which suggests that they are due, at least in part, to vitamin A deficiency.

Vitamin E: wounds that fail to heal, scar tissue that is consistently painful, or striae that will not disappear may be associated with vitamin E deficiency.

Vitamin K: Purple patches under the skin (known as purpura) may reflect a prothrombin deficiency, which in turn may result from lack of vitamin K.

Vitamin C: Small effusions of blood beneath the skin, known a petechiae, scattered in a diffuse manner over various skin areas, are characteristic of vitamin C deficiency. Hardened pimples that appear over hair follicles, particularly on the calves and buttocks, may indicate vitamin C deficiency. The hairs either fail to erupt or take on a spiral shape.

Pyridoxine: Deficiency causes scaly, dry skin, excessive looseness, and hence loss of body hair. Excessive secretion of the sebaceous glands, known as seborrhea, is seen about the eyes, nose, lips, and mouth, sometimes extending to the eyebrows and ears. Redness of the moist surfaces of the body is also a sign of pyridoxine deficiency. Scaly, pigmented dermatitis sometimes occurs around the neck, forearms, elbows, and thighs.

Riboflavin: Typical skin lesions include cracking of the lips and angles of the mouth, known as cheilosis; seborrhea of the nose and lips; scrotal and vaginal dermatitis; mouth and tongue ulcers.

Nicotinic acid: Gross deficiency causes pellagra, where the initial change is a temporary redness like sunburn. This clears to produce a more severe coloration in the form of deep red spots that coalesce to form a dark red or purple eruption, followed by scaling and loss of skin. Face, neck, hands, and feet are most affected, sometimes with concomitant edema and ulceration. Usually clearly defiend, rough patches on the hand are termed "pellagrous glove".

Patothenic acid: In animals deficiency symptoms are graying of the hair and ulceration of the skin, but there is no evidence that human beings show similar signs. "Burning feet" syndrome on soles of feet may be a nervous system rather than skin deficiency symptom. Some skin lesions like those noted with riboflavin deficiency have responded to pantothenic acid therapy, suggesting they are more likely due to multivitamin deficiency.

Biotin: A localized, scaly, shedding dermatitis is a symptom of deficiency in infants.

The mouth

Lesions of the mouth include those of the lips and are accepted as specific in some cases for certain deficiencies.

Riboflavin: A sore tongue with cracking of the lips and angles of the mouth, sometimes accompanied by intractable mouth ulceration, are features of deficiency. The tongue is magenta-colored with deep fissures and raised pimples (papillae).

Nicotinic acid: The tongue is swollen and the red color of raw beef. Deficiency produces inflammation of the gums, inflammation of the mouth, and an inflamed tongue.

Pyridoxine: Deficiency is characterized by cracking of

the lips and corners of the mouth, and inflammation of the tongue. Symptoms may be due to generalized B complex deficiency rather than specifically pyridoxine.

Vitamin B_{12}: The smooth, sore tongue associated with deficiency is almost diagnostic, since it is usually a feature of pernicious anemia.

Vitamin C: In a severe deficiency, there are bleeding gums, inflamed gums, and a loosening of the teeth. Small localized hemorrhages appear in the mouth.

Biotin: In infants suffering from the specific dermatitis associated with deficiency, there is also rawness of the surface of the mouth.

The gastrointestinal tract

The digestive tract can be affected by vitamin B complex deficiency at any level.

Thiamine: Deficiency is characterized by diarrhea, accompanied by abdominal distension and stomach pains.

Nicotinic acid: Deficiency invariably gives rise to diarrhea.

Pantothenic acid: Paralysis of parts of the intestinal tract, including post-operative paralytic ileus, may be associated with deficiency. Symptoms are abdominal distress and distension, sometimes with the inability to move the bowels.

The eyes

Deficiencies can affect both sight and eye tissues.

Vitamin A: Specific symptom of deficiency is night blindness characterized by poor adaptation of the eye to low-intensity light conditions. Eye tissue is also thickened and dry, particularly that of the sclera (white of the eye) and conjunctiva (mucous membranes).

Riboflavin: The white of the eye (sclera) develops prominent redness due to blood vessels, and conjunctivitis (inflammation of the mucous membranes) is common in the lower lid. Feelings of grittiness in the eye and constant watering and failing vision are other symptoms of deficiency.

Thiamin: Most common symptom of deficiency in eye is dimness of vision not associated with a specific lesion of the eye. Other ocular signs include involuntary rhythmic movement of the eyeballs, known as nystagmus; eye muscle fatigue; paralysis of the eye with loss of visual acuity (acuteness or clearness).

Nicotinic acid: Symptoms are very similar to those associated with thiamin deficiency, suggesting they are multivitamin-deficient in origin.

Vitamin C: Hemorrhages inside the eye often appear before those on the skin.

Vitamin K: In the newborn, deficiency often induces hemorrhages in the retina.

The central nervous system

Deficiency of most of the B vitamins causes symptoms associated with the nerves.

Thiamin: Gross deficiency causes mental confusion leading to coma. Milder deficiency gives rise to nystagmus (involuntary rhythmic movement of the eyeballs) and sometimes mental confusion. Other mental symptoms include narration of fictitious experiences (confabulation) and polyneuritis (nerve inflammation). Nervous consequences include foot and wrist drop when motor nerves are involved.

Pyridoxine: In infants, deficiency has been found to produce convulsions due to inadequate level of gamma-aminobutyric acid (GABA) in the brain. In adults, the most usual symptom is generalized inflammation of the nerves (peripheral neuritis), characterized by tingling, numbness, burning pain, and loss of vibratory sensation.

Nicotinic acid: Early signs are peripheral neuritis (see

above) and encephalopathy (brain disease or inflammation). Later symptoms are due to progressive dementia characterized by apprehension, confusion, derangement, and maniacal outbursts.

Vitamin B$_{12}$: Symtoms of deficiency are pins and needles in the feet and hands, weakness in the limbs, leg stiffness, unsteadiness, lethargy, and fatigue. Delirium and confusion are seen in advanced cases. Tactile (touch) sensation is impaired and the reflexes are depressed.

Folic acid: The only mental deficiency symptom is psychosis characterized by mental derangement, in which the patient is confused, lacks ability to describe events, and is unaware of symptoms.

The blood

Various vitamin deficiencies give rise to anemias of different types. Symptoms of all anemias are similar and include paleness, tiredness, lethargy, breathlessness, weakness, vertigo, headache, tinnitus (ringing in the ears), spots before the eyes, drowsiness, irritability, amenorrhea, loss of libido, and sometimes low-grade fever. Occasionally gastrointestinal complaints and even heart failure may develop.

The particular type of anemia requires blood and sometimes bone marrow examination for correct diagnosis and must be left to medical practioner.

Hypochromic anemia: Characterized by red blood cells depleted of hemoglobin. May be caused by deficiency of pyridoxine or riboflavin. Sometimes complicated by small red blood cells, when it is known as microcytic hypochromic anemia.

Megaloblastic anemia: Characterized by excessive numbers of immature red cells in the blood that cannot function as oxygen carriers. May be caused by deficiency of folic acid or vitamin B$_{12}$.

Iron-deficiency anemia: Characterized by the inability

to produce hemoglobin because of lack of iron. If vitamin C is deficient, iron cannot be absorbed or incorporated into hemoglobin. Vitamin C deficiency also casues hemorrhage and this too may contribute to the anemia.

Hemolytic anemia: Characterized by unstable red blood cells that burst readily and have a short life. May be caused by Vitamin E deficiency in infants and adults.

The heart and blood vessels

The later stages of thiamin deficiency cause severely weakened heart muscles leading to circulatory failure. The heart is grossly enlarged. Vitamin B_6 deficiency may give rise to massive deposition of fats in the heart and blood vessels, known as atherosclerosis.

The bones

Changes in the bones due to vitamin deficiency can usually be detected by x-ray diagnosis and clinical diagnosis only. Some changes, such as those produced by deficiency of vitamin A, riboflavin, pyridoxine, and pantothenic acid, have been noted only in animals.

Vitamin C: Deficiency produces irregular calcification, but this is obvious only from x-ray examinations.

Vitamin D: Deficiency in infants causes rickets. The most obvious signs are: restlessness and inability to sleep; retarded ability to sit, crawl, or walk; and retarded closure and hardening of the skull bones due to lack of mineralization. The long bones fail to ossify and are unable to stand the weight of the child, so that they bend, leading to bowlegs and knock-knees. Pigeon-breast deformity is sometimes obvious. These changes are detected earlier in x-ray examination.

Deficiency of vitamin D in adults leads to osteomalacia, different from rickets because in the adult the bones are already formed. Demineralization occurs, rather than a failure to mineralize the bones. Bones affected are the spine, pelvis, and lower extremities. As the bones soften, the legs may become bowed, the vertebrae shorten (reducing the height), and the pelvic bones flatten.

The reproductive system

Vitamin deficiencies in most animal species induce changes in the reproductive organs and process. In females, fetal abnormalities sometimes resulting in abortion are symptoms of deficiency. No exact parallel is shown in humans, but there are scattered reports that vitamin B_{12} or vitamin E deficiency can produce sterility in males and miscarriage in females, which is reversible by appropriate vitamin therapy.

Deficiency tests, deficiencies of vitamins are usually determined by blood tests, but these are normally taken only in conjunction with clinical signs before a medical diagnosis of deficiency is accepted. Hair analysis cannot indicate the vitamin status of an individual, but it does give a clue to possible mineral deficiencies. Tests for vitamin deficiency are as follows:

Vitamin A: The level of this vitamin and of carotene can be determined in the blood, but neither measurement is a good indication of body status of these vitamins, since there is considerable storage of each in the body. Normal vitamin A concentration is between 15 and 60 μg per 100 ml blood serum; that of carotene is between 8 and 40 μg per 100 ml blood serum.

Vitamin D: The best diagnostic procedure to determine vitamin D deficiency is to estimate 25-hydroxycholecalciferol in the blood, but it is a specialized assay. Radiographic examination is a good way to detect rickets and osteomalacia in individuals, particularly x-ray pictures of the ends of the long bones. A third test is to measure the blood concentration of the enzyme alkaline phosphatase—

high levels may indicate rickets even before the x-ray changes prove it, but this test is not specific.

Vitamin E: There are three tests that can indicate a possible vitamin E deficiency. First, the measurement of blood serum tocopherol levels is simple and a reliable index of the circulating vitamin. Normal values lie between 1.0 and 3.0 mg per 100 ml blood serum.

The second test involves measuring the creatine content of the urine. Usually, this only appears when vitamin E is deficient. Creatine, usually excreted as creatinine, comes from the muscles and excess amount in the urine is indicative of muscle breakdown, which is a function of vitamin E deficiency.

The third test involves measuring the fragility of the red blood cells in the presence of hydrogen peroxide. Normal red blood cells are resistant to hydrogen peroxide, but when they are vitamin E-deficient they readily burst in the presence of the peroxide. Such tests are carried out on isolated blood.

Vitamin K: This is impossible to measure directly in the blood, but an indication of vitamin K status comes from assay of the levels of the clotting factors of the blood. The usual test is to measure prothrombin time, which gives a reasonable estimate of the vitamin K present. This test is also used to monitor the effect of the vitamin K antagonists like warfarin on the clotting of the blood when the drugs are being taken regularly.

Vitamin C: Possible deficiency can be indicated by a combination of blood plasma levels and the extent of urinary excretion of the vitamin. White blood cell levels of vitamin C are a better indication of blood levels than those of plasma, but the technique is time-consuming and is used more in research than as a standard technique. Normal blood levels of vitamin C are from 0.4 to 1.5 mg per 100 ml, but white blood cells contain from 25 to 38 mg per 100 ml. A level of below 7 mg per 100 ml white blood cells indicates a high risk of scurvy.

Normally only 13 to 15 mg of vitamin C is excreted daily in the urine; less than this indicates a possible deficiency. Confirmation usually comes from a saturation test, where multiple small doses of the vitamin are given over a period of time. Four to six hours afterward, the urine level of the vitamin is measured. If the individual is suffering from vitamin C deficiency, urine levels will not rise because the body saturates its tissues before excreting any. Hence the appearance of greater-than-normal amounts of the vitamin in the urine suggests the body is saturated and thus there is no deficiency. If none is excreted, vitamin C intakes are increased until the vitamin appears in the urine. Individuals can easily determine if they need vitamin C by carrying out the above test on themselves. A dose of 300 mg every four to six hours is taken in water. Vitamin C is assessed in the urine by adding a dye to a sample of the urine. If the dye is decolorized, vitamin C is present. A suitable dye is 2,4-dinitrophenylhydrazine, available impregnated into paper dipsticks. A mass screening test involves introducing a harmless blue dye, 2, 6-dichlorophenolindophenol, onto the tongue or just beneath the surface of the gum. The time taken for the dye to decolorize reflects the vitamin C status of the body—the longer the time, the more chance of deficiency of the vitamin. The test is simply a preliminary one and must be confirmed by other means before a diagnosis can be made of true vitamin C deficiency.

Thiamin: This can be measured directly in the blood and urine or indirectly by assaying an enzyme dependent on the vitamin for activity. Blood plasma levels are very low under normal conditions at concentrations between 0.5 and 1.3 μg per 100 ml. Measurement of the vitamin excreted in a 24-hour urine sample is a reliable indication of thiamin deficiency. It can be improved in sensitivity by measuring urinary excretion after taking an oral dose of the vitamin. If this stays low, there is a good chance that the individual is lacking thiamin.

Riboflavin: The usual criteria for determining if a patient is deficient in riboflavin are the medical history, clinical examination, and response to therapy with the vitamin. Red blood cell determinations are not easy because the normal level is very low, between 20 and 28 μg per 100 ml. For this reason an enzyme, glutathione reductase, that requires riboflavin, is usually assayed to indicate riboflavin levels.

Pyridoxine: The amount of pyridoxal phosphate present in the blood before and after an oral dose of the vitamin can be indicative of deficiency of the vitamin. Normal levels are at least 5 μg per 100 ml. A second test involves measuring xanthurenic acid in the urine. Normally this is less than 25 mg per day but, if an oral dose of the amino acid tryptophan is given to an individual who is deficient in pyridoxine, xanthurenic acid is excreted at levels greater than 50 mg per day. Pyridoxine is necessary to convert xanthurenic acid further in body metabolism, so in the absence of the vitamin, this compound builds up and is readily excreted.

Nicotinic acid: Blood measurements are not reliable because no test is sufficiently sensitive or specific. Assay is usually carried out by measuring the ratio of methyl-nicotinic derivatives to creatinine in the urine.

Vitamin B_{12}: Blood levels can be measured directly using the fact that some bacteria need the vitamin for normal growth. The extent of growth of the microorganism indicates the amount of vitamin B_{12} present in a sample of blood. Normal blood levels are 0.015 to 0.03 μg per 100 ml blood plasma. Levels below 0.01 μg per 100 ml are indicative of vitamin B_{12} deficiency.

The more usual test for deficiency involves radioactivity-labeled B_{12} to measure its absorption. *See* Schilling test.

Folic acid: A diagnosis of deficiency is usually assessed on the basis of a macrocytic anemia (in the absence of B_{12} deficiency), a megaloblastic bone marrow, and leukopenia (low white blood cell count). Blood serum levels can be measured, but are difficult and time-consuming on a routine basis. Normal values are 0.5 to 2.0 μg per 100 ml serum and 16 to 64 μg per 100 ml red blood cells. When the amino acid histidine is given orally, the quantity of formiminoglutamic acid (FIGLU) in the urine is increased dramatically in folic acid deficiency. This test is usually carried out in conjunction with the other tests mentioned above.

Pantothenic acid: Measurement of the pantothenic acid level in the blood alone is usually indicative of deficiency of this vitamin. Confirmation usually comes from measuring coenzyme A activity, which contains and is dependent upon pantothenic acid levels.

Dehydroretinol, *see* A_2 (vitamin).

Delta-tocopherol, *see* E (vitamin).

Dental caries, a gradual disintegration and dissolution of tooth enamel and dentin that eventually affects the pulp. Results from interaction of three factors: a susceptible tooth surface; acid-forming bacteria; and high sugar concentration. Increased intakes of selenium, usually in areas where soil selenium is high, can also induce dental caries in children.

Signs and symptoms include: sensitivity to heat and cold; discomfort after eating sugar-based foods; a darkened area between the teeth; and softened enamel or dentin, which becomes obvious on dental examination.

Prevention is a combination of good dental hygiene with

adequate intakes of fluoride and calcium. Supplementary fluoride level depends upon concentration of the mineral in the drinking water, but a daily total intake up to 1.0 mg should be aimed for. Dietary calcium intakes of between 500 and 700 mg per day are necessary in children; in adults 800-1,000 mg calcium may help prevent caries. Children who live in areas of high soil content of molybdenum have low incidence of dental caries, so this trace mineral too may prevent the condition from developing.

Deodorants, contains vitamin E as an antioxidant to retard degradation of the oxygen-containing components of sweat.

Deoxyribonucleic acids, DNA. Nucleic acids, constituents of all cells, essential for synthesis of protein and transmission of hereditary characteristics to offspring. The basis of life's processes. Lack of DNA production has profound effects on health, the first sign of which is megaloblastic anemia, and on the process of aging.

Vitamins essential for DNA synthesis are A, folic acid, B_6, B_{12}, E, and choline. Abnormal DNA metabolism may be related to cancer.

Depression, a mild variety can be related to vitamin B_6 deficiency induced by drugs, the contraceptive pill, or premenstrual syndrome (PMS). Treated with 25 to 50 mg B_6 daily or 50 to 100 mg from the tenth day of one menstrual cycle to the third day of the next when due to PMS or the contraceptive pill. When associated with drugs, at least 25 mg B_6 daily is needed.

Dermatitis, an inflammation of the skin characterized by redness, oozing, crusting, scaling, and sometimes blisters. May be related to lack of vitamin B complex, vitamin

A, or polyunsaturated fatty acids. Treated with: whole B complex at high potency; vitamin A, both oral and topical; and PUFA orally, especially safflower oil or oil of evening primrose.

Desiccated liver, concentrated beef liver powder that has been dried in a vacuum at a low temperature to conserve the original nutrient value of the liver.

Vitamins present are (in mg per 100 g): vitamin A (20 mg); thiamin (1.0); riboflavin (9.57); pyridoxine (2.31); nicotinic acid (44.9); pantothenic acid (24.1); folic acid (1.09); vitamin B_{12} (0.363); biotin (0.109); vitamin C (75.9); vitamin E (1.39); and carotene (5.08).

Dextriferron, an iron dextrin injection. Provides 100 mg iron in 5 ml dextriferron solution. May be injected directly into the bloodstream. Toxic effects include flushing, nausea, unpleasant taste, headache, abdominal pain, and transient diarrhea. Allergic reactions have been reported. Normally used when oral treatment is ineffective. Total dose of iron in this form over the whole treatment should not exceed 2 g.

Diabetes insipidus, a disorder induced by lack of production of vasopressin, causing excessive thirst and the production of large volumes of very dilute urine (up to 30 liters per day).

Diabetes mellitus, associated with high blood sugar level that persists long after meals because of lack of the hormone insulin. Long-term consequences are arteriosclerosis, heart disease, gangrene, and blindness that may be related to specific vitamin deficiencies. Increases the daily requirements for vitamin B_6 (25 mg), C (500 mg), E

(400 IU), and A (7,500 IU) (because diabetics cannot produce it from carotenes).

Minerals

Diabetics tend to lose more zinc in their urine than nondiabetics, suggesting that simple replacement of zinc by diet or by supplementation can be beneficial. Chromium also tends to be low in the blood of diabetics. This trace mineral is an essetial component of glucose tolerance factor, which controls blood sugar. Supplementation with this mineral, preferably in the organic form (i.e., in yeast or amino acid-chelated) can also be beneficial. Studies of people suffering from diabetic neuropathy have indicated that their blood magnesium levels are significantly lower than those of people who are not diabetics. Those with the most advanced and severe retinopathy had the lowest blood magnesium levels of all. The significance of these observations is not known, but every diabetic should ensure adequate intakes of all three minerals.

Diarrhea, specifically associated with severe deficiency of nicotinamide, but may respond to supplementation with whole vitamin B complex.

Dicumarol, an anticoagulant. Acts by inhibiting the action of vitamin K.

Dieting, regimens that reduce daily calorie intake to 1,000 calories or fewer will usually cause a concomitant decrease in the vitamins and minerals in the diet to levels below the recommended daily intake. A multivitamin and multimineral supplement is essential on a daily basis while dieting.

Digestive tract, the gastrointestinal tract. The part of the stomach and intestines where the digestion of food and absorption of nutrients takes place.

Nicotinamide (at doses up to 3,000 mg daily) has been used to treat malabsorption diseases of the intestine, such as sprue. Folic acid deficiency can destroy the lining cells of the small intestine and impair the absorption process. Lack of pantothenic acid can cause abdominal distension. Supplementary vitamin can reduce postoperative distension and nausea, including the effects of paralytic ileus. Thiamin promotes good digestion and better functioning of the digestive tract. Improves the muscles of the tract and can cure stubborn cases of constipation.

Vitamin C, when taken with aspirin, can prevent the gastric bleeding induced by the drug. Gastric ulcers can be prevented by high doses of vitamin E (up to 600 IU daily). Better results are obtained with vitamin A, which at high doses (150,000 IU daily for four weeks) has been used to treat gastric ulcers. There are indications that prevention of stomach cancer may be helped by vitamin A supplementation.

Disease resistance,   depends on the efficiency of the development of immune response, which requires adequate vitamin A, folic acid, vitamin B_{12}, vitamin C, pantothenic acid, and choline.

Diuretic drugs,   substances that promote the excretion of water and electrolytes by the kidneys. They are used in the treatment of congestive heart failure and of liver, kidney, or lung diseases that give rise to salt and water retention leading to edema. The disease process in these conditions is not usually affected by the removal of excess water, but the edema is relieved. Diuretics are used to: counter salt and water retention induced by other drug treatments; enhance the effects of drugs given to reduce high blood pressure; and treat drug overdosage or posioning by enhancing the excretion of the toxic materials. The groups of diuretics are:

1. Thiazides, which inhibit sodium and chloride reabsorption in the kidney and hence promote excretion of these minerals. As a side effect they also cause excretion of potassium to such an extent that supplementation with the mineral becomes essential, and lowered excretion or uric acid, which builds up in the joints to cause gout.

2. Frusemide type, which act by stimulating the excretion of sodium, potassium, and chloride by the kidney, thus increasing water loss. Side effects are the same as for thiazides.

3. Mercurial drugs, which act by inhibiting sodium reabsorption but at different sites in the kidney than other diuretics. Also promote potassium excretion, necessitating supplementation with the mineral.

4. Aldosterone inhibitors, which function by preventing the action of natural aldosterone. These are potassium-sparing diuretics, decreasing its excretion but promoting that of sodium and chloride. Normally used in conjunction with 1., 2., and 3. above, where they counteract the potassium-losing effects of these diuretics.

5. Carbonic anhydrase inhibitors, which act by decreasing the rate of carbonic acid formation and hence acid production. Kidney secretion of acids and reabsorption of bicarbonate and sodium are thereby inhibited. Normally used in conjunction with other diuretics to compensate for increased potassium loss.

6. Some diuretics that diminish the excretion of potassium, and thus are used with other diuretics to counter their potassium-depleting effects.

7. Caffeine, which is a weak diuretic and is found in coffee, tea, and other beverages.

8. Herbal diuretics, which are milder than synthetic drug varieties and are less likely to cause potassium loss.

In addition to the potassium loss induced by some of the above diuretics, calcium, magnesium, and zinc excretion may also increase under their influence.

Dolomite, mixed calcium and magnesium carbonates. Provides 21.7 mg calcium and 13.0 mg magnesium in 100 mg. Usual supplementary dose is 3-6 tablets daily, providing 295-591 mg calcium and 177-354 mg magnesium. Taken in the evening, four tablets have been claimed to help induce sleep. Also available as amino acid-chelated dolomite tablets, which are claimed to be better absorbed.

Drinking water, can vary from soft through various grades of hardness. Extent of hardness usually reflects the amount of calcium carbonate in the water, but some authorities express water in terms of total dissolved mineral content. Technically, water is regarded as hard if it contains more than 75 mg of dissolved solids per liter.

Adults drink on average about 2 liters of water daily and more than half of this can be tap water. This quantity in a hard-water area can therefore supply a significant proportion of the daily requirements of minerals—more than 10 percent of calcium, magnesium, copper, iron, and zinc, but all in the ionized inorganic form. A typical daily intake from hard tap water would be (in mg per day): calcium—250; magnesium—50; iron—3, silicon—20; zinc—2; copper—1; fluorine—1 or more; sulfur—0.05; iodine—0.04; chromium—0.01; lithium—0.01; and traces of arsenic, lead, and mercury. The benefits of hard water over soft water (from epidemiological studies) are: lowered mortality rates from cardiovascular disease; a protective effect of calcium in preventing absorption of toxic trace minerals; lower rates of sudden heart failure because of the protective action of the magnesium content; a possible connection between the low magnesium levels in tap water and sudden-infant-death syndrome; and lower death rates from coronary heart disease related to the high silicon content of hard water.

Studies have also showed that: waters containing significant amounts of fluoride also appear to protect against calcification of the aorta as well as dental caries; iodine from water may contribute up to 20 percent of daily requirements of the mineral; areas where tap water contains 2.6 mg chromium per liter had a higher incidence of coronary heart disease than those where the chromium content was 8.6 mg per liter; areas where the lithium content of tap water is high (8 mg per liter) have been reported to have a less aggressive and less competitive population than those where the lithium level is low. Other epidemiological studies indicate that in hard water areas, there are lower cardiovascular mortality rates, and decreased incidence of gastric and duodenal ulcers. Smaller number of admissions for mental diseases and a lower rate of violent behavior are reported in areas where the drinking water contains 100 mg per liter lithium. So many minerals are present in hard water that it is likely that its protective action against heart disease is a result of them all being presented together in meaningful amounts. No one has determined with certainty that any one is more significant than another.

Soft water can contain more toxic trace minerals than hard water because it tends to dissolve them from pumping machinery and pipes. All water can be contaminated by industrial effluents like cadmium and mercury or with nitrates from heavily fertilized agricultural land. Water containing high levels of nitrates or nitrites should not be used to make up formula for babies, since these minerals increase the risk of methemoglobinemia, a disease where the blood has a decreased capacity to transport oxygen.

Some waters are so hard that they have to be partially softened at the source before being fed into domestic and industrial water supplies. Domestic softening of water has many advantages for household functions, but the water should be kept separate from that used for drinking. The reasons are:

1. Hard water is more conducive to health.
2. The act of softening water with ion exchange resins exchanges the desirable calcium ions for the less desirable sodium ions. Softened water will therefore have an increased sodium content.

Drugs, may increase requirements for certain vitamins; may cause malabsorption of vitamins; and may interfere with the utilization and activation of vitamins. *See* the entries for individual drugs.

Dry skin, treatment is to increase intake of vitamin A (7,500 IU daily), PUFA (safflower oil, wheat germ oil, or oil of evening primrose, up to 3 g daily), and lecithin (up to 6 capsules daily). Treat affected area with vitamin E cream.

E

E, a fat-soluble vitamin. Known as d-alpha-tocopherol (natural) and available in supplements as d-alpha-tocopheryl acetate and d-alpha-tocopheryl succinate. Also available as synthetic dl-alpha-tocopherol. Natural forms also include d-beta-tocopherol, d-gamma-tocopherol, and d-delta-tocopherol, all less active than d-alpha-tocopherol. The word tocopherol comes from "tokos" birth and "phero" to bear. All four natural types are found in food.

Functions	Best Food Sources in mg per 100 g	
Antioxidant		
Reduces oxygen needs of muscles	Wheat germ oil	190.0
Anti-blood-clotting agent	Soybean oil	87.0
Blood vessel dilator	Corn oil	66.0
Maintains healthy blood vessels	Safflower oil	49.0
Protects:	Sunflower oil	27.0
polyunsaturated oils	Peanut oil	22.0
amino acids	Cod-liver oil	20.0
vitamin A	Roasted peanuts	12.0
thrombosis	Potato chips	11.0
atherosclerosis	Shrimps	6.6
thrombophlebitis	Olive oil	4.6
Increases "safe" cholesterol	Green leafy vegetables	2.3
Acts with selenium	Legumes	1.7
Promotes ability of white blood cells to resist infection	Tomatoes	1.4
	Meats	0.6
	Fruits	0.5
	Root vegetables	0.1

Symptoms of Excess Intake

Recommended Daily Intake

Should be at least 30 mg. *See* recommended daily intakes

Nausea
Diarrhea
Muscle weakness
Transient increase in blood pressure
Palpitations
Blood pressure increase is rare and does not occur in those already taking heart drugs

Stability in Foods

Unstable—*see* losses in food processing

Deficiency Caused By	Therapeutic Uses
Malabsorption of fats	Intermittent claudication
Consistent use of liquid paraffin	Cerebral thrombosis
Gastric or intestinal surgery	Coronary thrombosis
Alcoholism	Atherosclerosis
Cirrhosis of the liver	Arteriosclerosis
Obstructive jaundice	Varicose veins
Cystic fibrosis	Thrombophlebitis
Celiac disease (gluten sensitivity)	Menstrual problems
Excessive intake of polyunsaturated oils lacking the vitamin	Low fertility
Excessive oxygen (as in oxygen tents)	Skin ulcers
	Diabetic gangrene
	Nerve, joint, and muscular complaints
	Hemolytic anemia of the newborn
	Thalassemia
	Sickle-cell anemia
Deficiency Symptoms	Cystic breast disease
	Oxygen excess in premature babies
In children: Irritability	Direct application to:
Water retention	scar tissue
Hemolytic anemia	stretch marks
In adults: Lack of vitality	sunburn
Lethargy	burns
Apathy	scalds
Lack of concentration	
Irritability	
Decreased sexual interest	
Muscle weakness	

Eczema, an acute or chronic noncontagious itching, inflammatory disease of the skin. Can be due to essential fatty acids (EFA) deficiency, but more specifically that of gamma linolenic acid (GLA).

Infantile eczema may be due to the lack of GLA in cow's milk. Treat with oral oil of evening primrose (1,500 to 3,000 mg daily).

Atopic eczema may be due to allergic reaction. Shown to respond to oral oil of evening primrose (up to 3,000 mg daily).

Other vitamin treatment includes vitamin A (7,500 IU), vitamin C (up to 1,000 mg), and high potency vitamin B complex including inositol (500 mg daily).

Minerals

Some cases respond to oral zinc therapy. The usual dose is 50 mg elemental zinc three times daily that can be reduced to 25 mg of the mineral three times daily as the condition responds. More effective if taken in conjunction with daily vitamin C (1,000 mg) and essential fatty acids in the form of safflower oil or oil of evening primrose capsules (three 500 mg strength daily). Response can be slow, perhaps needing several months for complete remission.

Edema,   the retention of excessive water in the body. Not a disease in its own right but a symptom of some other condition. Has been claimed that high potencies of certain vitamins have a diuretic effect in removing excess water: vitamin C at levels of 1 g or more; vitamin E at levels greater than 500 IU; and pyridoxine at levels of 200 mg. May be effective for mild edema, e.g., in premenstrual syndrome, but most edema requires stronger acting drugs (medicinal or herbal).

Eggs,   a moderate source of all vitamins except vitamin C (*see* Figure 15). Egg white is devoid of all fat-soluble

Figure 15: Vitamin content of eggs

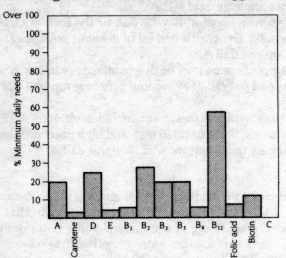

vitamins. The vitamin B complex occurs mainly in the yolk. A good source of all essential minerals.

The vitamins remaining after the various cooking methods for eggs are shown in Figure 16. The vitamins not mentioned show zero loss. The mineral content of eggs is shown in Figure 17.

Elderly, the largest single population group prone to mild deficiency of vitamins, particularly B complex, C, and K. Reasons include: aversion to salads and meats because of poor dentition; reluctance to shop frequently for a variety of food due to lack of mobility or emotional reasons; less care in preparing food due to loss of marital partner; undue reliance on refined carbohydrates and simple beverages as staple diet; dependence on restaurant

Figure 16: Vitamins remaining in eggs after cooking

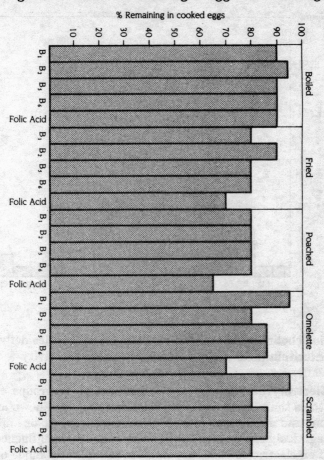

% Remaining in cooked eggs

or institutional cooking; and inefficient absorption of food micronutrients.

Most elderly persons will benefit from a daily multi-vitamin supplement with extra vitamin C (250-500 mg)

Figure 17: Mineral content of eggs

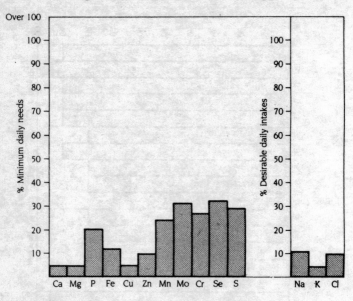

plus choline as phosphatidyl choline (3-6 capsules daily) or lecithin (5-15 g) daily to improve mental activity.

Electrolytes, electrically charged atoms or groups of atoms that exist in aqueous solution. They are known as ions and are divided into anions and cations. Anions are negatively charged (so-called because under the influence of an electric current they migrate towards the anode or positive end). Examples are: chloride (Cl^-); phosphate ($PO4^=$); bicarbonate (HCO_3^-); and sulfate (SO_4^-). Cations are positively charged (because under the influence of an electric current they migrate towards the cathode or negative end). Examples are: sodium (Na^+); potassium (K^+);

calcium (Ca^{++}); and magnesium (Mg^{++}). All metals may be regarded as cations when they are present as salts in solution within the body. Hydrogen when positively charged (H^+) confers acidity in solution.

The principle cation inside body cells is potassium (K^+), but magnesium (Mg^{++}) is also present. In fluids that bathe the cells (extracellular fluids), the principle cation is sodium (Na^+), but a small amount of calcium (Ca^{++}) is also present. Because ions can move freely across cell membranes, the maintenance of potassium inside and sodium outside cells is an energy-requiring process (*see* sodium pump). Maintaining this balance is very important to ensure the correct volume of water inside and outside the body cells. Imbalance can lead to dehydration or, conversely, edema (water retention). All positively charged cations are neutralized by an equal number of negatively charged anions so that the acidity of the fluid of body cells is maintained near neutral.

The transmission of nerve impulses and the contraction of muscles depend upon the correct electrolyte equilibrium at the cell membrane. Whenever a nerve or muscle is active, there is a charge of impulse that allows sodium and calcium to enter the appropriate cell; at the same time potassium and magensium move out of the cell. Once the impulse has passed, the ionic pump comes into play to restore the original equilibrium.

The nerves (called motor nerves) that actually stimulate muscle contraction are dependent on the correct calcium-magnesium ionic ratio in the blood. When calcium is lacking these nerves become oversusceptible to stimuli. The result is a condition called tetany, characterized by spasm and twitching of the muscles, particularly those of the face, hands, and feet.

Functions of electrolytes are: maintenance of water balance in the body (*see* sodium; potassium); maintenance of nerve-impulse transmission; maintenance of smooth muscle contraction; maintenance of acid-base (or alkali) balance of the body (*see* acid-base balance); and participation in some enzymatic and hormonal reactions.

The presence of an electrical charge (either positive or negative) on a mineral changes its fundamental properties.

Sodium (Na): As a pure metal is highly reactive, being violently decomposed by water, producing caustic soda and hydrogen, which can ignite spontaneously. As the cation sodium (Na^+), it is perfectly stable in water and exists as such in salt solutions and within the body.

Potassium (K): Also reacts violently with water, producing caustic potash and hydrogen. As the cation potassium (K^+), it is perfectly stable and exists as such in the body.

Calcium (Ca): Reacts with water but less violently than sodium or potassium. As the cation calcium (Ca^{++}) with two positive charges, it is present to a small extent in body fluids as a stable substance necessary for nerve-impulse transmission, muscle contraction, and clotting of the blood.

Magnesium (Mg): As a pure metal reacts only very slowly with water and is far more stable than sodium, potassium, and magnesium. Heat causes spontaneous ignition with a blinding light, which is why it was once used in flash photography. As the cation magnesium (Mg^{++}), it carries two positive charges, which stabilize the mineral for its functions within the body.

Phosphorus (P): Is a very reactive substance that ignites spontaneously at temperatures above 86°F (30°C). As the free metal, it is highly toxic, causing gastrointestinal irritation, liver damage, skin eruptions, circulatory collapse, coma, convulsions, and death with as little as 50 mg. On the skin, it causes severe burns. When combined with oxygen to form phosphate (PO_4) and in its anionic form phosphate ($PO_4^=$), it is innocuous and performs its functions within the body, as insoluble calcium phosphate in the bones and teeth and as ionic phosphate in body fluids.

Chlorine (Cl): Is a highly dangerous, yellow gas with a suffocating odor. As the charged atom chloride (Cl⁻), it comprises half of common salt and acts within the body as an important anion that neutralizes the cations sodium and potassium.

Embolism, an obstruction or occlusion of a blood vessel, especially an artery, by a transported clot. *See* blood clot.

Endurance, is increased by vitamin E. Optimum daily intake is 100-150 IU for a training period of 1.5-2.0 hours and 250-300 IU for a training period of 3-4 hours. In racehorses, daily intakes of 5,000-10,000 IU vitamin E have increased performance and calmed nervous animals.

Enteritis, a regional condition. *See* Crohn's disease.

Epilepsy, convulsive seizures. Large amounts of folic acid may neutralize the action of anticonvulsive drugs, particularly phenytoin.

Estrogen Replacement Therapy (ERT), *see* Hormone Replacement Therapy.

Etretinate, a vitamin A-related, synthetic derivative of retinoic acid used in treating psoriaisis and other skin disorders by the oral route.

Side effects include dryness of the mucous membranes and hair loss. Teratogenic (causing an abnormal fetus), so pregnancy must be avoided during use. Use only under medical supervision.

Exophthalmia,   the abnormal extrusion of the eyeball. Also known as popeyes. A symptom of Graves' disease due to excessive production of thyroid hormones.

Extrinsic factor,   *see* B_{12} (vitamin).

Eyes,   the sight process depends upon adequate vitamin A (2,500 IU daily). Bloodshot eyes are prevented by vitamin B_2 (10 mg daily). Heavy smoking causes tobacco amblyopia (reduced vision) due to the inactivation of vitamin B_{12}.

F

Farnoquinone,   *see* K_2 (vitamin).

Fatigue,   mental or physical tiredness that may follow prolonged or intense activity, or tiredness that cannot be associated with any measurable medical cause. Can produce tearfulness, depression, and irritability. An early sign of a deficiency of: pantothenic acid; thiamin; vitamin C; or vitamin E. May be associated with a generalized mild deficiency of vitamins. Treat with a multivitamin preparation. If there is no improvement after one month, seek medical advice.

Minerals
Studies indicate that in the absence of any other cause fatigue may be associated with mild deficiency of magnesium and potassium. Supplementation with these minerals is more likely to help in cases of tiredness due

to muscle fatigue. Studies indicate that taking extra quantities of magnesium (500 mg daily) and potassium (1,500 mg daily) overcame waking tiredness in a high proportion of individuals suffering from chronic fatigue. Potassium was found to be best taken as increased intakes of fresh fruits and vegetables, dried fruit, and vegetable and fruit juices, as part of the diet rather than as tablets. Fatigue caused by lack of iron is usually associated with anemia. *See* anemia.

Fats, complexes of fatty acids, both polyunsaturated and saturated, and glycerine. Hard fats usually contain mainly saturated and mono-unsaturated fatty acids (e.g., fats of animal origin); oils usually contain mainly poly-unsaturated with some monounsaturated fatty acids (e.g., vegetable oils). Hard margarines are mainly saturated and monounsaturated fatty acids; soft margarines contain more polyunsaturated fatty acids.

All fats and oils of whatever origin provide 9 kilo-calories per g. Dietary fats in the Western world provide about 40 percent of total calorie intake. Most authorities now recommend reduction to between 25 and 35 percent of total calorie intake. Some suggest replacement of saturated fats in the diet by polyunsaturated fats, by switching from animal fats to vegetable oils. High polyun-saturated fat intake requires a concomitant increase in vitamin E.

High blood fats can be reduced with vitamin E (400 IU), vitamin C (500 mg), and soy lecithin granules (15 g) daily. Lecithin provides 120 kilocalories in 15 g that must be counted against fat intake. High blood fats associated with high-fat intake are regarded as increasing the chances of developing cancer, gout, coronary thrombosis, stroke, and complications of diabetes. *See also* polyunsaturated fatty acids.

Fatty acids, metabolism is dependent upon vitamin B_2 and vitamin C (via carnitine in muscle cells). *See* fats; polyunsaturated fatty acids.

Fertility, is measured in men by the number and the mobility of spermatozoa in semen. There is no definite association in men between infertility and vitamin deficiency, but some evidence shows that vitamins A, B_{12}, and E are needed for normal sperm production. These vitamins are definitely required by many species of animals for reproduction. There is no strong evidence that vitamin E can help infertile human females, but 200 IU daily has prevented miscarriage in those prone to it. Vitamin B_{12} can also help some women who are unable to conceive.

Fish, *white varieties* include cod, haddock, Atlantic halibut, lemon sole, plaice, saithe, and whiting. Contain traces only of fat-soluble vitamins and negligible vitamin C. A good source of vitamin B_{12} with moderate amounts of the rest of the B complex.

Fatty varieties include eel, herring, bloater, kipper, mackerel, pilchard, salmon, sardines, sprats, trout, tuna, and whitebait. Contain higher potencies of the fat-soluble vitamins than white fish, but similar quantities of the vitamin B complex. Negligible vitamin C is present.

The vitamin content of fish is shown in Figure 18.

All types of fish provide only moderate amounts of the essential minerals (*see* Figure 20). Vitamins left after cooking fish in various ways are shown in Figure 19.

Fish oils, fish body oils as well as fish liver oils are rich sources of PUFA and two fatty acids that are not found in vegetable seed oils. These are eicosapentaenoic acid (EPA) and docosahexaenoic acid (DHA). Both are members

Figure 18: Vitamin content of fish

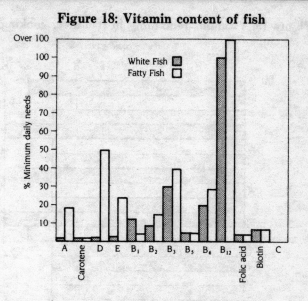

Figure 20: Mineral content of fish

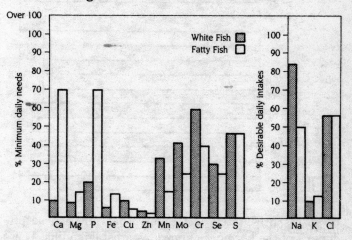

Figure 19: Vitamins remaining in fish after cooking

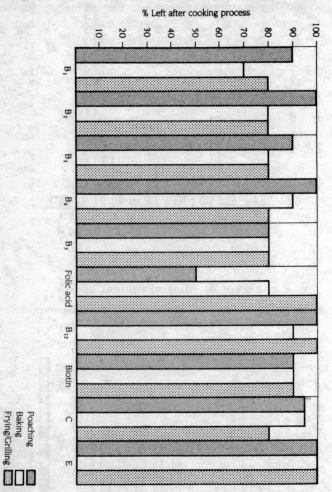

of an essential fatty acid family that function as precursors of the hormones known as prostaglandins. These
prostaglandins are believed to: inhibit formation of blood

clots in the circulatory system; reduce blood fat levels; increase HDL-cholesterol levels; and reduce risk of heart disease and stroke. They effectively thin the blood. Daily intake of ½-1 lb of oily fish (such as mackerel or herring) supplies sufficient EPA and DHA for protective effect. Cod-liver oil will supply them but is too risky because of its vitamin A and D content.

Supplements are now available that provide EPA (180 mg) and DHA (120 mg) that doubles the usual daily intake. Preventive therapy requires up to 3 capsules daily (900 mg total EPA and DHA). For those with angina or who have suffered heart attacks or stroke, 5 capsules daily is sufficient (1,500 mg total EPA and DHA) to help prevent further attacks.

Fluoridation, is the addition of fluoride to a water supply that lacks the trace element in order to raise its concentration to a level that will reduce the incidence of dental caries.

It has been known since 1916 that fluoride in drinking water can help prevent dental caries in the teeth of growing children. Since then many epidemiological studies have indicated that where the drinking water contains at least 1 mg fluoride per liter water (1 ppm), the incidence of childhood dental caries is lower than in comparable areas where only traces of fluoride are present in the water. The fluorides are believed to be deposited on the enamel surface of developing teeth and this appears to be where they exert their anticariogenic action. These observations have led to campaigns by various local authorities to add fluoride to the water supply if it is deficient in fluoride. However, fluoridation has not been generally accepted with enthusiasm because many believe that the process is neither safe nor essential.

There seems little doubt from various studies that

there is a decline in the incidence of children's dental caries where water previously low in fluorine has had fluoride added to it. What is in doubt is how much this action has contributed to dental health in view of: improvement in dental-health awareness among the population as a whole; the knowledge that prevention is possible; better health education; the application of fluoridated gel to the teeth of children; mouth rinses containing fluoride; better dental care by dentists; and widespread use of fluoridated toothpaste. Fluoride is now generally accepted as an anticariogenic agent; controversy rages over the best way to ensure an adequate intake.

One objection to fluoridation is the possibility of supplying too much fluoride to children, and some cases of fluorosis have been noted in those drinking treated water. A more serious objection was raised in the US where a 5 percent increase in the cancer death rate in some 20 cities with fluoridated water has not been seriously challenged by fluoridation supporters. The only hard fact to arise from fluoridation of water is that, if there are any benefits to be gained, they are confined to a lower incidence of dental caries in children.

Fluorides used to fluoridate drinking water include: hydrofluorosilicic acid; sodium fluoride; and sodium silicofluoride.

Fluorine, chemical symbol F. Atomic weight 19.0. A halogen that occurs as fluoride in the earth's crust at an abundance of 65 mg per 100 g. Most important natural sources are fluorite, cryolite, and florapatite. It is an essential trace element for animals and humans. First detected in animals by Gay-Lussac in 1805.

As fluoride, fluorine is now known to be present in trace amounts in the bones, teeth, thyroid gland, and skin of animal and human tissues. When eaten in food or obtained by drinking water, ingested fluorides are all present as negatively charged atoms (anions), so there is no barrier to absorption. They are rapidly absorbed and distributed in a manner similar to that of chlorides and, like these, fluorides tend to stay in the extracellular fluid. Much of the fluoride finds its way to the skeleton (e.g., in animal studies 60 percent ended up in the bone after two hours), and any excess is efficiently excreted via the urine. Some is also deposited in the teeth but, whereas a sufficient amount is protective to the teeth, excess can be harmful. Blood levels of fluoride are between 14 and 19 μg per 100 ml, of which 15-20 percent is ionic. The mineral does not appear to cross the barrier from blood plasma to breast milk, so increasing maternal intake during lactation is unlikely to provide more for the baby. More fluoride is retained by the body during childhood than in the adult state.

Food sources of fluoride are widespread, and drinking water supplies appreciable amounts. Total dietary intake is thus estimated at 1.82 mg fluoride per day. To this must be added the amount contained in the water supply. Assuming an intake of 1.1 liters daily, unfluoridated water will supply an extra 0.11-0.21 mg; fluoridated water will supply 1.1 mg extra fluoride. The richest source of dietary fluoride is tea; particularly the Chinese variety, which contains up to 10 mg fluoride in 100 g dried leaves. Six cups of this daily will provide about 3 mg fluoride from the infused dried leaves alone. Indian tea will provide about half this quantity.

Functions of fluoride are not known with certainty, but it appears to confer strength and stability to the bones and teeth, probably by forming insoluble fluorophosphates. It acts as an anticariogenic agent in the developing teeth of children, probably by reducing the solubility of tooth minerals or by discouraging the growth of acid-producing bacteria in the mouth. It may play a part in preventing osteoporosis in the elderly.

Deficiency in animals causes: anemia in mice; infertility in mice; stunted growth in rats and chicks; and lack of skeletal development in rats and chicks. In human beings, deficiency gives rise to dental caries in children, and to osteoporosis in elderly adults (possibly) where it may be associated with low calcium intakes.

Signs of deficiency are probably confined to the appearance of caries in the teeth of children. *See* dental caries.

Therapy of deficiency can be: fluoridation of drinking water supplies, *see* fluoridation; use of fluoride toothpaste; oral fluoride tablets; direct application to teeth of fluoride gel; and mouth rinses with fluoride solutions. All have been claimed to be effective in reducing the incidence of dental caries in children.

Therapy with sodium fluoride has been use to treat osteoporosis, Paget's disease, bone pain, and otosclerosis. *See* entries for specific conditions.

Excess intake of fluoride causes fluorosis. In cattle and sheep, excessive intakes may be taken when they graze on land contaminated with fluoride-containing dust. Both teeth and skeleton are affected. Signs are first seen in the teeth of young, growing animals as white mottled patches and a rough enamel surface. In adult animals, the surfaces of the large bones and lower jaw become thickened and the bone density thickens with extra calcification. Sometimes bony outgrowths appear. Weakness and reduced milk yield are also signs of excessive fluoride intake in dairy animals.

In humans, the first and most obvious sign is mottling of the teeth caused when the chalky-white irregular patches on the surface of the enamel become infiltrated by yellow or brown staining. Severe fluorosis weakens the enamel, resulting in surface pitting. All teeth may be affected, but fluorosis is most often seen on the incisors of the upper jaw. Dental fluorosis does not mean that skeletal fluorosis is present, but the latter can occur with extremely high intakes of fluoride taken over long periods.

When the water supply contains more than 10 mg fluoride per liter of water (10 ppm) or when excessive amounts of fluoride are inhaled, e.g., from smelting aluminum, fluorosis affects more than the teeth: appetite is depressed; there is increased density (sclerosis) of the bones of the spine, pelvis, and limbs; the supple ligaments of the spine become calcified, resulting in the so-called "poker back"; calcium is deposited in muscles and tendons; and nerve disturbances following the changes in the spinal column can appear. All of these changes are classed as osteosclerosis.

Treatment of fluorosis is to reduce the intake of dietary fluoride.

Recommended dietary intake of fluoride depends on the concentration of fluoride in the drinking water. The American Dental Association recommends the following intakes of fluoride (in mg per day) in areas where the water concentration is less than 0.3 parts per million: birth to 2 yrs—0.25; 2 to 3 yrs—0.50; 3 to 13 yrs—1. In areas where the water concentration is 0.3 to 0.7 parts per million, the recommended intake is as follows: birth to 2 yrs—none; 2 to 3 yrs—0.25; 3 to 13 yrs—0.50. Where the water concentrations exceeds 0.7 parts per million, no supplementation is recommended. The level of fluoride in drinking water should not exceed 1 part per million. While this may be suitable for growing children who drink milk, which has very little fluoride content, it is additive for those who drink tea, which is rich in the mineral.

Fluorosis, excessive deposition of fluoride in the teeth causing mottling. Can also apply to large amounts of fluoride deposited in bone. *See* fluorine.

Folacin, *see* folic acid.

Folates, a group of folic-acid-related compounds that occurs in foods, only some of which show vitamin activity.

Folic acid, a water-soluble member of the vitamin B complex. Also known as: vitamin Bc; vitamin M; pteroylglutamic acid (PGA); liver lactobacillus casei factor; and folacin. Antianemia vitamin. A yellow-orange crystalline powder.

Isolated in 1939 from liver; then in 1940 found to be a growth factor for bacteria. In 1945, Dr. Tom Spies demonstrated that it cured the anemia associated with pregnancy. The active form is folinic acid, produced from folic acid with the aid of vitamin C in the liver.

Best Food Sources in μg per 100 g

Food	μg
Dried brewer's yeast	2,400
Soy flour	430
Wheat germ	310
Wheat bran	260
Nuts	110
Pig liver	110
Green leafy vegetables	90
Wheat grains	80
Legumes	80
Pig kidney	42
Whole-grain bread	39
Citrus fruits	37
Eggs	30
Brown Rice	29

Functions

Needed for metabolism of RNA (ribonucleic acids) and DNA (deoxyribonucleic acids) in protein synthesis.

Blood formation

Genetic code transmission

Builds up resistance to infection in newborn and infants

Recommended Daily Intake

Should be at least 400 μg. *See* recommended daily intakes

Folic acid cont.

Deficiency Symptoms	Deficiency Results in
Weakness Fatigue Breathlessness Irritability Sleeplessness Forgetfulness Mental confusion	Possible spina bifida Premature birth Toxemia of pregnancy Premature separation of 　placenta from uterus Habitual abortion
Deficiency Caused by:	**Stability in Foods**
Pregnancy Contraceptive pill Old age Many drugs	Destroyed by light and air— *see* losses in food processing
Therapeutic Uses	**Symptoms of Excess Intake (more than 15 mg daily)**
Preventing deficiency 　consequences Megaloblastic anemia Schizophrenia Mental deterioration Psychosis Malabsorption diseases 　e.g., sprue	Loss of appetite Nausea Flatulence Abdominal distension Sleep disturbances No problems with lower 　intakes

Folinic acid,   the active form of folic acid produced under the influence of vitamin C in the liver.

Food preservatives,   the vitamins C and E are the only

recognized natural food preservatives, but bioflavonoids have some function.

Fortification of foods, falls into three categories as far as vitamin addition is concerned:

1. Restoring original vitamin content. In the countries where this is carried out on white flour, restoration is statutory at present, but the extent of adding vitamins varies. The recommended additions for white wheat flour (in mg per kg flour) are given in Figure 23. Where rice is the staple diet of a country, this also is fortified with vitamins.

Vitamin C is added to most brands of dehydrated potato to restore that lost during the drying process, but this restoration is not obligatory.

Vitamin E is added to some vegetable oils to replace that lost during the refining process. Many cooked cereals have thiamin, riboflavin, and nicotinic acid added to them to replace those vitamins lost during refining and processing, but this is not obligatory.

2. Enrichment, where the vitamin is added to give concentrations greater than in the original food. Examples are: the addition of vitamin C to fruit juices and drinks; the addition of vitamins A and D to liquid milk; and the addition of vitamins A and D to dried milk.

3. Vitaminization is the addition of vitamins to a food that does not normally contain them. The process is carried out to ensure that the foods are equal in vitamin content to those for which they are being substituted. One example is margarine, which is produced by the hardening of vegetable oils (hard type), or by the blending of vegetable oils with partially hardened oils (soft type). As produced, margarines are devoid of vitamins A and D; these are added

Figure 23: Recommended vitamin additions to white wheat flour

Country	Thiamin	Riboflavin	Nicotinic acid
Brazil	4.50	2.50	—
Canada	4.18	2.42	30.5
Denmark	5.00	5.00	—
Germany	3.00-4.00	1.50-5.00	20.0
Great Britain	2.40	—	16.0
Sweden	2.60-4.00	1.20	23.0-40.0
Switzerland	4.18	2.53	50.0
US	4.18	2.42-2.53	30.5
USSR	4.00	4.00	20.0

to give the margarine a similar content of these vitamins to that of butter. Sometimes vitamin E and polyunsaturated fats are added to increase the intake of these essential nutrients. Addition of vitamin A is required in the US; that of other vitamins is optional.

The substitution of expensive animal proteins with cheaper protein is likely to require extensive vitaminization, since soy protein is highly refined and processed. To make the two sources of protein equivalent, most vitamins must be added, but particularly vitamin B_{12} since this is completely lacking in soy protein.

Frostbite, injury to the skin induced by extreme cold and characterized by redness, swelling, and pain that can reach deep tissues. In cold climates, vitamin C (425 mg daily) can help prevent frostbite by maintaining skin temperature.

Fruit juices, include apple, black currant, grape, grapefruit, lemon, lime, orange, and pineapple.

As well as being a refreshing drink, fruit juices of all varieties (fresh, reconstituted, or frozen) should be regarded as moderate providers of carotene, vitamin E, and the vitamin B complex. Vitamin C content can vary depending upon how much has been added, since the vitamin is lost during the production process. Only in freshly squeezed juices is the full content retained.

Black currant juice is particularly high in vitamin C level.

All fruit juices are low-sodium drinks and supply excellent intakes of potassium along with useful quantities of trace minerals.

Vegetable juices (e.g., carrot) tend to provide more carotene than fruit juices, but contents of other vitamins are similar. While vegetable juices also provide excellent potassium levels, they are often salted to improve their taste, so sodium levels can be increased.

Fruits, *see* separate entries for bananas, apples, pears, and melons.

Fruits, citrus, include oranges, lemons, limes, mandarins, tangerines, and pineapples.

Supply some carotene, vitamin E, and the vitamin B complex, but their most important contribution is their vitamin C content (*see* Figure 24). Should be regarded as low-sodium foods that provide high intakes of potassium with useful quantities of the trace minerals (*see* Figure 25).

Fruits, dried, include apricots, currants, dates, figs, peaches, prunes, and raisins.

Figure 24: Vitamin content of citrus fruits

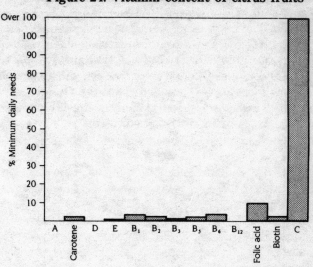

Carotene and the vitamin B complex are higher than in the original fruit because of a concentration effect, but the drying process destroys the vitamin E and most of the vitamin C (*see* Figure 26).

All are low-sodium foods that are also excellent sources of potassium, calcium, magnesium, iron, and copper (*see* Figure 27).

Fruits, soft, include blackberries, black currants, cranberries, gooseberries, grapes, loganberries, mulberries, passion fruits, raspberries, red currants, and strawberries.

A useful source of carotene and vitamin E with small amounts only of the vitamin B complex. An important provider of vitamin C with black currants an extremely rich source. *See* Figure 28.

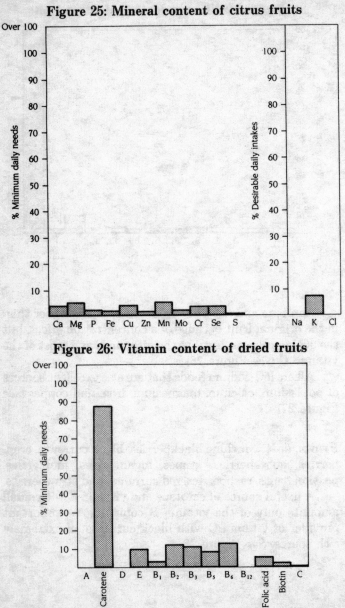

Figure 25: Mineral content of citrus fruits

Figure 26: Vitamin content of dried fruits

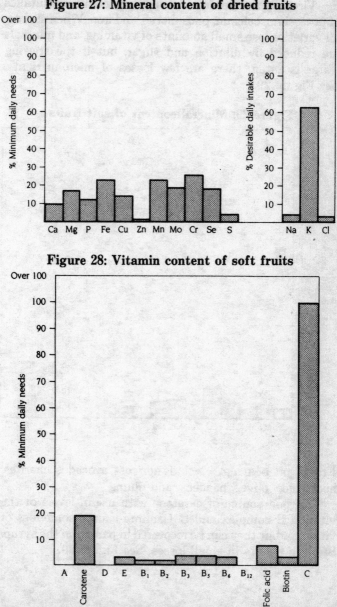

Figure 27: Mineral content of dried fruits

Figure 28: Vitamin content of soft fruits

Virtually sodium free. All supply good dietary intakes of potassium, calcium, phosphorus, and iron. When stewed, all varieties lose small amounts of vitamins, and minerals are reduced by dilution and sugar, but if the stewing water is eaten, there are few losses of micronutrients. *See* Figure 29.

Figure 29: Mineral content of soft fruits

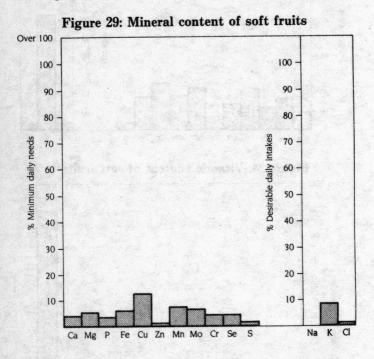

Fruits, pit-bearing, include apricots, avocados, cherries, nectarines, olives, peaches, and plums.

A good source of carotene with useful levels of the vitamin B complex and C. Canning causes some loss of vitamins, but they can be recovered in part from the syrup. Stewing results in small losses. *See* Figure 30.

Figure 30: Vitamin content of pit-bearing fruits

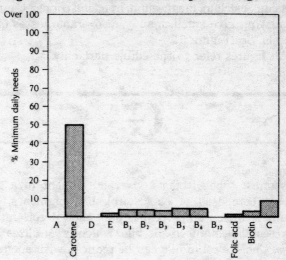

Figure 31: Mineral content of pit-bearing fruits

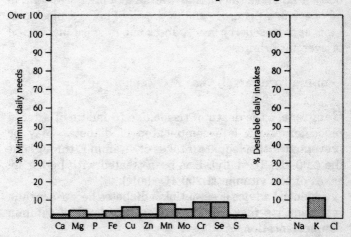

All are low-sodium foods that are excellent sources of potassium, calcium, magnesium, iron, and copper. Canning and stewing give small, mainly recoverable losses of all minerals. *See* Figure 31.

All figures refer to the edible part only.

G

Gallstones, cholelithiasis. Over 80 percent of a gallstone is composed of cholesterol, bile pigments, and calcium; a further 10 percent is pure cholesterol. Caused by excess cholesterol in the bile, which crystallizes into stones. Cholesterol in bile can be reduced with adequate vitamin C intake (up to 1,000 mg daily).

Gamma-linolenic acid (GLA), usually formed in the body from linoleic acid. Substantial amounts are found in oil of evening primrose and in the oil of borage, black currant, and gooseberry seeds, and some in spirulina. *See* oil of evening primrose.

Gamma-tocopherol, *see* E (vitamin).

Gangrene, the death of tissue due to failure of arterial blood supply. A late complicaton of diabetes. May be prevented with adequate intakes of vitamin E throughout life (200-400 IU daily). Has been treated with higher intakes of the vitamin (1,200 IU daily).

Medical advice is essential in diabetes because insulin requirements may be reduced at this level of vitamin supplementation.

Gastrointestinal tract, *see* digestive tract.

Gelatin, provides traces only of all B vitamins except B_{12}.

Geophagia, also known as clay eating. The habit of eating clay is common in rural areas of the United States, in the Middle East, and in some areas of Africa. The practice is considered normal during pregnancy in many places throughout the world, usually among communities in the lower economic strata, and is believed to supply calcium. Clay is eaten for its mineral content; to relieve hunger; to relieve gastrointestinal discomfort; to overcome diarrhea; and to detoxify harmful minerals. Among people on poor diets, clay eating can provide substantial quantities of essential minerals. There is no evidence that the practice is harmful, but once diets are improved, the habit usually stops. It has also been associated with an attempt to cure iron deficiency by some researchers; others believe that geophagia causes malabsorption of iron, inducing anemia. Zinc too is supplied in clay, but the chelating effect of clay on zinc may make it unavailable and at the same time immobilize zinc from other dietary sources.

Gingivitis, inflammation of the gums. Has been treated with very high doses of vitamin A (500,000 IU) and vitamin E (30 IU) daily by injection for six days; then 50,000 IU vitamin A three times daily with 200 IU vitamin E twice daily for three weeks orally. A complete cure is claimed with no relapses.

Glandular fever, also known as infective mononucleosis. Caused by Epstein-Barr virus, one of the herpes type, and characterized by high fever, sore throat, and swelling of the lymph glands.

Supplements should include high intake of vitamin C

(up to 1,500 mg daily), high-potency vitamin B complex and amino acid L-lysine (1,500 mg daily).

Glaucoma, a disease of the eye characterized by increased pressure within the eyeball causing restricted field of vision, a colored halo around lights, and lessening of visual power eventually resulting in blindness. Ensure adequate daily intakes of vitamin A (7,500 IU) and riboflavin (10 mg) for good sight. In addition, pressure may be reduced with vitamin C (500 mg per kg body weight) taken daily over several months.

Glossitis, inflammation of the tongue. A symptom of vitamin B_{12} and/or riboflavin deficiency. When due to other causes, may respond to nicotinamide at doses up to 300 mg daily.

Gluconates, complexes of minerals with glucose-like residues that are better absorbed than conventional mineral salts. The glucose-like residue is gluconic acid, a natural substance that the body makes and is able to utilize for energy purposes. This enables the minerals combined with it to pass from the intestine into the bloodstream at a more efficient rate, so that less of the mineral is wasted by malabsorption. Gluconates are under body control like any other type of mineral supplement, so excessive amounts are not absorbed; the body simply takes what it needs. A full daily complement of mineral needs as gluconates would supply only 10 calories.

A recent comprehensive report prepared for the Food and Drug Admininstration has concluded that mineral gluconates are safe and effective mineral supplements. They were found to be superior to mineral salts in the amounts absorbed from the diet. Potassium gluconate is of particular interest because it was found that it had less tendency than potassium chloride to cause small bowel ulceration when presented in tablet form.

Gluconates available include calcium, magnesium, iron, zinc, manganese, potassium, and copper (*see* entries for individual minerals for potencies).

Glucose tolerance factor, usually abbreviated GTF. The only active form of chromium known to function in the body. It is present in foods and can be synthesized in the body from trivalent chromium, nicotinic acid, and certain amino acids. It is a complex whose exact structure is not known, so only natural source material is available.

Its history goes back to 1929 when yeast extracts were found to potentiate the action of the hormone insulin. This action was attributed to the vitamins in yeast, and interest waned until 1955, when rats fed on torula yeast were found to develop diabetes and liver degeneration. No known nutrients were able to reverse these conditions, so the existence of a new dietary agent, GTF, was postulated. In the early 1960s, GTF was identified as a complex of trivalent chromium, nicotinic acid, and protein-like material. Animals fed diets deficient in the complex developed a diabetes-like condition.

In the mid-1960s, many adults and elderly people with glucose intolerance (a factor in diabetes) were found to improve on a supplement of 150-250 μg chromium daily in the form of chromic chloride. Similar benefits were noted in malnourished children in Jordan, Nigeria, and Turkey, but not in Egypt. This suggested that children in Egypt, unlike the others, did not lack chromium. Many experiments and observations then led to the conclusions that:

1. Simple chromium salts did not meet the criteria of an essential element.
2. Chromium salts did not cross the placental barrier.

3. Chromium salt supplementation in humans always took several days or weeks to become noticeable.

4. Chromium salts did not equilibrate with the body pool of organic chromium.

5. Calculations of chromium balance in humans indicated a very wide deficit when the absorption rate for chromic chloride was assumed to be the same as for food chromium. For example, if food chromium were absorbed at the same rate as chromic chloride, its calculated dietary intake of 50-100 μg per day would lead to only 0.25-0.5 μg in the urine. The usual daily excretion via this route is 7-10 μg, suggesting that more food-origin chromium is absorbed and more excreted.

Chromium in the form of brewer's yeast is better absorbed, can be transported across the placenta, is quickly distributed to the tissues, and has a faster action in reducing blood sugar than does chromic chloride in rat experiments. Studies in isolating the factor thus yielded GTF, albeit in a crude form.

GTF is far superior to chromium salts as a therapeutic or supplementary form of chromium. Attempts to synthesize it from chromium, nicotinic acid, and amino acids have not been successful. Twenty-five percent of the chromium of GTF in brewer's yeast is absorbed compared with 1 percent of chromium salts. Yeast can be enriched with chromium by adding the mineral salt to growing yeast, removing the excess chromium salt and drying the yeast. In this way yeast is available containing up to 60 μg chromium per g of yeast, all of it presented as GTF. Although precise quantitative assessment of GTF is difficult, the following foods are known to be rich in it (in descending order of biological activity): dried brewer's yeast; black pepper; calves liver; cheese; and wheat germ. Moderate sources are: whole wheat bread; cornflakes; white bread; spaghetti; beef; whole wheat grain;

butter; rye bread; margarine; oysters; chilli peppers; wheat bran; and shrimp. Poorer but nonetheless useful sources are: lobster; mushrooms; chicken legs; haddock; beer; egg white; chicken breasts; and skimmed milk.

The toxicity of GTF is low. Studies suggest that human beings can tolerate up to 1 mg per kg body weight, or 60 mg in the average adult. The corresponding figure for chromium salts is 18 mg.

Glutamic acid, an amino acid, usually supplied by the food, but can be synthesized within the body. A precursor of gamma-aminobutyric acid (GABA), a natural calming agent produced by the central nervous system. Vitamin B_6 is essential for GABA synthesis, lack of which causes convulsions in infants.

Glutethimide, a hypnotic drug. Prevents absorption of folic acid and prevents conversion of vitamin D to 25-hydroxyvitamin D.

Glycerophosphates, introduced into medicine on the grounds that lecithin contains phosphorus in the form of glycerophosphate and therefore these compounds would be more easily assimilated into body tissues and particularly the brain. There is no evidence to support this, but glycerophosphates were widely used in the past and are still used as general tonics rather than as suppliers of phosphorus.

Goiter, a swelling of the neck due to enlargement of the thyroid gland, where the gland enlarges in an attempt to increase the output of hormone.
    Endemic: Goiter due to lack of iodine in the soil and thus in the diet.

Sporadic: Usually due to simple overgrowth of the gland or to a tumor.

Exophthalmic: The swelling is associated with overactivity of the gland. *See* Graves' disease. The condition may also be due to increased intake of certain foods. *See* goitrogens.

Goiters are particularly apt to occur at puberty and during pregnancy.

Endemic goiter occurs mainly in three types of terrain:

1. Mountainous areas of Europe, Asia, North and South America, the Alps, Himalayas, Andes, Rockies, Cameroon mountains, and Highlands of New Guinea.
2. On alluvial plains once covered by glaciers, e.g., the area around the Great Lakes of North America, and some areas of New Zealand.
3. In isolated localities where the water originates in limestone, e.g., Derbyshire and the Cotswolds of England.

Simple goiters in nonendemic areas also occur, e.g., in Glasgow where iodine intake was found to be only 60 percent of the norm.

Treatment of endemic goiter with iodine has been known since the mid-eighteenth century, but it was not until 1920 that American researchers D. Marine and O.P. Kimball demonstrated unequivocally that sodium iodide reduced the incidence of goiter in children. Confirmation of the presence of thyroxine in the thyroid gland came from E.C. Kendall and A. E. Osterberg of the US in 1919; that of triiodothyronine came from J. Gross and R. Pitt-Rivers of the UK in 1952.

Endemic goiter responds to iodide therapy. A simple goiter in nonendemic areas rarely requires treatment, and iodides are unlikely to cause it to shrink. Only if the goiter becomes disfiguring is thyroxine used. If this is unsuccessful, surgery is usually considered. When the goiter is due to intakes of goitrogenic foods, these should be discontinued.

Goitrogens, substances found in some foods that inhibit formation of hormones by the thyroid gland. They occur principally in the seeds of cabbage, mustard, and rape, and also in cabbage leaves, kale, and turnips. The active substances are glucosinolates and thiocyanates, which respectively prevent the synthesis of thyroxine and reduce the amount of iodine in the thyroid gland. There is no strong evidence that these foods cause goiter in humans—probably because not enough is eaten. It is possible in farm animals who have large intakes of these foods and some of the goitrogens may find their way into the milk, but not enough to cause goiter in the humans who drink it. Peanuts, cassava, and soybeans are also goitrogenic, but the active principles are not known. Cooking methods tend to destroy goitrogens.

Gold salts, include gold thioglucose, sodium aurothiomalate, and sodium aurothiosulfate. All are used in treating rheumatoid arthritis, but are ineffective in osteoarthritis. Given by deep intramuscular injection, either in aqueous solution or in oil suspension. Toxic effects include: mouth ulceration; itching; urticaria; eczema; seborrheic dermatitis; alopecia; inflamed gums; gastritis; and colitis. Skin reactions are the most common. Blood abnormalities and kidney damage may also occur.

Gout, a recurrent acute arthritis of toe and finger joints that results from deposition in the joints and tendons of crystals of sodium urate (uric acid). Has been treated with orotic acid (4 g daily for six days), which dissolves uric acid crystals and removes pain and swelling.

Graves' disease, *see* hyperthyroidism.

Gray hair, caused by loss of natural pigment. In animals, development of gray hair is a symptom of pantothenic acid and/or biotin deficiency. There is no hard evidence that these vitamins prevent graying of the hair in humans, but cases are on record where they have restored natural color. PABA deficiency in animals causes premature graying of hair. Color has been restored with oral PABA, but there is no hard evidence that it has this effect in humans.

Growth, depends on adequate supply of protein, fats, carbohydrates, and calories. Transformation of these into growing tissues requires adequate thiamin, riboflavin, pantothenic acid, biotin, vitamin B_{12}, and vitamin A during prenatal and postnatal growth.

Gum disease, characterized by a progressive inflammation and infection of the gum tissue and underlying jawbone. Also known as periodontal disease. Believed to be due to residual food, bacteria, and tartar deposits that collect in the tiny crevices between the gums and the necks of the teeth. As the bacterial infection spreads deeper into the tissue surrounding the jaw/tooth connection, the gums recede until teeth loosen and fall out. Resistance to gum disease may be increased with correct diet. Extra calcium has been shown to reduce the onset of the condition and in some cases reverse it. Typical intakes were 500 mg calcium twice daily. It has been found important at the same time to maintain a low dietary phosphorus: calcium ratio. The ideal ratio is 1:1 but most popular foods have a high ratio, e.g., meat—20:1; refined cereals— 6:1; and potatoes—5:1. Soft drinks are high in phosphorus. Bone meal has a 1:2 ratio but, since much phosphorus is supplied in other foods, the ideal calcium supplement for periodontal disease is that with no phosphorus. Dolomite, amino acid-chelated calcium, calcium gluconate, calcium lactate, and calcium orotate are all suitable.

Gums, *see* gingivitis.

H

Hair analysis, the assay of a sample of hair for its mineral content. After preparation and dissolution of the hair, the resulting liquid is measured for minerals using atomic absorption spectroscopy, neutron activation analysis, or electron microprobe analysis, which allow accurate determinations of many trace minerals at concentrations down to 0.1 μg per g, and less in some cases. Hair analysis offers certain advantages over the more usual blood and urine analysis for minerals. These are:

1. Hair provides a better assessment of normal trace mineral concentrations because these reflect average levels over the period of growth.
2. Hair allows long-term variations in trace mineral concentrations to be assessed. As hair grows, it reflects the body status of minerals during the period of growth so, if long hair is subdivided into lengths, measurement will show the variation in mineral content over that period. The technique has been used to determine mineral status during pregnancy.
3. Hair is an inert, chemically homogenous substance that is a permanent record of the minerals in it. Once a mineral has been deposited in hair it stays there.

4. The concentrations of most trace elements are higher in hair than those in blood and most tissues of the body. Chromium levels are 50 times higher in hair than in blood; cobalt levels are 100 times higher.

5. Hair provides a record of past as well as recent trace mineral levels. Body status can therefore be measured in retrospect.

6. Collection of hair is painless, is not an invasive technique, can be carried out by untrained people, and the product can be kept indefinitely without deterioration.

Against the value of hair analysis are the objections that:

1. There is a possibility of variations across the scalp. Any variation can be minimized by always taking hair from the same part of the head, usually the short hair at the back.

2. Procedures for washing and preparing the hair sample before analysis can differ among those carrying out the assays. The washing stage can be with solvents or with detergents, but studies suggest that the two are compatible and the problem is not serious.

3. Hair may have been treated with bleach or dye, which can leach out trace elements. Shampooing and conditioning do not have this effect.

4. Zinc and selenium are used extensively in hair shampoos, coloring agents, and conditioners, and these may be absorbed into the hair. There is no clear evidence that this happens.

5. There is no correlation between concentrations of trace elements in hair and in blood. This is not surprising in view of the differing time-scales that each type of assay reflects. Comparative hair analyses, carried out by the same procedures by the same analyst on the same individual over a particular time-scale, could give useful information about body changes in mineral status.

Interpretation of hair analysis is not straightforward and should be left to an expert. It has been suggested that hair examination in this way is of more use in determining toxic minerals, and the significance of levels of essential minerals is debatable. There do appear to be correlations between low levels of hair copper and high levels of hair zinc with higher blood pressure in humans. There is a strong positive correlation between some toxic elements in hair and the incidence of high blood pressure in children. Low hair zinc levels are known to be associated with dwarfism. It has also been claimed that certain patterns are emerging; for example:

1. Schizophrenics have high calcium, low iron, high copper, and low zinc levels in their hair.
2. Arthritics have high lead, low iron, and low copper levels in their hair. Sometimes they show low manganese and a high calcium level that may depress magnesium concentration.
3. Diabetics often have low chromium, low manganese, and low zinc, with excessively high calcium levels in their hair.

The significance of these findings has not yet been determined. They cannot be regarded as diagnostic of these conditions without accompanying biochemical analyses and clinical signs.

For most individuals it is safe to treat low levels of essential minerals in hair with a change in diet or with supplements to supply those minerals that are low. Essential minerals that are present in high quantity may then be reduced to normal levels. High levels of toxic minerals should be treated by a qualified practitioner who will assess their significance by carrying out other tests. High calcium intakes combined with vitamin C and pectin is one combination that may help remove small amounts of toxic trace minerals.

Hashimoto's disease, the most common cause of hypo-thyroidism. Also known as Hashimoto's thyroiditis; Hashimoto's struma; chronic lymphatic thyroiditis; and auto-immune thyroiditis. More prevalent in women (8 times as often as in men) and between the ages of 30 and 50 years. It is an autoimmune disorder where the body produces disordered immunological response against itself to such an extent as to cause tissue injury.

Symptoms are painless enlargement of the thyroid gland or a feeling of fullness in the throat.

Treatment is the same as for myxedema (*see* myxedema).

Hay fever, a condition characterized by oversecretion of the nasal and eye mucous membranes, caused by hypersensitivity to pollen. Prevention has been claimed with high doses of vitamin B complex plus extra calcium pantothenate (100 mg), and pyridoxine (100 mg) in some cases. Treatment includes vitamin C (500 mg every 6 hours), which has a recognized antihistamine effect. It is also claimed that vitamin E (300 IU) and bioflavonoids (200 mg) daily may bring relief in some people.

Headache, a pain or ache anywhere in the head. It is a symptom rather than itself an illness. Causes include: disease of the eye, nose, or throat; sinuses that are blocked or infected; head injury; air pollution or poor ventilation; medications; alcohol; tobacco smoking; fever; infections; disturbances of the digestive tract and circulatory system; brain disorders; iron-deficiency anemia; low blood sugar; overdose of vitamin A; deficiency of nicotinamide, pyridoxine, or calcium pantothenate; and allergies.

Treatment depends upon the underlying cause, so professional advice must be sought. Adequate intakes of nicotinamide, pyridoxine, calcium pantothenate, and vitamin A may help relieve some headaches.

See also migraine.

Heart, edible, traces only of vitamins A, D, and carotene and a poor source of vitamin E (0.37-0.70 mg per 100 g). A good source of B vitamins, supplying the following (in mg per 100 g): thiamin (0.21-0.48); riboflavin (0.8-1.5); nicotinic acid (10.6-14.7); pyridoxine (0.11-0.38); and pantothenic acid (1.6-3.8). A good source of vitamin B_{12}, providing 13-15 μg per 100 g. A poor source of folic acid (4 μg) and biotin (3 μg). Vitamin C levels vary from 5 to 11 mg per 100 g.

Heart disease, coronary heart disease (CHD) or ischemic heart disease (IHD) are synonymous terms for diseases arising from a failure of the coronary arteries to supply sufficient blood to the heart muscle. These diseases are in most cases associated with atherosclerosis of the coronary arteries. They include myocardial infarction, angina pectoris, and sudden death without infarction.

Myocardial infarction is death of part of the heart muscle due to failure of the blood supply (ischemia). Usually due to blockage of the supplying blood vessel with a clot, or by fat deposition on the vessel wall. *See* atherosclerosis; blood clot.

Angina pectoris, see angina.

Sudden death may occur in those who have had myocardial infarction and angina.

Heart disease can be prevented and cured by dietary and supplementary means. The following may help reduce the chances of heart disease and decrease the possibility of further problems in those who have the condition: regular vitamin B complex plus high potencies of vitamin E (400-1,200 IU daily); vitamin C (500-1,000 mg daily);

vitamin B_6 (100 mg daily); lecithin (15-45 g daily); replacement of saturated animal fats in the diet by PUFA; and regular intakes of fish oil containing EPA and DHA.

Minerals

Adequate intakes of certain minerals appear from epidemiological and other studies to protect against heart disease, and in some cases can benefit the individual with the condition. The minerals are:

1. Calcium and magnesium. Observations suggest that those communities living in hard-water areas have fewer cases of heart disease than those living in soft-water areas. Hard water contains many minerals, but the main ones are calcium and magnesium and these are believed to exert a protective effect.
2. Calcium, which in adequate quantities tends to reduce blood cholesterol levels. Low body calcium levels result in high blood cholesterol levels. Calcium may act in the intestine by combining with fatty acids to form insoluble calcium soaps that are excreted. This reduces fat absorption and lowers blood fats. Both fat and cholesterol levels can be reduced with intakes of calcium between 1,025 and 1,200 mg per day. The mineral appears to function by reducing LDL (low-density lipoprotein) cholesterol levels, but allows HDL (high-density lipoprotein) cholesterol levels to be maintained. The end result is reduction in the severity of atherosclerosis.
3. Magnesium, which in adequate quantities appears to prevent cardiac spasms. Postmortem studies on those who have died from heart disease indicate lower heart-muscle levels of magnesium than in those who have died of other causes. Magnesium is believed to dilate blood vessels in the heart; calcium causes constriction. Correct balance of both minerals ensures that the heart beats smoothly.

When magnesium is short, the imbalance can cause constriction, which in turn gives rise to cardiac spasm. Diet and supplementation should ensure adequate intakes of both minerals.

4. Potassium, which helps to counteract the negative effects of sodium on the blood pressure. Postmortem studies indicate that, in those dying suddenly from heart attacks, potassium levels in the heart muscle are also low. Low potassium concentration is associated with angina. Low magnesium and potassium levels may be localized because of heart problems (rather than causing them), but a sensible insurance against heart attacks is adequate intakes of potassium as well as the other minerals.

5. Selenium, which when deficient in animals gives rise to heart problems and high blood pressure. In human studies, those who live in areas where soil selenium and hence selenium intakes are low have the highest rates of coronary disease. Where selenium intakes are highest, rates of coronary disease are lowest. The largest trial was in China, involving more than 45,000 people, in an area where selenium is low. In this area heart disease is rife, affecting much of the population; supplementation with selenium in thousands of children reduced the rate of heart disease from 40 per 1,000 to zero. The death rate in those already afflicted was reduced from 50 percent to 6 percent, simply by feeding small amounts of selenium (200 μg per day). *See* Keshan disease.

6. Chromium, which is usually low in the heart tissues of those dying from heart disease. Chromium appears to play a significant role in increasing the highly desirable HDL-cholesterol levels at the expense of the less desired LDL-cholesterol levels. This alone helps reduce the chances of development of heart failure.

7. Manganese, which has been found in low concentration in the heart tissue of those dying from cardiac problems.

Heavy metal poisoning, excess lead, mercury, and cadmium in the body can be detoxified with high doses of vitamin C (up to 3,000 mg daily) plus supplementary essential minerals.

Hemorrhoids, commonly known as piles. Characterized by dilated veins of the rectum. Treated with high intakes of bioflavonoids (lemon bioflavonoid complex plus rutin— up to 1,000 mg daily), plus vitamin C (500 mg daily).

Hepatitis, inflammation of the liver. When due to viral infection, can be relieved by very high doses of vitamin C (25-30 g) for a few days, preferably by intravenous injection but also orally, by taking 5 g every four hours. Medical supervision is recommended.

High-potency multivitamin complex is needed to restore vitamins lost from the liver both during and after an attack of hepatitis.

Herpes simplex, cold sores. May respond to daily intakes of essential amino acid L-lysine (0.5-1.5 g). The same treatment is suitable for genital herpes.

Herpes zoster, *see* shingles.

High blood pressure, may be assoicated with high-sodium, low-potassium, and high-cadmium intakes. *See* heart disease; salt.

High-cadmium intakes antagonize the uptake and metabolism of selenium in the body, so the effect of this toxic mineral may be mediated through these effects or in a direct action of its own.

Hormone replacement therapy (HRT), the treatment of symptoms of menopause with natural or synthetic female sex hormones. Have a similar effect on vitamins to those of the contraceptive pill. *See* contraceptives, oral. Treated with similar supplements.

Hydralazine, a blood pressure-reduction drug. Enhances the excretion of pyridoxine.

Hydrochloric acid, a mineral acid, produced by the parietal cells of the stomach, that provides the acidic medium of the gastric juices needed for the early stages of food digestion. Gastric juice contains between 0.2 and 0.5 percent hydrochloric acid. The acid is a combination of hydrogen ions (which determine acidity) and chloride ions. Hydrogen ions arise by the dissociation of carbonic acid, itself produced from carbon dioxide and water in the blood. Carbonic acid production is under the control of an enzyme, carbonic anhydrase, which contains zinc. Only the hydrogen ions from the dissociation of carbonic acid pass from the blood to the parietal cells of the stomach (bicarbonate ions are unable to do so), where they combine with the readily available chloride ions to form hydrochloric acid.

Excessive production of hydrochloric acid causes heartburn, and gastric and duodenal ulcers.

Deficiency of hydrochloric acid production (known as hypochlorhydria), or complete lack (known as achlorydria), can lead to malabsorption of some minerals that are usually solubilized by hydrochloric acid, and to chronic gastritis due to destruction of the parietal cells. The condition is associated with pernicious anemia, gastric cancer, and other cancers of the gastrointestianl tract, possibly because in the absence of hydrochloric acid certain cancer-forming substances can be produced from normal food ingredients.

Supplementary forms of hydrochloric acid are:

1. Dilute hydrochloric acid. Two to 5 ml of 10 percent

hydrochloric acid are diluted with 200-250 ml of water and sipped through a straw during the course of a meal. No more than 20 ml of the 10 percent hydrochloric acid should be taken over 24 hours.

2. Betain-hydrochloride, which provides 23.8 mg hydrochloric acid in 100 mg. The usual dose is 60-500 mg dissolved in water, which is drunk after meals. Also available in tablet form.

3. Glutamic acid hydrochloride, which provides 19.9 mg hydrochloric acid in 100 mg. The usual dose is 600-1,800 mg, which is dissolved in water and drunk after meals. Also available in tablet and capsule forms.

Hydrocortisone,   a natural corticosteroid hormone present in adrenal glands. *See* corticosteroids.

Hydrofluorsilicic acid,   provides 13.2 mg fluoride in 100 mg acid. Used in controlled amounts for the fluoridation of drinking water.

Hydroxocobalamin,   vitamin B_{12b}. *See* B complex.

Hyperactivity,   usually occurs in children; characterized by excessive or abnormal activity. Often benefits from high doses of vitamins including: nicotinamide (1-3 g); pyridoxine (100-300 mg); vitamin C (1 g); and vitamin E (up to 400 IU) daily. Constant monitoring is essential.

Hypercalcemia, infantile,   high blood level of calcium that may lead to excess calcification of bones, hardening of the arteries, and possibly mental retardation. Symptoms of excessive vitamin D intake. May also occur in adults, causing deposition of calcium in the soft tissues.

Hyperkeratosis, rough, bumpy skin, once known as "toad skin". Most obvious sign of vitamin A deficiency.

Hypertension, high blood pressure. *See* blood pressure.

Hyperthyroidism, characterized by an excessive secretion of thyroid gland hormones, which increase the metabolic rate. Also known as thyrotoxicosis; Graves' disease; Basedow's disease; Plummer's disease; toxic diffuse goiter; and toxic modular goiter.

All forms of hyperthyroidism give rise to the following signs and symptoms: goiter; fast heartbeat; warm, fine, moist skin; tremor; eye signs that include stare, lid lag, lid retraction, eye pain, excessive tears, irritation, and sensitivity to light; nervousness; increased activity; increased sweating; heart sensitivity; palpitations; fatigue; increased appetite; weight loss; insomnia; weakness; and excessive bowel movements sometimes leading to diarrhea. In addition, symptoms confined to Graves' disease include abnormal extrusion of the eyeball (exophthalmia), and an itchy, red, coarse, and thick skin.

Treatment consists of:

1. Iodine in high doses usually in the form of potassium iodide or sodium iodide, orally or by intravenous injection. Lasts only up to a week and functions by inhibiting the incorporation of iodine into the thyroid hormones.
2. Antithyroid drugs that inhibit the incorporation of iodine into thyroid hormones.
3. Radioactive iodine, used in female patients past their child bearing years, and in males. No evidence of increased incidence of tumors, leukemia, or cancer of the thyroid after this treatment. The therapy of choice in those above 40 years of age with Graves' disease.
4. Surgery, in all age groups, to remove the whole or part

of the thyroid. Sometimes hypothyroidism occurs and can be treated with thyroxine. After complete removal of the thyroid, thyroxine therapy is needed for life.

Hypothyroidism, *see* cretinism; Hashimoto's disease; myxedema.

I

Immigrants, those from Asia are particularly prone to vitamin D deficiency, producing rickets in children and osteomalacia in adults. Reasons are not known with certainty. Change to Western diet, including dairy products, more exposure of skin to sunshine, and supplementary vitamin D are recommended.

Immune system, the defense mechanism that the body develops against bacterial and viral infections. Cells responsible arise in the thymus gland, spleen, and lymphatic system. The immune system is impaired by malnutrition and certain vitamin deficiencies. *See* disease resistance.

Impotence, the inability of the male to attain or sustain an erection satisfactorily for normal sexual intercourse. More common in diabetics because they appear to lack the ability to convert carotenes to vitamin A, which is essential for sex hormone production. Adequate intakes of vitamin A as the preformed vitamin help the condition.

Minerals

Impotence has been noted in patients undergoing kidney dialysis who were found to have low blood levels of zinc because the dialyzing fluids lacked the mineral. Remedying this restored normal sexual function. Earlier studies on zinc-deficient populations in the Middle East and elsewhere found that lack of dietary zinc gave rise to retarded sexual development in growing children. Increasing zinc intakes allowed normal development to continue. Zinc has been shown to help in some cases of sexual dysfunction in adult males. Low testosterone (male sex hormone) levels were associated with low blood zinc concentration resulting in low sperm counts. Increasing dietary zinc from the food and by supplementing with 30 mg of the mineral daily restored sexual function to normal.

Inborn errors of metabolism, a term introduced by Sir Archibald Garrod in 1908 to describe conditions caused by a deficiency of, or an error in, a single gene. This is the result of a spontaneous or induced mutation in one or both parents, and so it becomes part of the genetic makeup of the fetus. These diseases are thus potentially present at the moment of conception. They are completely different from acquired congenital diseases that are due not to genetic errors, but to defects arising in the uterus.

Several hundred inborn errors of metabolism have been described, and probably as many more are as yet undiscovered. Some of these respond to treatment with a specific vitamin, usually at levels far in excess of normal dietary intakes. The defect is usually: in an enzyme that requires the specific vitamin in order to function; defective absorption of a vitamin; an inability to transport a vitamin; or an inability to convert a vitamin to its active form.

Thiamin:
1. Certain types of maple syrup urine disease. Character-

ized by delayed nervous system development. Due to a defective enzyme that requires thiamin pyrophosphate as a coenzyme. Responds to 10 mg thiamin daily.

2. Lactic acidosis. Characterized by persistent low blood sugar and acidosis due to accumulation of lactic acid. The deficient enzyme is pyruvate carboxylase. Responds to 10 mg thiamin daily.

Nicotinamide:

1. Hartnup disease. Characterized by intermittent skin rash and mental disturbance; symptoms similar to pellagra. Appears to be partly due to impaired intestinal absorption of tryptophan, an amino acid that is a precursor of nicotinamide. Skin and mental symptoms respond to 100 mg of nicotinamide daily.

2. Hydroxykynureninuria. Symptoms are: mild, mental deficiency; short stature; rash on buttocks; and ulceration of the mouth. Responds to 100 mg of nicotinamide daily.

Pyridoxine:

1. Infantile convulsions. Symptoms are convulsions, excessive irritability, and an acute sense of hearing immediately after birth. Responds to 10 mg pyridoxine daily by mouth. Treatment must continue for many years.

2. Cystathioninuria. Symptoms are mental retardation and congenital defects with an increased tendency to bleed. Pituitary gland abnormalities result from large amounts of the amino acid cystathionine in the blood and urine, because the body cannot metabolize it. Pyridoxal phosphate is a coenzyme for the enzyme cystathioninase, which is defective. Responds to high doses (more than 10 mg per day) of pyridoxine.

3. Hypochromic anemia. Anemia with high blood serum iron and increased iron stores. Due to a defect of the enzyme delta-aminolevulinic acid synthetase. Usually, but not always, responds to large doses of pyridoxine, at levels of 20-100 mg per day.

4. Homocystinuria. Characterized by an excessive excretion of the amino acid homocystine in the urine. Some cases respond to very large doses of pyridoxine, at levels of 200-500 mg per day.

5. Xanthurenic aciduria. Characterized by excessive excretion of xanthurenic acid after a high tryptophan meal. Symptoms are defective mental states. Sometimes responds to large doses (up to 200 mg per day) of pyridoxine.

Biotin:

1. Propionic acidemia. Acidosis in the newborn due to the accumulation of propionic acid in the blood. Caused by a defect in the enzyme propionyl CoA carboxylase, which requires biotin. Responds well to 10 mg biotin daily.

Folic acid:

1. Congenital defect in folate absorption. Deficiency of folic acid caused by a defect in its absorption from food and an inability to transport the vitamin. Characterized by: anemia; mental retardation; seizures; involuntary movement; and impairment of voluntary movement. Anemia responds to doses of folic acid of 40 mg per day, but may not alleviate seizures.

2. Formiminotransferase enzyme deficiency. Symptoms are retarded mental and physical development and increased folic acid level in the blood. Condition involves the vitamin but does not respond to it.

Vitamin B_{12}:

1. Malabsorption of the vitamin that is not due to lack of intrinsic factor. Characterized by megaloblastic anemia that responds only to injections of vitamin B_{12}.

2. Congenital lack of intrinsic factor. Occurs early in life and is due to nonproduction of intrinsic factor for reasons unknown. Responds completely to injections of vitamin B_{12}.

3. Megaloblastic anemia due to lack of one of the specific

transport proteins (transcobalamin II) of vitamin B_{12} in the blood. Usually occurs in newborns. Responds to injections of 1 mg vitmain B_{12} on a regular and prolonged basis.

4. Lack of the other specific transport protein (transcobalamin 1) of vitamin B_{12} in the blood. Characterized by low vitamin B_{12} blood levels but no other signs of deficiency.

5. Methylmalonicaciduria. Acidosis in the blood of the newborn. Large amounts of methylmalonic acid in the urine. Due to an inability to form the coenzyme form of vitamin B_{12} called 5-deoxyadenosylcobalamin. Responds to frequent injections of high-dose (1 mg) vitamin B_{12} or the coenzyme B_{12} itself.

Vitamin A:

The condition is due to an inability to convert carotene to vitamin A. One case only has been described, and the symptoms include night blindness, dry eyes (Bitot's spots), and low blood plasma vitamin A with high blood carotene level. Can be treated by administration of preformed vitamin A.

Vitamin D:

1. Hereditary vitamin D-resistant rickets with hypophosphatemia. Low phosphate levels in the blood but calcium levels are normal. Primary abnormality is the inability to reabsorb phosphate in the kidney. Main disease is rickets or osteomalacia and dwarfism. Treatment is very high doses of the vitamin daily (2.5 mg or 100,000 IU), but this can cause intoxication. May respond better to high oral intakes of phosphate.

2. Fanconi syndrome. Rickets or osteomalacia with low blood phosphate that is resistant to normal vitamin D intakes. Due to an inability of the kidney to acidify urine, resulting also in low blood potassium levels. The amino acid cystine accumulates in the blood and excessive amino acids are excreted in the urine. May respond to massive doses of vitamin D but possible toxic effects must be monitored.

3. Primary renal tubular acidosis. Usually affects females in late childhood. Characterized by chronic acidosis, osteomalacia, calcium deposits in the kidneys, and stones in the kidneys. Increased excretion of calcium and phosphate in the urine lead to low blood levels of the minerals. Treatment of the acidosis is with citrate; in some cases vitamin D is required, but it is not a standard therapy.

Indian childhood cirrhosis, a rapidly progressive disorder and an important cause of death in the Asian subcontinent. Characterized by excessive copper deposits in the liver and kidneys of the children affected. Onset is earlier than Wilson's disease, but treatment is similar (*see* Wilson's disease).

Indomethacin, an antiarthritic drug. Impairs vitamin C and thiamin utilization.

Inositol, a water-soluble member of the B complex. Not a true vitamin, as the body can make it in limited quantities. There are high concentrations in the brain, stomach, kidney, spleen, liver, and heart. Also known as bios I; myoinositol; mesoinositol; and lipotropic factor.

Present in cereals and vegetables as phytic acid, which is a combination of inositol and phosphorus. A major constituent of lecithin. A colorless, crystalline substance.

Functions	Recommended Daily Intake
As fat-solubilizing agent Mild antianxiety agent Maintains healthy hair Controls blood cholesterol level	Difficult to assess because of body synthesis. Probable daily intakes between 500 and 1,000 mg

Inositol cont.

Best Food Sources in mg per 100 g

Lecithin granules	2,857
Beef heart	1,600
Desiccated liver	1,100
Wheat germ	690
Lecithin oil	360
Liver	340
Brown rice	330
Cereals	320
Beef steak	260
Citrus fruits	210
Nuts	180
Molasses	180
Legumes	160
Green leafy vegetables	100
Whole wheat bread	100
Soy flour	70

Deficiency Symptoms

None that are specific

Stability in Foods

Very stable to all cooking processes

Therapeutic Uses

Reducing blood cholesterol
Restoring healthy hair
With vitamin E to treat nerve damage
Antianxiety agent
Treating irritability
Treating schizophrenia

Symptoms of Excess Intake

None reported
When present as phytic acid, it may immobilize some minerals but has no effect on vitamins

Insect repellant, thiamin in daily doses of 75-100 mg acts in those who are prone to insect bites, probably because the odor of the vitamin in the skin is repugnant to insects.

International units (IU), a means of expressing vitamins in terms of biological activity. Now mainly superseded by expressing them as weight (milligrams or micrograms). Only three are still measured in units:

Vitamin A, 1 IU = 0.30 micrograms retinol
Beta-carotene, 1 IU = 0.10 micrograms retinol
Vitamin D, 1 IU = 0.025 micrograms
Vitamin E, 1 IU = 1.0 milligram dl-alpha-tocopheryl
    acetate, or 0.91 mg
  dl-alpha-tocopherol, or 0.74 mg d-alpha-tocopheryl
    acetate, or 0.67 mg
  d-alpha-tocopherol, or 1.12 mg dl-alpha-tocopheryl
    succinate, or 0.83 mg
  d-alpha-tocopheryl succinate.

Other vitamins that were once expressed in international units are:

thiamin hydrochloride, 1 IU = 3 micrograms
pantothenic acid, 1 IU = 13.33 micrograms
vitamin C, 1 IU = 50 micrograms

Intestinal surgery, postoperative nausea and distension can be reduced by 250 mg calcium pantothenate daily. Vitamin C (1,000 mg per day) before and after an operation will accelerate the healing process.

Intrauterine devices, known also as the coil or IUD. Copper has been known to be toxic to spermatozoa since the mid-eighteenth century and the metal is incorporated into intrauterine devices. A typical copper T-shaped IUD has a copper surface of 135 square millimeters and releases about 29 μg of copper daily into the uterine fluid. Localized high concentration of the mineral is believed sufficient to cause a contraceptive effect, although local irritations by the device may also play a part. Some devices do not contain copper but exert their protective effects in some other way. The end-result is inhibition of implantation of the fertilized ovum. IUDs are now used with caution because of the risks of side effects or injury.

Intrinsic factor, a specific protein secreted by the stomach that forms a complex with vitamin B_{12} in the diet. The complex is then absorbed in the ileum, the lower part of the small intestine. Lack of intrinsic factor gives rise to pernicious anemia, because B_{12} in the diet cannot be absorbed. The factor may also be deficient in those who have had part or all of the stomach removed.

Giving intrinsic factor with vitamin B_{12} may help absorb the vitamin, but eventually the factor may no longer be effective, as it is derived from animals. No more than 8 μg oral vitamin B_{12} is absorbed by the intrinsic factor mechanism at one time.

Iodine, chemical symbol I. Atomic weight 126.9. An essential trace element for animals and humans.

Geographical Distribution

Worldwide soil distribution extremely variable

Areas lacking mineral are described as "goiter belt" since goiter is most prevalent disease caused by iodine lack

In the US, it stretches across the middle of the country

In the UK, it is in the Midlands and South West England, thus the name for the disease "Derbyshire Neck"

Prevalent also in areas of China, Africa, Continental Europe, Russia, and South America

Food grown in these soils lacks iodine, and those who rely mainly on locally grown produce will not receive the mineral in their diets.

Recommended Daily Intake

Difficult to assess in view of varying iodine content of foods but should be about 200 μg
See recommended daily intakes

Iodine cont.

Functions

The functions of iodine reside solely in its presence in the thyroid hormones triiodothyronine and thyroxine

These hormones determine the level of metabolism in the body, i.e., essentially the rate at which we live. They are necessary for converting food into energy, and the way we dissipate that energy

Deficiency Caused by

Reduced dietary intakes
Excessive intakes of anti-thyroid foods including:
  brassica
  cabbage
  cassava
  kale
  peanuts
  soy beans
  turnips and seeds of
    cabbage
  mustard and rape
Some medications

Body Content

The adult contains between 20 and 50 mg iodine and most of it is concentrated in the thyroid gland, situated in the base of the neck. The rest is the blood as the thyroid hormones triiodothyronine (T_3), and thyroxine (T_4).

Food Content

This depends upon the soil content of iodine, so food analyses are meaningless. As a general guide the following foods tend to provide our daily intakes of iodine as μg per 100 g food:

Fruits, vegetables, cereals, and meats	2-5
Haddock	659
Whiting	65-361
Herring	21-27

Dried kelp is the richest
  source at 535 μg per g

Deficiency Results in	Deficiency Symptoms

Deficiency of iodine is an important world health problem. At least 200 million people suffer from diseases traced to lack of the element. Intakes less than 50 μg per day induce deficiency.
 	
   Lack of iodine gives rise to goiter; underactive thyroid; cretinism
   Lack of thyroid hormone (when iodine is adequate) gives rise to myxedema.
	Apathy
	Drowsiness
	Sensitivity to cold
	Lethargy
	Muscle weakness
	Weight gain
	Coarse skin
	All can be due to lack of
	   iodine or lack of thyroxine

Symptoms of Excess Intake	**Iodine Supplements** **in μg per 100 μg**
Unlikely to happen under normal circumstances but may occur in medical treatment with iodine as iodides. Treat as medical matter requiring professional help	Ammonium iodide (87.6); calcium iodide (43.2); calcium iodobehenate (23.5); potassium iodide (76.5); potassium iodate (59.3); sodium iodide (84.7); iodized table salt *see* separate entry; kelp *see* separate entry; and sea salt (4).

Iodine poisoning,   symptoms of acute poisoning from ingestion of elemental iodine are mainly due to its corrosive effects on the gastrointestinal tract. It causes: a disagreeable metallic taste; vomiting; abdominal pain; and diarrhea. Eventually the kidneys fail to produce urine, and swelling of the throat due to edema, or edema of the lung, follows.

The fatal dose is 2 to 3 g of elemental iodine. The maximum permissible atmospheric concentration is 0.1 ppm. Large volumes of milk and starch solutions with 1 percent solution of potassium thiosulphate are needed in the emergency treatment of swallowed iodine.

Iodism, the hypersensitivity to iodine itself or, more rarely, iodides after prolonged oral administration. Symptoms are: a severe cold in the head (coryza); headache; pain in the salivary glands; watery eyes; weakness; conjunctivitis; fever; laryngitis; bronchitis; skin eruptions; skin rashes; and exacerbation of acne.

Iodized table salt, sodium or potassium iodide or potassium iodate is added to table salt to ensure no lack of iodine in the general population. It is carried out in the US, Switzerland, Yugoslavia, New Zealand, and some countries of South America. Salt is not iodized in the UK.

In the US, iodized salt must contain 76 μg iodine per g salt. Daily consumption of table salt is estimated at between 2 and 6 g, providing 152-456 μg iodine. New Zealand suggests 84.7 μg iodine per g salt. Other countries recommend lower levels in table salt that appear to be just as effective. Salt used in the processing and refining of foods is not usually iodized.

Iron, chemical symbol Fe, from the Latin word ferrum. Atomic weight 55.85. Exists as ferrous iron and ferric iron. An essential trace mineral that is present in the body to the extent of 3.5 to 4.5 g. Two-thirds is present as hemoglobin, the red oxygen-carrying pigment of blood. The remainder is stored in the liver, spleen, bone marrow, and muscles (where it is present as myoglobin, which acts as an oxygen reservoir within the muscle fibers). In these organs and in the blood plasma, iron exists as a protein complex.

Iron cont.

Best Food Source
in mg per 100 g

Dried brewer's yeast	20.0
Wheat bran	12.9
Cooked liver	12.5
Cooked kidney	11.5
Cocoa powder	10.5
Oysters	8.1
Soy flour	8.0
Parsley	8.0
Dried fruits	5.8
Sardines	4.6
Cereals	4.1
Clams	3.9
Corned beef	2.9
Whole wheat bread	2.5
Kidney beans	2.5
Beef	1.9

Body Content

Depend upon iron absorbed from diet. Losses via all routes are about 1 mg daily. Menstruation increases this by about 0.8 mg daily. Losses during breast-feeding about 0.4 mg daily. About 24 mg iron released daily from normal blood breakdown but most is conserved by the body.

Functions

In hemoglobin, acts as oxygen carrier in red blood cells
In myoglobin, acts as oxygen reservoir in muscles
In body cells, acts in oxygen transfer in cytochromes
Present in enzyme catalase, which protects against peroxide poison
In developing resistance to infection

Absorption from Food

Only 1 to 1.5 mg absorbed daily (i.e., 10 percent) from 15 to 20 mg in the diet. Absorption is highest in childhood, reducing in later years. In food, iron is present in organic heme form and inorganic nonheme form. Heme iron is in meats and is absorbed unaided. Nonheme iron needs vitamin C for efficient absorption. Iron must be in ferrous form to be absorbed.

Iron cont.

Relationship with Vitamin E

Only iron in the ferric form will destroy vitamin E. When in the ferrous form, the mineral is compatible with the vitamin. Use iron supplements only in the ferrous form (look on the package).

Symptoms of Excess Intake

Most people reject high intakes of iron and excrete it in the feces. However the unabsorbed iron may induce constipation or even diarrhea.

Excessive deposition of iron in the tissues can occur in hemochromatosis, a rare hereditary disease. It also happens when the body cannot rid itself of excess iron, due to certain disease conditions.

Increased body levels resulting from consistent high intakes in the diet or by supplementation are very rare.

Iron Supplements in mg per 100 mg

Iron amino acid chelate (10); ferrous aspartate (14.2); ferrous carbonate saccharated (24); ferrous citrate (23.8); ferrous fumarate (31.3); ferrous gluconate (12.5); ferrous glycine sulfate (17.8); ferrous lactate (19.4); ferrous orotate (15.2); ferrous oxalate (31.1); ferrous succinate (32.6); ferrous sulfate (20.1); ferrous tartrate (22.5); and ferrocholinate (12.5).

Ferric salts are also widely used but are not recommended, as they must be converted first to ferrous salts by the digestive system to be absorbed. Vitamin C appears to be essential in this respect but it can also aid the absorption of ferrous salts.

Iron cont.

Deficiency Symptoms

Related to the anemia
that results from reduced
hemoglobin levels:
    tiredness
    lack of stamina
    pallor
    breathlessness
    giddiness
    headaches
    insomnia
    palpitations
Ultimate test of deficiency
is blood hemoglobin con-
tent. Should be within
range of 12-16 g per 100
ml blood. A level less
than 12 g is considered
anemic. In the United
States, an estimated 20
million people are iron
deficient; 35-50 percent of
women show signs of iron
deficiency anemia, and 60
percent or more of infants
and pregnant women are
affected. Less than 8 g
per 100 ml may affect the
heart output of blood

Deficiency Not Related to Anemia

Low blood plasma levels of
    iron can cause general-
    ized itching (pruritus)
    especially in the aged
In children, iron deficiency
    can depress growth and
    impair mental
    performance

Therapeutic Uses

Iron-deficiency anemia
Generalized itching
Impaired mental per-
    formance in the young

Poisoning with Iron

Accidental poisoning with
ferrous sulfate, usually in
children, can be fatal. As
little as 3 g of this
substance taken as one
dose has caused death in
a small child

Iron cont.

Recommended Daily Intake	*Recommended Daily Intake Cont.*
Varies with the authority—*see* recommended daily intakes	Usually in the region of: 10-12 mg for children 15-18 mg for adults

Isoniazid, an antituberculosis drug. Enhances excretion of pyridoxine.

Isotretinoin, an isomer of retinoic acid, less toxic than tretinoin, and given orally.

Itai-itai, also known as "ouch-ouch", a disease reported in Japan that is probably associated with high intakes of cadmium from eating rice grown on land irrigated with high-cadmium-containing water. Characterized by kidney and gastrointestinal lesions together with bone softening and severe bone pain similar to that in osteomalacia. Symptoms occurred mainly in older women, particularly those who had borne many children, and in those consuming diets low in protein, vitamin D, and calcium. Cadmium may be antagonistic to dietary calcium, causing severe deficiency of it.

Itching, also known as pruritus. A generalized form is sometimes associated with old age. Blood plasma iron levels are usually low even though no iron-deficiency anemia is present. The condition is apparently due to a response of skin nerves to local iron deficiency. Treatment is with 60 mg of elemental iron three times daily. Response is usual within a few days of therapy.

IUD, *see* contraceptives; intrauterine devices.

J

Jaundice, obstructive, yellow skin due to excessive bile pigments overflowing from liver because of bile duct blockage. Causes deficient absorption of fat-soluble vitamins, particularly vitamin K, which is given by injection. Water-solubilized vitamin E is required.

K

K, a fat-soluble vitamin, derived from, koagulation (Danish). Occurs naturally in foods as vitamin K_1, also known as phytomenadione, phyloquinone, phytylmenadione, and antihemorrhagic vitamin. Also produced by intestinal bacteria as vitamin K_2. The synthetic vitamin is K_3, also known as menadione and menaphthone.

K_1 ws isolated from alfalfa by Dr. Henrik Dam in 1935 at the University of Freiburg; K_2 was isolated from decayed fish meal by Dr. Edward Doisy of St. Louis University in 1939.

Function	Symptoms of Excess Intake
Sole function is in control of blood clotting	None have been reported

Vitamin K cont.

Best Food Sources
in µg per 100 g

Cauliflower	3,600
Brussels sprouts	800
Broccoli	800
Lettuce	700
Spinach	600
Pig liver	600
Cabbage	400
Tomatoes	400
String beans	290
Beef liver	200
Meats	100
Potatoes	80
Legumes	30

Stability in Foods

Survives most domestic cooking methods. Some losses in commercial processing of foods, including deep-freezing

Therapeutic Uses

Hemorrhagic disease of newborns
Inability to absorb fats
In long-term antibiotic treatment
Treating toxic effects of anti-coagulant drops, e.g., warfarin

Deficiency Caused by

In infants: Poor transfer of vitamin across placenta in pregnancy
Low levels in human milk
Sterile intestine
In adults: Malabsorption of fats
Lack of bile salts
Celiac disease
Surgery on intestine
Persistent liquid paraffin intakes
Antibiotic therapy
Liver disease of all kinds

Deficiency Symptoms

Usually in the deficient newborn and include excessive bleeding from stomach, intestine, and umbilical stump

Recommended Daily Intake

Not established because of adequate production by intestinal bacteria in healthy person
Probably need 500-1000 µg in diet

Kanamycin, an antibiotic. Prevents absorption of vitamins K and B_{12}.

Kelp, the popular name for the seaweed *Ascophylum nodosum*. Also known as tangle, and knotted wrack. Grows in abundance on the west-facing coasts of Europe, which are exposed to the Gulf Stream, as well as in the North Temperate Zones on both the Atlantic and Pacific coasts of North America. It feeds through its fronds (leaves) and is attached to rock by holdfasts. Minerals from sea water are concentrated in the body of the plant. After collection from the sea the plant is dried at temperatures between 167 and 185 °F (75-85 °C), then ground to a fine powder. It may be added in this form to foods, but is usually taken in the form of compressed tablets. Sometimes the powder is extracted with water and only the aqueous extract is used. The solids content of the extract is usually about 10 percent.

Kelp is an excellent source of many minerals, but it is usually taken for its iodine content. A typical analysis of kelp is (in mg per g): potassium—19.8; sodium—16.4; calcium—12.3; nitrogen—12.1; sulfur—4.6; magnesium—2.5; and phosphorus—1.0. Levels of trace minerals present are (in μg per g): iodine—535; iron—220; zinc—43; manganese—38; nickel—10; copper—4; cobalt—3; bromine, chromium, lead, strontium, and vanadium,—1; and molybdenum—0.1.

Another species, *Laminaria hyperborea*, is particularly rich in iodine, containing from 5.8-6.8 mg per g, i.e., it is approximately ten times more potent than kelp. *See* kelpware.

Kelpware, the popular name for the dried thallus (filament without a root) of *Fucus vesiculosus, Fucus serratus,* and *Fucus siliquosus*. Also known as bladder wrack, sea wrack, bladder fucus, black tang, cut weed, and sea oak.

Found in the Atlantic and Pacific oceans. Mineral contents are similar to those in kelp. *See* kelp.

Keratinization, the formation of hard, dry, scaly cells in place of normal healthy cells in wet surfaces of the body, particularly around the eyes, mouth, and lining of reproductive tract. A symptom of vitamin A deficiency.

Keshan disease, a congestive heart disease that is potentially fatal, affecting children and prevalent in vast areas of rural China. Clinical studies indicate that when given 1,000 μg selenium per week, affected children were cured of heart disease. When the selenium supplement was given to all members of a commune, incidence of the disease became zero.

Kidney, as a food is the second richest source of vitamin A, B complex, and C next to liver (*see* Figure 32). Also provides excellent amounts of trace minerals (*see* Figure 33).

Figure 32: Vitamin content of kidney

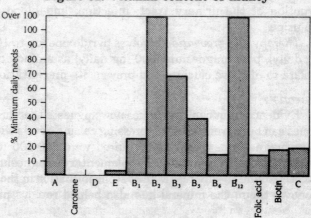

Figure 33: Mineral content of kidney

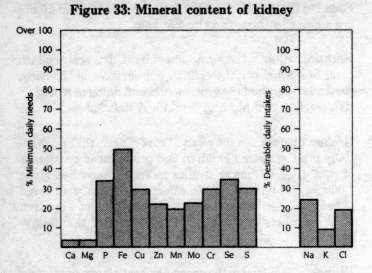

Kidney stones, also known as renal stones, renal calculi, or urinary calculi. Common causes of back pain, obstruction, and secondary infection. Over 90 percent are composed of calcium salts. The stones cause pain, fever, obstruction of the urinary tract, infection, and blood in the urine.

Therapy and prevention involves pyridoxine (up to 100 mg daily), plus magnesium (300 mg daily) as amino acid chelate to dissolve calcium and prevent its precipitation.

Minerals

Evidence from clinical studies now suggests that such stones can be prevented by suppressing calcium levels with extra magnesium. Quantities required were 200-300 mg elemental magnesium daily. Supplementary magnesium has been found to suppress kidney-stone formation in those prone to them; the mineral has also helped remove preformed stones in some cases. Vitamin B_6 supplementation may complement the action of magnesium since the vitamin is concerned in the mineral's metabolism.

L

Lactoflavin(e),   *see* B_2 (vitamin).

Laetrile,   a water-soluble factor present in vitamin B complex. Also known as amygdalin, B_{17}, and vitamin B_{17} (incorrectly). Full name levo-mandelonitrile-beta-glucuronoside. First isolated from apricot pits in the early 1950s by the father and son team of Drs. E.T. Krebs and E.T. Krebs, Jr. A white crystalline powder. Present in supplements as laetrile.

Richest sources are apricot pits (average 5 mg per kernel); peach pits; apple seeds; bitter almonds; cherry pits; plum pits; lime seeds; pear seeds; some grasses; and some berries (figures not known).

Unstable to heat, so pits are usually eaten raw.

Functions as a source of organic cyanide. Cancer cells are believed to convert organic cyanide to inorganic cyanide but they are unable to detoxify it. Hence inorganic cyanide specifically destroys cancer cells.

Deficiency in humans has not been reported.

Deficiency in animals has not been reported.

Recommended dietary intake is not set by any authority.

Toxicity is due entirely to cyanide content.

Toxic symptoms are cold sweats, headaches, nausea,

lethargy, breathlessness, blue lips, and low blood pressure—all associated with excess cyanide. Injectable laetril is less toxic than oral dosing.

Prescription is legal in some US states, but the Interstate Commerce Commission forbids interstate transportation of Laetrile.

Therapy with laetrile is confined to cancer, but its benefits are very controverisal. The injectable preparation is preferred, but is regarded as only part of a holistic approach.

Lead, chemical symbol Pb, from the Latin plumbum. Atomic weight 207.2. One of the metals known to the ancient world. Occurs in the earth's crust to the extent of 0.002 percent, mainly as the mineral galena in which it is combined with sulfur.

Traces of lead appear to be essential for the health of some animals, but it has never been shown as a necessary trace mineral for humans. Problems have arisen because of excessive intake rather than deficiency.

Excess intakes may occur from food, drinking water, and the air. Exhaust fumes from gasoline driven vehicles are the main source of atmospheric lead, which has a maximum permissable concentration of 1.5 mg per cubic meter. In Los Angeles, air concentration was 4.5 μg per cubic meter in 1969, which contributed significant extra intake. In the UK, a survey of drinking water in 43 districts indicated that 96 percent of the population in those districts consumed water with a pH less than 7.8, which was sufficiently acid to dissolve lead from piping. In softwater areas, lead piping can give rise to levels of 108 μg lead per liter water. The main water supply was only 17.9 μg per liter, indicating significant dissolution of lead. Food levels of lead reflect the extent of the metal in the water that irrigates the land on which the food is grown. Homemade beer and wine made in pewter vessels can also contribute significant amounts of lead by dissolution.

Total dietary intake of lead in industrialized societies is between 200 and 400 μg daily. Ninety percent of this is unabsorbed and excreted in the feces; most of the remainder is excreted through the kidneys. Some stays behind, and a blood level above 42 μg per 100 ml is associated with lead poisoning.

Toxic effects are well documented in children who are more susceptible to lead poisoning than adults. Poisoning has come from accidental ingestion of lead salts; from lead toys; and from sucking lead-painted articles. Acute poisoning causes: intense thirst; a metallic taste in the mouth; burning abdominal pain; vomiting; diarrhea; black stools; lack of urine formation; shock; and coma. Chronic poisoning is insidious, causing loss of appetite; constipation; headache; weakness; a blue or black lead line on the gums; and anemia. Later there is: vomiting; irritability; incoordination; neuritis, leading to unsteady gait, visual disturbance, and delirium; paralysis (with wrist and foot drop); and kidney failure. Acute abdominal pain may result; in pregnancy the uterus violently contracts, inducing abortion. Organic lead compounds like those in gasoline exhaust fumes have a specific action on nervous tissues. Mental disturbances are often a feature, and convulsions may occur.

Anemia is often the first sign of lead intoxication, but it is seldom severe and is characterized by large numbers of immature red blood cells.

Learning disabilities, the inability to learn and concentrate in children and adolescents. Usually associated with hyperactivity. For megavitamin therapy, *see* hyperactivity.

Lecithin, a complex mixture of choline, inositol, fatty acids, and phosphorus. May be presented as liquid oil (50 percent lecithin) in capsules or as dry granules (98 percent lecithin). Color varies from light yellow to dark brown depending on the source, crop variation, and treatment. It is odorless or has a slight nut-like odor and bland taste.

There are high concentrations in the brain, liver, kidneys, and bone marrow, but it is present in all animal and vegetable cells.

Best Food Sources in mg per 100 g

Liver	850
Meats	650
Fish	580
Eggs	350
Butter	150
Wheat	2,820
Soybean	1,480
Peanuts	1,113
Corn	953
Oats	650
Rice	580

Fatty Constituents

Vegetable lecithins provide polyunsaturated fats
Animal lecithins provide saturated fats

Recommended Daily Intake

Impossible to assess because of synthesis in the body

Symptoms of Excess Intake

None have been reported

Functions

Solubilizes fat
Mobilizes fat
Prevents fat build up in organs
Constituent of fatty membranes
Constituent of myelin sheath (insulator around nerves)
Provider of choline
Provider of inositol

Therapeutic Uses

Reducing high blood pressure
Reducing blood cholesterol levels
Reducing blood fat levels
Solubilizing gallstones
Treating atherosclerosis
Preventive treatment following:
    angina
    heart attack
    stroke
Treating senile dementia
Treating Alzheimer's disease

Leg cramps, *see* cramps.

Leg ulcers, caused by a breakdown of healthy skin resulting from poor blood circulation. Often a feature of deep vein thrombosis, varicose veins, and diabetes. Have been treated successfully by a combination of oral zinc supplements (200 mg three times daily), and directly applied zinc ointment containing zinc, silver (as silver nitrate), and allantoin (from comfrey) at the 1 percent strength. *See also* ulcers.

Legumes, include beans, lentils, and peas.

All legumes are good sources of carotene, vitamin E, and the vitamin B complex. They also contribute good levels of vitamin C but, as all water-soluble vitamins are lost into the cooking water, this should be utilized in some way to recover the vitamins. Lentils, however, are lower in carotene and vitamin C contents. *See* Figure 34.

Figure 34: Vitamin content of legumes

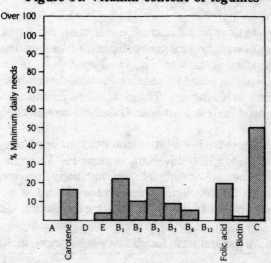

All are virtually free of sodium (unless it is added during cooking) but supply important quantities of potassium and the trace minerals to the diet. Figure 35 indicates the contribution of legumes to the daily intakes of minerals.

Figure 35: Mineral content of legumes

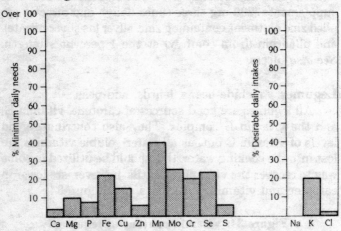

Leucocytes, white blood cells. Function as phagocytes that engulf invading microorganisms. Efficiency depends upon mobility of the leucocytes and upon their antimicrobial action. Both factors require adequate vitamin C concentration in leucocytes. Those with low resistance to infection need up to 3 g vitamin C daily to ensure adequate levels.

Lymphocytes are white blood cells that produce antibodies to neutralize invading organisms. Vitamin C in lymphocytes are essential for antibody production. Children with deficient lymphocytes exhibit a normal defense response to infection with 1 g of vitamin C daily.

Lipids, a general term for all fatty substances, including fats, oils, phospholipids (lecithin), cholesterol, triglycerides, and fatty acids. *See* individual entries.

Lipoic acid, known also as thioctic acid. Regarded as vitamin for bacteria, protozoa, plants, and some animals. Essential for pyruvate oxidation in these species. Not regarded as essential in humans but has been used as a therapy in the treatment of liver disease and poisoning by nonedible mushrooms.

Liquid paraffin, an anticonstipation agent. Prevents absorption of vitamins A, D, E, and K, and the carotenes.

Lithium, chemical symbol Li. Atomic weight 6.9. An alkali metal. Occurrence in the earth's crust is 0.005 percent by weight as the minerals spodumene, lepidolite, petalite, and triphylite.

Lithium is not considered to be an essential trace mineral in animals or humans but it is usually supplied to the body in drinking water. Studies on communities differing in lithium content of their drinking water suggest that higher intakes of the mineral result in: lower death rates from heart attacks; lower numbers of admissions for mental disorders; lower suicide rates; lower murder rates; lower incidence of gastric and duodenal ulcers; lower incidence of gout; and lower incidence of rheumatism. Low lithium levels in water were found to be 8 mg per liter; high levels were 100 mg per liter. Some South American Indian communities known for their quiet, peaceful ways and reduced incidence of arthritic conditions, gastroduodenal ulcers, and heart disease, have been found to have lithium intakes from their drinking water some 50 times more than the average Western community.

Absorption of lithium is very efficient and is passive, requiring no specific absorption process. It is rapidly distributed throughout the body with highest concentrations occurring in the bones, the thyroid gland, and the brain. Most excretion occurs through the kidneys into the urine and there are also losses in the sweat and saliva. The mineral crosses the placenta in the pregnant female and also appears in the breast milk of the nursing mother. All information on distribution throughout the body has come from studies on people given high doses of lithium. It cannot be detected easily in the body when the sole source is dietary.

Food sources of lithium are not known, as levels have not been measured. Concentrations in drinking water can range from 4-150 mg per liter and this represents the main source for most people.

Functions of lithium include that of a mood stabilizer. This has been utilized in psychiatry where the mineral is given as a treatment for mania and in the prevention of manic depression and depression. It could also be acting in a similar manner in those communities where there is a high intake from water supply, but the evidence is based only on epidemiological studies.

How it functions is unknown. Observed effects of lithium when given in drug doses are:

1. Increased turnover of the hormone noradrenaline.
2. Displacement of sodium from extracellular fluids.
3. Reduction of bone mineral content.
4. Increased blood serum concentrations of magnesium, calcium, and phosphate.
5. Increased blood plasma level of parathormone (from the parathyroid glands), which controls calcium and phosphorus metabolism.
6. A reduced synthesis and release of thyroid hormones.
7. An increased release of insulin, enhancing formation of muscle glycogen.
8. Increase in blood plasma level of antidiuretic hormone (vasopressin).

9. Transient increase in blood plasma level of aldosterone.

Therapy with lithium in acute mania requires constant monitoring of the plasma concentration to ensure that this lies close to 0.7 mg per 100 ml. At this level there is no interference with sodium and potassium levels. If lithium concentration rises above 1.4 mg per 100 ml, adverse effects will appear. Treatment must therefore be left in the hands of a medical practitioner who has access to a blood plasma monitoring service.

In the past, lithium has also been used to treat leukopenia (low white blood cell count), hyperthyroidism, Meniere's disease, tardive dyskinesia, and Huntington's chorea. It has also been used in the management of migraine, cluster headache, epilepsy, and premenstrual syndrome. Many of these nonpsychiatric uses are anecdotal and need to be investigated further. Doses of blood serum concentrations of lithium for use in these disorders have not been standardized.

Therapeutic forms of lithium are: lithium carbonate; lithium citrate; lithium chloride; lithium sulfate; lithium aspartate; lithium gluconate; lithium orotate; and lithium acetate. All are classed as prescription drugs only.

Excess intakes give rise to nausea; vomiting; diarrhea; coarse tremor; sluggishness; and defective speech at blood plasma levels greater than 1.05 mg per 100 ml. At higher levels, i.e., greater than 1.4 mg per 100 ml, the mineral gives rise to manifestations of impaired consciousness; abnormal muscle tenseness; coarse tremor; twitchings; increased reflex action; epileptic fits; and "coma vigil," where the individual can react when spoken to only by moving the head or eyes.

Liver, the largest gland in the body, forming one-fortieth of the body weight.

Storage depot for vitamins A, D, riboflavin, pantothenic acid, biotin, folic acid, pyridoxine, vitamin B_{12}, and vitamin C. Contains sufficient vitamin A, D, and B_{12} to last 6 months to 2 years in a well-fed person. Other vitamins must be replenished regularly every day or so.

Site for activation of all vitamins, i.e., the conversion of thiamin, riboflavin, nicotinamide, pyridoxine, pantothenic acid, and biotin into phosphate complexes; the conversion of folic acid to folinic acid; the conversion of vitamin B_{12} into its coenzyme forms; the conversion of vitamin D into 25-hydroxyvitamin D; and the conversion of vitamin A into retinoic acid. All these transformations are essential before the vitamins can perform metabolic functions. Also the site for: the synthesis of choline and inositol and their further incorporation into lecithin; the conversion of cholesterol into bile salts, dependent upon vitamin C; and the production of proteins needed for blood clotting, dependent upon vitamin K.

Figure 36: Vitamin content of liver

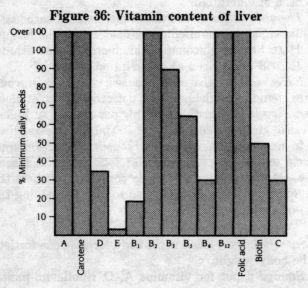

Diseases of the liver can: cause excessive loss of all vitamins, but especially the B complex; prevent the uptake of vitamins by the liver; and reduce the efficiency of the activation of vitamins into metabolic forms.

Alcohol and some medications can have similar effects on vitamins.

Fatty liver is due to deficiency of choline and inositol.

As a food, liver from all sources supplies large quantities of vitamin A and carotene, with some vitamin D and E. A rich source of the B vitamins and, unlike most foods of animal origin, provides some vitamin C. An excellent source of all minerals, including trace elements. *See* Figures 36 and 37.

Figure 37: Mineral content of liver

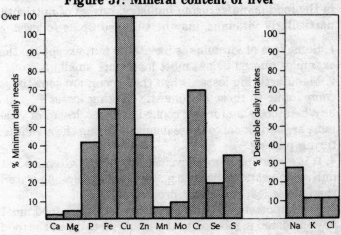

LLD factor, *see* B$_{12}$ (vitamin).

Loss of taste, a symptom associated with many conditions, e.g., head colds, pregnancy, and old age. Also known as hypogeusia. Associated also with copper deficiency, zinc deficiency, and vitamin deficiencies (especially vitamins A, B_6, and B_{12}). Loss of taste perception may be associated with a deficient protein in the saliva, known as gustin, that is a zinc-containing protein. Treating gustin-deficient people with zinc supplements (25 mg of the element daily) restored gustin contents of the saliva to normal and the sense of taste returned. Studies have indicated that about one-third of those with hypogeusia are zinc deficient. It is worthwhile, therefore, to take extra zinc as first-line treatment in any case of taste loss.

Losses in food processing, the term "food processing" includes domestic cooking techniques as well as those used in the food manufacturing industry. Losses of nutrients, particularly vitamins, may be summed up as follows:

1. Some loss of vitamins is inevitable but, except for the examples quoted below, most losses are small.
2. Manufacturing losses, when they occur, are sometimes comparable to those in domestic cooking losses.
3. When foods are further cooked at home, losses of vitamins are additional to those incurred during the manufacturing process.
4. It is easier and more convenient to recover vitamins lost during domestic cooking (e.g., by utilizing cooking water) than those lost in factory processing.
5. The importance of the losses in a particular food must be considered in relation to the whole diet. When the food makes only a small contribution to the intake of vitamins, processing losses may not be significant. However, losses from foods that make up a significant part of the diet, like milk and cereal products for infants and cereals in some countries, can cause serious deficiencies in those relying on such diets.
6. Some processing methods confer nutritional advantages

on the vitamin content of food, e.g., trypsin inhibitors in some vegetables are destroyed by cooking, and nicotinic acid is liberated from its inactive bound form by the cooking of cereals.

7. Underprocessing of some foods may not destroy harmful microorganisms in those foods. Processing can improve appearance and flavor of some foods and allow preservation for year-round availability. The ideal conditions of food processing allow these advantages with only minimal destruction and loss of vitamins.

Vitamin A: Both vitamin A and carotene are insoluble in water and so do not suffer from losses through extraction into processing and cooking water. The main destructive agent is oxygen, but in foods they tend to be protected by natural antioxidants like vitamin E.

Destruction of vitamin A and carotenes is accelerated by peroxides and free radicals formed from accompanying fats, particularly those of the polyunsaturated variety. Peroxides and free radicals in turn are formed by high temperatures and oxygen, and are promoted by light, traces of iron, and the presence of copper.

The amounts of vitamin A left after boiling margarine in water and frying in the fat are shown in Figure 38.

Canning green vegetables causes a 15-20 percent loss in vitamin A activity; yellow vegetables lose 30-35 percent. Drying vegetables and fruits under mild, controlled conditions produces up to 20 percent loss; traditional open-air drying methods destroy the vitamin completely.

Thiamin: Apart from vitamin C, thiamin is the least stable of the vitamins. Stable only under acid conditions, its destruction is catalyzed by copper. It is completely inactivated by sulfur dioxide, a widespread preservative added to foods; e.g., ground beef containing sulfur dioxide loses 90 percent of its thiamin in 48 hours. Protein and amino acids protect thiamin in foods, and starch assists

Figure 38: Vitamin A remaining in margarine after cooking

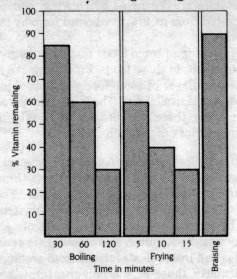

by absorbing the vitamin. Cereals are added to pork to help stabilize thiamin in cooked meats.

Principal losses of thiamin are due to its water solubility; the more finely ground the food the greater the loss. Chopped and minced foods can lose from 20-70 percent of their thiamin, which can be recovered by eating the extracted liquors. Cooking meat at temperatures up to 300°F (150°C) causes no destruction of the vitamin but considerable losses into the exuded juices. At temperatures of 400°F (200°C), 20 percent of the thiamin is destroyed.

The vitamin is not lost by leaching when boiling rice in distilled water, but 8-10 percent is lost in tap water and 36 percent is lost in well water, indicating the effects of alkalinity. Baking processes cause 15-25 percent loss of the vitamin but adding baking powder increases it to 50 percent.

Among vegetables, only potatoes contribute significant amounts of thiamin (about 15 percent of the daily intakes) to the diet. Pre-peeled potatoes and potato chips are kept white by adding sulfite solution, causing 55 percent destruction of the vitamin present. Further frying results in a 10 percent additional loss from the unpreserved variety, and 20 percent from the vegetable soaked in sulfite solution. Commercial processing causes 24 percent losses in potatoes dipped in sulfite solution after three days' storage at 40 °F (5 °C); further losses due to frying can be 30 percent.

Meats, poultry, and fish represent important sources of thiamin in the diet, but much of the vitamin can be lost depending upon the cooking method used. These are indicated in Figure 39.

The baking of bread gives rise to losses of up to 30 percent of the thiamin in the finished loaf, but no further breakdown occurs. Toasting of bread causes further losses up to 30 percent.

Riboflavin: Stable to oxygen, acid, and heat up to 266 °F (130 °C). Unstable to alkalis and light. Readily lost by leaching from chopped foods in wet processing and cooking.

Light in the presence of alkali converts riboflavin to lumiflavin, which in turn destroys vitamin C. In milk, 5 percent lumiflavin can cause a 50 percent loss in the vitamin C content. Under any conditions, however, light remains the great destroyer of riboflavin, as shown in Figure 40, which refers to the vitamin in milk and bread after only two hours exposure:

In the dark, under slightly acid conditions, riboflavin is completely stable; e.g., after 48 days in cold storage, beef has the same vitamin content as that immediately after slaughter.

Milk loses riboflavin when heated. On boiling there are

Figure 39: Thiamin remaining in meats, poultry, and fish after cooking

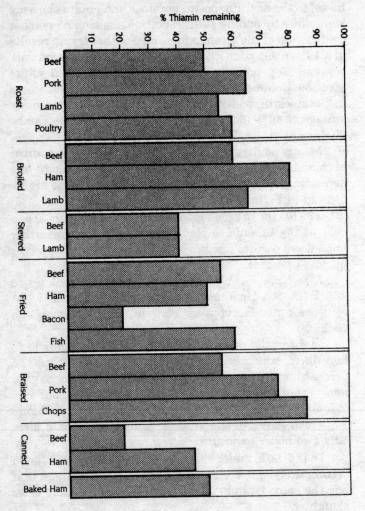

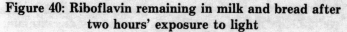

Figure 40: Riboflavin remaining in milk and bread after two hours' exposure to light

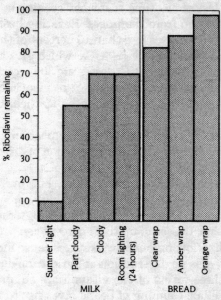

losses of 12-25 percent; in pasteurization these losses are 14 percent. Similar losses occur in meat cooking, and in all cases losses are greater in the presence of light. Dry curing of meat gives rise to 40 percent loss of riboflavin content; wet curing causes similar losses.

Nicotinic acid: Very stable, and leaching causes the only losses. It is unaffected by heat, air, light, acidity and alkalinity, and by sulfite. One of the few vitamins to be liberated by cooking processes, since in many cereals it is bound to starches and proteins in a complex called niacytin, which is not digested in the gastrointestinal tract. In wheat flour, 77 percent of the nicotinic acid is in a bound form that is completely liberated by baking with alkaline baking powder. In Mexico, corn is soaked overnight in lime water before making tortillas, in order to free the vitamin.

Some loss of nicotinic acid when cooking meat, but all can be recovered from the juices. Roasting beef and pork at 302°F (150°C) loses less than 10 percent of the vitamin; at temperatures of 401°F (205°C), which give an internal temperature of 208°F (98°C), losses are 30 percent. Dry curing of meat gives rise to no losses of nicotinic acid; wet curing causes 20 percent of it to be leached, but this is recoverable.

No nicotinic acid is lost in the pasteurization and sterilization of milk, or in the production of dried milk and dried egg.

Pyridoxine: Very stable to heat, but pyridoxal and pyridoxamine are more sensitive. Stability in milk during sterilization or drying is reduced due to interaction with milk proteins. Losses of up to 20 percent can occur during milk sterilization; higher temperatures cause more serious losses. There is no destruction of pyridoxine during cooking. The three forms of the vitamin are all stable to air, acid, and alkali. Canning of beans gives rise to 20 percent loss into blanching water and 15 percent in steam, but all can be recovered by utilizing the water. Losses into thawed fluids of 20-40 percent can occur when frozen vegetables are cooked.

Folic acid: Unstable only in the free form. Losses are 10 percent in steam blanching, 20 percent in pressure cooking, and 25-50 percent in boiling vegetables. Can be destroyed by oxidation. Losses from sterilized milk can vary from 20-100 percent depending on time of contact with air. If vitamin C is present, there is a protective effect and no folic acid is lost. If vitamin C is destroyed by subsequent reheating, folic acid is also oxidized.

Folic acid is sensitive to sunlight and its destruction is catalyzed by riboflavin, so store foods in a dark place. Cumulative losses of folic acid occur in food processing, and total losses can be as high as 65 percent. Vegetables, fruits, bread, and dairy products can be left with as little as 30 percent of their original folic acid content when finally eaten.

Viamin B$_{12}$: Unstable in the presence of alkali but stable under all other conditions of cooking. Light may destroy some, but proteins in the food appear to protect the vitamin. Leaching represents the main loss in food preparation.

Pantothenic acid: Stable under most cooking methods that are carried out in neutral conditions, but destroyed by heat, both on the acid and alkaline side of neutrality. Wheat suffers a 60 percent loss during manufacturing procedures involving baking powder. Meat losses are 30 percent during cooking but most is recoverable, as it is due to leaching. Six to 8 percent is lost from meats over periods up to twelve months in a deep-frozen state.

Biotin: Nothing is known about its stability in cooking processes.

Vitamin C: The most unstable of all the vitamins. Soft fruits like strawberries, raspberries, and black currants lose up to 60 percent of the vitamin when processed and stored. Vitamin C in fruit juices is very unstable, and losses of up to 50 percent are common once the container is opened. Virtually all is lost after two weeks in the refrigerator, particularly if the container is shaken after each opening. Figure 41 indicates how much vitamin C remains after cooking various vegetables under different conditions.

All the vitamin C leached out into the water can be recovered by utilizing the water in sauces, gravies, etc.

Vitamin D: Regarded as being very stable, but few studies have been carried out. It withstands smoking of fish, pasteurization and sterilization of milk, and drying of eggs. Probably loses between 25 and 35 percent of activity during the spray-drying of milk, but this is allowed for in fortification.

Figure 41: Vitamin C remaining in vegetables after cooking

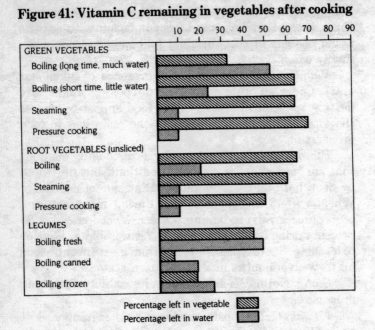

Percentage left in vegetable
Percentage left in water

Vitamin E: Very sensitive to oxidation, particularly in the presence of heat and alkali. Serious degradation in frozen foods. Even at deep-freeze temperatures (10°F or −12°C) vitamin E losses can total 68 percent after two weeks. French-fried potatoes at the same low temperature can lose 68 percent and 74 percent of the vitamin after one month and two months, respectively.

Processing and refining of cereals lead to wholesale losses of vitamin E. The most serious is the decrease in the vitamin content of white flour (92 percent) when it is produced from whole wheat grains. Whole wheat bread provides 2.2 mg per 100 g compared with only 0.23 mg in the white variety, because the wheat germ is removed and bleaching agents destroy vitamin E.

Cooking food in fats destroys 70-90 percent of the vitamin E content. Greatest losses happen in the presence of rancid fats and oils and these cannot always be detected by taste. Continual use of cooking fats and oils (e.g., in a deep fryer) consistently destroys the vitamin in the food being fried.

Tocopherol esters are most stable than the free tocopherol. Only 10-20 percent of the ester was destroyed under conditions that completely inactivated the free vitamin.

Boiling destroys 30 percent of the vitamin E in sprouts, cabbages, and carrots. Canning of vegetables leads to even greater losses, up to 80 percent of the original content.

Losses of vitamin C in cooking, depend upon the cooking method:

Boiled, peeled and mashed: 30-50 percent lost.
Boiled, unpeeled: 20-40 percent lost.
Baked: 20-40 percent lost.
Roast: 20-40 percent lost.
Steamed: 20-40 percent lost.
French fried: 25-35 percent lost.

Losses can be minimized by keeping the volume of water low. Much of the vitamin C can be recovered from the cooking water by utilizing it in sauces, gravy, etc.

Losses of vitamin C in storage, vitamin C is lost steadily from potatoes once they leave the ground and are stored:

Main crop, freshly dug: 30 mg per 100 g.
After 1-3 months storage: 20 mg per 100 g.
After 4-5 months storage: 15 mg per 100 g.
After 6-7 months storage: 10 mg per 100 g.
After 8-9 months storage: 8 mg per 100 g.

Lumbago,   pain, tenderness, and stiffness in the back muscles. Has been relieved by high doses (up to 600 mg) of thiamin. May also respond to 2 g calcium pantothenate daily.

Lung cancer,   *see* cancer.

M

Magnesium,   chemical symbol Mg. Atomic weight 24.31. Name is derived from the Greek city Magnesia, where there are large deposits of magnesium carbonate. The human body contains about 25 g of magnesium, of which half is found in the bones. The rest is distributed among the organs, nerves, and blood.

Best Food Source in mg per 100 g	
Soy beans	310
Nuts	250
Dried brewer's yeast	230
Whole wheat flour	140
Brown rice	119
Dried peas	116
Shrimps	110
Whole wheat bread	93
Rye flour	92
Seafood	90

Best Food Sources cont.

Dried fruits	80
Vegetables	60
Meats	50
Bananas	42
Green leafy vegetables	25

Recommended Daily Intake

Vary with authority, but in the region of 400 mg. *See* recommended daily intakes.

Magnesium cont.

Functions

Cofactor in many body processes including energy production and cell replication

Cofactor for vitamins B_1 and B_6

Stabilizes body cell structure

In growth

In repair and maintenance of body cells

Cofactor in hormones

Component of chlorophyll

Nerve impulse transmission

Deficiency Symptoms

Weakness

Tiredness

Vertigo

Convulsions

Nervousness

Muscle cramps and tremors

Tongue jerks and tremors

Involuntary eye movements

Unsteady gait

Hyperactivity in children

Irregular heartbeat

Palpitations

Low blood sugar

Painful swallowing

Deficiency Caused By

Reduced dietary intake due to poor diet, malnutrition, anorexia nervosa, high fiber intake, loss of appetite

High dietary intake of phosphate calcium, vitamin D, and saturated fats

Reduced absorption due to laxative abuse, infections, or allergies (celiac disease)

Kidney disease; diabetes; cancer; alcoholism; diuretics; antibiotics; and heart drugs

Contraceptive pill

High milk intake in diet

Heart Disease

May be related to low body magnesium levels because death rates from coronary heart disease are higher in soft water areas worldwide. Missing mineral in soft water is magnesium, which is decreased in the heart muscle of those dying from heart attacks

Magnesium cont.

Magnesium Supplements in mg per 100 mg

Magnesium amino acid chelate (18); dolomite (13); magnesium carbonate (25.2); magnesium acetate (11.2); magnesium chloride (11.8); magnesium citrate (16.2); magnesium gluconate (5.3); magnesium orotate (6.9); magnesium oxide (59.5); and magnesium sulfate (9.7)

Therapeutic Uses

Premenstrual tension
Menstrual cramps
Toxemia of pregnancy
Morning sickness
Hypoglycemia (low blood sugar)
Atherosclerosis, arterio-sclerosis
Angina

Therapeutic Uses cont.

Abnormal and irregular heartbeats
Epilepsy
Alcoholism
Kidney stones
Insomnia
Hyperactivity in children

Symptoms of Excess Intake

Flushing of skin
Thirst
Low blood pressure
Loss of reflexes
Shallow breathing
Can act as a purgative

These are highly unlikely in normal individuals who take too much magnesium because intestines reject excess mineral. Most likely in those with kidney disease

Magnesium stearate, consists of a mixture of magnesium stearate and magnesium palmitate, prepared from magnesium and vegetable oils (or sometimes animal fats). Used in dusting powders for skin diseases and in cosmetics. Acts as mechanical barrier in barrier cream. Added to tablets as a lubricant to prevent tablets from sticking during manufacture, but quantity used is usually only up to 5 mg per tablet.

Provides about 4.5 mg magnesium in 100 mg stearate, so when used as a lubricant adds only 0.2 mg magnesium to tablet. Not used as a supplement because of its water insolubility. Inhalation of magnesium stearate by babies can cause toxic effects, but no evidence that small amounts used as tablet lubricant are harmful.

Used also as a food additive. Functions as an emulsifier, an anticaking agent, and a release agent. Acceptable daily intake not limited. Permitted as a miscellaneous additive.

Magnesium sulfate, a common ingredient of laxative mineral waters. Also known as Epsom salts. Rarely used as a supplement although, when taken for its mild purgative effect, significant amounts may be absorbed. Should not be taken by those with impaired kidney function, or by children with intestinal parasitic diseases. Acts in dilute solution when swallowed by reducing the normal absorption of water from the intestine, with the result that the bulky fluid contents distend the bowel, and evacuation of the contents of the intestine follows in 1 or 2 hours.

Provides 9.7 mg magnesium in 100 mg sulfate. As a purgative, the dose is 5-15 g sulfate in 250 ml water, preferably before breakfast. For children, the dose is 100-250 mg sulfate per kg body weight.

Used also as a food additive. Functions as a dietary supplement; as a firming agent; and in brewing. Acceptable intake has not been determined.

Manganese, chemical symbol Mn. Atomic weight 54.9. An essential trace element for human beings.

Manganese cont.

Best Food Sources in mg per 100 g

Cereals	4.92
Whole wheat bread	4.21
Nuts	3.54
Legumes	2.01
Fruits	1.05
Green leafy vegetables	0.78
Liver	0.64
Root vegetables	0.58
Meats and fish	0.02
Black tea (0.5 mg per cup)	

Recommended Daily Intake

Suggestions are from 2.5 to 5.0 mg. Usually easily obtained from good diets. Tea can provide up to half required intake in tea-drinking countries like UK and Australia

Deficiency Caused By

Usually related to poor dietary intake when processed and refined foods form large part of diet

Rarely may be due to excessive copper intakes

Functions

Growth

Maintains healthy nervous system

Cofactor for enzymes for energy production and health of joints

Cofactor for female sex hormones

Cofactor for nucleic acid synthesis

Production of thyroxine

Cofactor for vitamins B, C, and E

Synthesis of structural proteins of body cells

Development and maintenance of healthy bones

Stimulates glycogen (animal starch) storage in liver

Therapeutic Uses

Schizophrenia

Myasthenia gravis

Anemia (improves utilization of iron)

Benefits claimed in the above conditions

Supplementation is also wise in other conditions mentioned under Deficiency Symptoms

Manganese cont.

Deficiency Symptoms	Body Content and Turnover

No specific symptoms associated with deficiency, but low blood and tissue levels reported in:
  diabetes
  heart disease
  schizophrenia
  atherosclerosis
  myasthenia gravis
    (muscle wasting and
    weakness)
  rheumatoid arthritis
  infants before weaning
	An adult contains between 12 and 20 mg
	Highest concentrations in skeleton, liver, kidneys, and heart
	Daily losses in feces are about 4 mg (via bile)
	Only 3 to 5 percent of dietary manganese is absorbed

Symptoms of Excess Intake	**Manganese Supplements in mg per 100 mg**
These are very rare from oral ingestion of manganese but include: lethargy; involuntary movements; lack of control of voluntary movements; changes in muscle tone; postural changes; and coma	Manganese amino acid chelate (10); manganese sulfate (24.6); manganese gluconate (11.4); manganese orotate (315.2); manganese chloride (27.7); manganese glycerophosphate (24.4); and manganese hypophosphite (27.1).

Margarine, both hard and soft are fortified with vitamins A and D to contain (in μg per 100 g): vitamin A—900; vitamin D—7.94. A good source of vitamin E, providing 8.0 mg per 100 g. Traces only of all B vitamins but contains no vitamin C.

Marzipan, vitamins are provided by almonds, lemon juice, and eggs. Vitamin A content is 10 μg per 100 g, but carotene is absent. Vitamin D content is 0.13 μg per 100 g. A good provider of vitamin E at 9.1 mg per 100 g. B vitamins present are (in mg per 100 g): thiamin (0.12); riboflavin (0.45); nicotinic acid (2.4); pyridoxine (0.06); and pantothenic acid (0.35). The folic acid level is 45 μg per 100 g, and the biotin level is 2 μg per 100 g. Vitamin C content is 2 mg per 100 g.

Minerals

An excellent source of potassium that is low in sodium. A rich source of calcium, magnesium, and phosphorus. A good source of iron, zinc, and sulfur. Minerals present are (in mg per 100 g): sodium (13); potassium (400); calcium (120); magnesium (120); phosphorus (220); iron (2.0); copper (0.08); zinc (1.5); sulfur (81); and chloride (13).

Meats, all muscle meats, whether from beef, lamb, veal, or poultry (chicken and turkey), contain only traces of vitamins A, D, and carotene, and little vitamin E. They are completely devoid of vitamin C and provide very little folic acid and biotin. Pork is a better provider of the B vitamins, but these tend to be reduced a little in the curing process to produce bacon. Figures 42, 43, and 44 show the vitamins and mineral content of meats, and the vitamins remaining after cooking, respectively.

Megaloblastic anemia, characterized by the appearance of large, immature red blood cells with a shortened lifespan. May be due to deficiency of folic acid, vitamin B_{12}, or pyridoxine. The only treatment is to replace the specific deficient vitamin.

Megavitamin therapy, treating certain conditions with

Figure 42: Vitamin content of meats

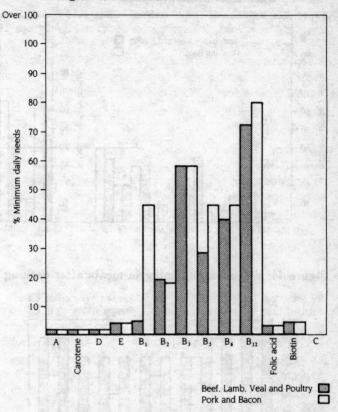

doses of vitamins far above the levels found even in good diets. The use of vitamins as medicines but without the side effects noted with drugs. Has been used successfully in treating arthritis, autism, colds, heart disease, hyperactivity, learning disabilities, respiratory infections, schizophrenia, and senile dementia. *See* individual condition for treatment.

Figure 43: Mineral content of meats

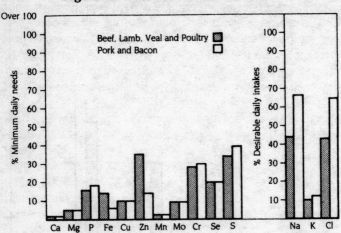

Figure 44: Vitamins remaining in meats after cooking

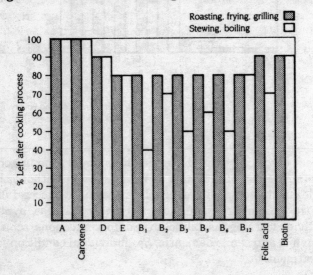

Melons, *Cantaloupe:* Raw, edible portion is a very rich source of carotene, providing also a good amount of vitamin C. The orange-colored flesh contains 2.0 mg carotene per 100 g plus 0.1 mg per 100 g of vitamin E. B vitamins present are (in mg per 100 g): thiamin (0.05); riboflavin (0.03); nicotinic acid (0.5); pyridoxine (0.07); and pantothenic acid (0.23). Folic acid level is 30 μg per 100 g; biotin has not been detected. Vitamin C content is 25 mg per 100 g.

Honeydew: Raw, edible portion is a moderate source of carotene but provides good amounts of vitamin C. Carotene content is 100 μg per 100 g for the green-colored flesh; vitamin E level is 0.1 mg per 100 g. B vitamins present are (in mg per 100 g): thiamin (0.05); riboflavin (0.03); nicotinic acid (0.5); pyridoxine (0.07); and pantothenic acid (0.23). Folic acid level is 30 μg per 100 g; biotin is absent. Vitamin C content is 25 mg per 100 g.

Watermelon: Raw, edible portion is a poor source of all vitamins except pantothenic acid and vitamin C. Carotene is 20 μg per 100 g; vitamin E level is 0.1 mg per 100 g. B vitamins present are (in mg per 100 g): thiamin (0.02); riboflavin (0.02); nicotinic acid (0.3); pyridoxine (0.07); and pantothenic acid (1.55). Provides small amount of folic acid (3 μg per 100 g) but no biotin. Vitamin C content is 5 mg per 100 g.

Minerals

All types are low in sodium and supply very good levels of potassium. Some trace minerals are present.

Cantaloupe: Levels for raw, edible portion are (in mg per 100 g): sodium—14; potassium—320; calcium—19; magnesium—20; phosphorus—30; iron—0.8; copper—0.04; zinc—0.1; sulfur—12; and chloride—44.

Honeydew: Levels for raw, edible portion are (in mg per 100 g): sodium—20; potassium—220; calcium—14; magnesium—13; phosphorus—9; iron—0.2; copper—0.04; zinc—0.1; sulfur—6; and chloride—45.

Watermelon: Levels for raw, edible portion are (in mg per 100 g): sodium—4; potassium—120; calcium—5; magnesium—11; phosphorus—8; iron—0.3; copper—0.03; and zinc—0.1.

Memory, when faulty may be a symptom of thiamin deficiency. Treat with adequate doses (up to 50 mg daily) of vitamin B₁. When associated with age may respond to choline. *See* senile dementia. It is claimed that RNA intake may help improve memory, particularly in the aged.

Menaphtone, *see* K₃ (vitamin).

Menaquinone, *see* K₂ (vitamin).

Ménière's disease, a disorder characterized by recurrent severe vertigo, deafness, tinnitus (ringing in the ears), nausea, and vomiting. Some relief is gained from the following regimen: thiamin (10-25 mg); riboflavin (10-25 mg); a 50:50 mixture of nicotinic acid and nicotinamide (100-250 mg); all four times daily for two weeks. If relief is obtained, reduce all vitamins to a dose that maintains relief and continue treatment.

Menkes' syndrome, a rare genetic disease of infants characterized by an inability to absorb copper, resulting in progressive degeneration of the nervous system. Deterioration starts with convulsions at three months of age, and death used to occur within three years. Symptoms and signs are: failure to keratinize hair, which looks like steel wool, thus the name "steely-hair syndrome"; mental retardation; low body temperature; low copper levels in blood plasma and in liver; weakened skeleton; and degenerative changes in the walls of the aorta. Provided diagnosis is made early in life, the condition can be controlled with intravenous copper.

Menopause, the period in a woman's life when her secretion of female sex hormones slows down and eventually ceases. Characterized by hot flushes, headaches, giddiness, nervousness, depression, excessive menstrual flow, increase in weight, and pruritus (itching) in sexual parts.

Vitamin E (100 IU with each meal) is claimed to relieve hot flushes, headaches, and nervousness. Pyridoxine (50-100 mg daily) may help relieve depression. Iron (15 mg) and vitamin C (200 mg) daily will help replace blood losses. Calcium (1,000 mg) and vitamin D (6.25 μg) will help prevent calcium loss from bones, induced by deficiency of estrogens.

Menstrual cramps, abdominal cramps that tend to occur a few days before menstruation and may continue through the first few days of the menstrual flow. Has been found to respond, along with associated leg and back cramps, to supplementary calcium, 500-1,000 mg in the few days preceding menstruation until it has finished.

Menstruation, the monthly breakdown of the lining of the uterus, leading to loss of blood in the menstrual flow.

Blood loss is replaced by adequate intakes of mineral iron (24 mg) with vitamin C (100 mg); vitamin E (100 IU); folic acid (200 μg), and vitamin B_{12} (5 μg). The mild depression that can occur just before menstruation often responds to pyridoxine. *See* depression. Irregular or painful menstrual periods may respond to bioflavonoids (1,000 mg daily).

Mental ability, may be increased in normal children with thiamin (10 mg), vitamin C (100 mg), and vitamin E (100 IU) daily to ensure adequate intakes and thereby maximize potential.

Mental disturbance,   can be related to mild deficiencies of vitamins, particularly thiamin, riboflavin, nicotinamide, pyridoxine, folic acid, and vitamin B_{12}. Sufferers may also be vitamin-dependent, requiring larger intakes than can be obtained from diet. *See* autism; depression; megavitamin therapy; schizophrenia; and senile dementia.

Mercury,   chemical symbol Hg, from the Latin *hydrargyrum*. Atomic weight 200.6. Also known as quicksilver and liquid silver. Occurs in nature as cinnabar (mercuric sulfide) with an abundance in the earth's crust of 0.5 mg per kg.

Not known to have any essential role in the metabolism of any living organism. In the form of liquid or gaseous mercury, it is toxic. Mercury salts and particularly organic forms of mercury are more poisonous than the element. Dental amalgams used for filling teeth cavities are so insoluble that they are usually not regarded as toxic, but some doubts have been expressed recently on the safety of the tiny amounts eroded from fillings. There have been claims that cancer, heart disease, menstrual, and thyroid problems are relieved by the removal of amalgam fillings. The most dangerous forms of mercury are the alkyl derivatives methylmercury and ethylmercury. They are usually introduced into the body from fish and grain foods.

Inorganic mercury salts, introduced by pollution into fresh and sea waters, are converted by microorganisms into methylmercury. This is introduced into the food chain via small plant-eating fish, to large carnivorous fish like tuna, swordfish, and pike. When these fish are eaten by humans, poisoning results. Fatal levels of contamination in such fish have been reported from Japan, where industrial pollution has introduced mercury salts into sea water.

Fish from inland freshwater lakes in Sweden and North America may contain as much as 503 μg mercury per 100 g, which is a toxic level. Canned tuna can contain 10-80 μg mercury per 100 g, half as methylmercury. Deep-sea fish caught off the UK fishing grounds contain only 8 μg mercury per 100 g, but nearer the coasts, where chemical effluents are discharged into the sea, fish may contain up to 50 μg mercury per 100 g. The highest tolerable weekly intake of mercury according to WHO recommendations is 300 μg, of which no more than 200 μg should be methylmercury.

Seeds that have been dusted with alkyl mercury compounds to prevent fungal contamination have caused poisoning in Guatamala, Iraq, and Pakistan. The poisoning was accidental since the seeds were not meant for human consumption, but 459 deaths resulted from 6,500 cases. Similar treated seeds fed to farm animals have given rise to mercury poisoning in humans who ate the meat from these animals.

Elemental mercury may arise from: accidental breaking of thermometers and barometers: discarded batteries, mercury vapor lamps, and mercury switches; coal burning, which can contribute 3,000 metric tons per year to the atmosphere; natural weathering of rocks and soils, which contribute 230 metric tons annually; the "silvering" of coins; and the manufacture of mercury amalgams.

Ingested mercury compounds accumulate in certain parts of the brain, eventually causing brain damage. Other affected organs include the colon and kidneys. Methylmercury causes: nerve degeneration; birth defects; genetic defects; chromosome damage; excessive salivation; loss of teeth; and gross muscle tremors. When applied to the skin, alkyl mercury compounds cause irritation, redness, and blistering.

In babies, dusting of the skin with powders or application of ointments containing mercury causes pink disease or acrodynia. Characterized by: lesions of the skin on the hands and feet; swelling of the extremities; digestive disturbances; itching of the hands and feet; pink coloration of hands, feet, cheeks, and tip of nose; weakness of the muscles; and arthritis.

Acute poisoning by soluble mercury compounds causes: metallic taste; thirst; severe abdominal pain; vomiting; ashy discoloration of the mouth and throat; and diarrhea contaminated with blood. Later, ulceration, kidney disease, and colitis with severe hemorrhage may develop. Mercury vapor, when inhaled, causes respiratory symptoms and kidney damage.

Chronic poisoning by mercury vapor, by soluble mercury salts, or by prolonged skin contact, causes: tremor; muscle instability; sensory disturbances; gastrointestinal symptoms; dermatitis; liver and kidney damage; anemia; and mental deterioration. A blue line on the gums may be indicative of chronic mercury poisoning.

Maximum permissible atmospheric concentrations of mercury are 0.1 mg per cubic meter of air and 0.01 mg alkyl mercury per cubic meter of air.

Medicinal compounds of mercury include:

1. Ammoniated mercury to treat impetigo and threadworm infections.
2. Oleated mercury, as ammoniated mercury.
3. Mercurial diuretics, used in cardiac edema.
4. Mercuric chloride, used in solution as a disinfectant for the skin.
5. Mercuric cyanide, used as a disinfectant in eye solutions.
6. Red mercuric iodide, used as a disinfectant in wounds; as a vaginal douche; as a skin disinfectant; to treat ringworm and lupus; and to treat syphilis.

7. Mercuric nitrate, used to treat syphilitic warts; eczema; and psoriasis.

8. Yellow mercuric oxide, used as an ointment to treat blepharitis and conjunctivitis. Prolonged use should be avoided, as mercury can be absorbed through the eye tissues.

9. Mercuric oxycyanide, preferred over mercuric chloride as a skin disinfectant and in eye lotions.

10. Mercurous chloride, once used orally as a purgative at doses of 30-200 mg, but now discontinued because of absorption. As an ointment or dusting powder, it has been used to treat itching, psoriasis, and eczema, and as a strong ointment (30-50 percent) in preventing syphilis.

Mesoinositol,   *see* inositol.

Metformin,   an antidiabetic drug. Prevents absorption of vitamin B_{12}.

Methods of food processing,   *Blanching:* Required to inactivate enzymes that cause deterioration of food. It always precedes freezing and drying and is a feature of canning. Leaching occurs into the blanching water and the extent of loss depends largely on the time the vegetable is in contact with water. Temperature must be high enough to inactivate the enzymes, i.e., at least 185°F (85°C). Garden peas need 1 minute; sliced beans 2 minutes; Brussels sprouts from 3.5 to 7 minutes, depending upon size. Temperatures vary from 200 to 210°F (93 to 99°C) and oxidation may contribute to some destruction of the vitamins.

Losses during blanching are estimated to be between 13 and 60 percent for vitamin C; 2-30 percent for thiamin; and 5-40 percent for riboflavin. Carotene losses are less than 1 percent but these ignore possible transformation into less active forms. Losses due to extraction into the water are lessened if the water is consumed. Canning retains all the leached vitamins in the liquor, so it should not be discarded when the vegetable contents are eaten. Similarly with canned meats. Microwave blanching is reported to cause less damage than steam, and a combination of microwave and hot water treatment is claimed to preserve more vitamins and produce a more palatable product. Fluidized-bed blanching, which is really hot gas treatment, is claimed to reduce vitamin C and carotene losses. In domestic blanching, losses of vitamin C, thiamin, and carotene can be prevented by rapid cooling after blanching. Cold air is best to prevent further leaching into the water.

Heat sterilization: Because oxygen is excluded, losses of vitamins are minimal during canning procedures. Thiamin is lost even so, particularly from meat. The best conditions to preserve vitamins are heating for a short time at high temperatures rather than longer periods at lower temperatures.

Losses are less for canned meats and fruits than for vegetables during heat sterilization, because the acid conditions are protective. Minor losses only of riboflavin and nicotinic acid occur during the heat sterilization of meats. Once the food has been sterilized in cans, stability of the vitamins is good. Only 15 percent of vitamin C is lost after two years' storage of vegetables in cans.

Freezing: One of the better methods of preserving foods, since only the fresh variety is frozen when at the peak of its vitamin content. In frozen meat, most of the vitamins are well preserved but the exudate from thawing can contain appreciable amounts of the water-soluble vitamins. Vegetables must be blanched before freezing, so losses are those mentioned under blanching. Similarly, during the thawing process the aqueous exudate will contain vitamins, so introducing frozen vegetables directly into the heating water will retain them all as long as this water is utilized in the meal. Pyridoxine, pantothenic acid, and vitamin E are most affected by deep freezing.

Irradiation: Causes some losses in vitamins but freeze-drying before treating with ionizing radiation reduces these losses. The most sensitive vitamins are thiamin, riboflavin, vitamin A, and vitamin E. The most stable is nicotinic acid.

Freeze-drying: This low-temperature dehydration is probably the best method of retaining vitamins in the preserved food. It is not, unfortunately, widespread.

Hot-air drying: Causes variable losses in the different vitamins. Under the most favorable conditions some 10-15 percent of vitamin C is lost during hot-air drying of vegetables.

Pressure cooking: The shorter time required plus the smaller volume of water used reduces vitamin losses compared with conventional boiling. The principal cause of loss is leaching rather than heat, but this is limited by the volume of water rather than by the time of cooking. In many vegetables it has been shown that losses of thiamin in pressure cooking are 25-50 percent, those in steaming are 50 percent, and those in boiling 75-80 percent. Vitamin C losses are of the same order but vary among different vegetables.

Microwave heating: Uses high-energy electromagnetic radiation (frequency 2450m Hz, wavelength 12cm) to produce very efficient cooking. Microwaves generate heat throughout the bulk of the food rather than simply applying it to the surface as in a conventional oven. Losses of vitamins may be less than or equal to those associated with conventional cooking methods, but they are never more.

General principles for retaining the highest vitamin content in foods cooked using domestic methods are:

1. Use fresh food rather than stored food.

2. Cook in a minimum amount of water.

3. Minimum cooking at a high temperature is preferable to long cooking at a lower one.

4. Cooked foods should not be stored before eating except when deep-frozen.

5. Remember that cooking of frozen foods represents the second process they have been through, so the whole of the food plus cooking liquids (or thawed exudate) should be utilized. *See* eggs; fish; meats; milk; and vegetables.

Methotrexate, an anticancer drug. An immunosuppressant. Impairs folic acid utilization.

Migraine, a particular type of headache caused by constriction of the blood vessels followed by their dilation, which gives rise to pulsating pain. Characterized by nausea, vomiting, and visual disturbances in severe cases.

Vitamin therapy includes whole vitamin B complex (10 mg potency) three times daily plus nicotinamide (100 mg), calcium pantothenate (100 mg), and pyridoxine (50 mg), all three times daily. If this regimen prevents attacks, reduce doses gradually to those that maintain relief.

Minerals

Extra magnesium taken at the rate of 400 mg daily, preferably as the amino acid chelate, has been claimed to prevent development of migraine headaches. A trigger factor in the development of those headaches may be high concentrations of sodium in some sufferers. One study has shown that migraine attacks can be precipitated in some people by sudden loads of common salt, as in potato chips, salted nuts, and high-sodium foods such as pickles, sauces, and preserved meats; or of sodium glutamate in highly spiced and oriental foods. Avoiding these foods led to a reduced incidence of migraines in these people.

Milk, a good source of all vitamins (*see* Figure 45), but seasonal variation with regard to the fat-soluble. A low-sodium food that is rich in potassium and calcium, but not a good source of iron (*see* Figure 46). Nonfat milk is devoid of fat-soluble vitamins, but its content of the water-soluble variety is similar to those of whole milk. Dried nonfat milk is very rich in all micronutrients because of the concentration effect.

Figure 45: Vitamin content of milk

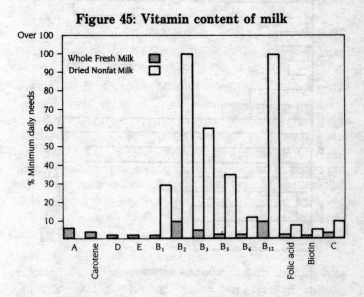

Milk of magnesia, an aqueous suspension of hydrated magnesium oxide containing the equivalent of 7.45-8.35 percent magnesium hydroxide. 10 ml contains the equivalent of 550 mg of magnesium oxide providing 300 mg magnesium.

Mineral, literally "mined from the earth." Divided into:

Figure 46: Mineral content of milk

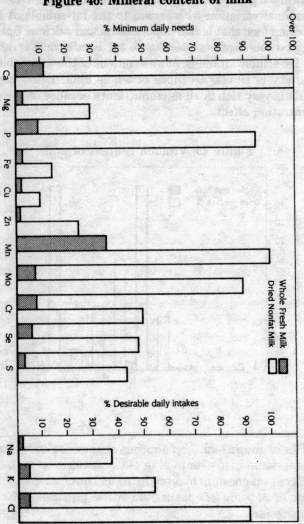

1. Metallic elements, present in high quantities in the body and diet when daily intakes are greater than 100 mg, e.g., calcium, magnesium, and potassium.
2. Nonmetallic elements, abundant in the earth, body, and diet when daily intakes are greater than 100 mg, e.g., carbon, phosphorus, and sulfur.
3. Metallic elements, present in very small amounts in the body and diet, that are essential for health, e.g., chromium, copper, iron, and zinc.
4. Nonmetallic elements, present in very small amounts in the body and diet, that are essential for health, e.g., fluorine, iodine, and selenium.

Any essential element not found in groups 1 and 2 is classed as a trace mineral or trace element.

Mineral absorption, the process whereby minerals are transferred from the food or from supplements into the intestinal cells and hence into the bloodstream. The main site of absorption of minerals is the small intestine, but some are transferred in other parts of the gastrointestinal tract. Simple minerals like sodium, potassium, chloride, and iodide that are present as electrically charged atoms (known as ions) are absorbed by simple diffusion from the gut contents into the intestinal cells and there is little or no control of their absorption. Control of their level in the body is through their excretion. Sodium, potassium, lithium, and ammonium ions are monovalent, i.e., they carry only one positive charge. They cannot be chelated for this reason. Calcium, magnesium, copper, zinc, iron, and manganese are all divalent, i.e., they carry two positive charges per atom. Small amounts of them may also be assimilated by simple diffusion, but usually they must be chelated with amino acids before they can be absorbed into the intestinal cells and hence into the bloodstream. Transport of divalent minerals within the body is mainly as complexes with amino acids or with proteins, but small amounts exist in the bloodstream as simple ions, e.g., calcium, which participates in the blood-clotting process. Absorption of divalent minerals therefore depends upon:

1. The quantity of protein or amino acids present in the digestive system.

2. The quality of protein or amino acids available, since the right sort of amino acids must be present.

3. Competition among minerals for the amino acids available and the specific sites of absorption in the small intestine. For example, lead and iron compete for the same sites; cadmium and zinc compete for the same sites. Any excess of one mineral over its competitor will increase its chances of absorption.

    Figure 47 shows the ratios of quantities of minerals absorbed from amino acid chelates compared with those from mineral salts and oxides.

Figure 47: Ratios of quantities of minerals absorbed from amino acid chelates compared with those from mineral salts and oxides

Mineral	Amino acid chelates: Carbonates	Amino acid chelates: Sulfates	Amino acid chelates: Oxides
Copper	5.8:1	4.1:1	3.0:1
Magnesium	1.8:1	2.6:1	4.2:1
Iron	3.6:1	3.8:1	4.9:1
Zinc	3.0:1	2.3:1	3.9:1

Mineral content of vegetables, in general the mineral content of vegetables reflects that of the soil in which they are growing. Studies have indicated that even in plants growing in adjacent areas, there is wide variation in mineral content because of differing soil concentrations. Other factors may also play a part (*see* minerals in soil). Figure

48 illustrates how vegetables may not always contain the concentrations of minerals expected. However, it must be pointed out that most mineral concentrations in vegetables sold commercially lie somewhere in the middle of the ranges.

Figure 48: Variation in mineral content of selected vegetables

Food	Content	Boron	Manganese	Iron	Copper	Cobalt
			Parts per million (ppm)			
Green beans	High	73	60	227	69	0.26
	Low	10	2	10	3	0.00
Cabbage	High	42	13	94	48	0.15
	Low	7	2	20	0.4	0.00
Lettuce	High	37	169	516	60	0.19
	Low	6	1	9	3	0.00
Tomatoes	High	36	68	1,938	53	0.63
	Low	5	1	1	0	0.00
Spinach	High	88	117	1,584	32	0.25
	Low	12	1	19	0.5	0.20

Mineral losses in freezing, consist of: the leaching of minerals during the thawing process; losses into the water during the blanching stage; and losses into the water or fat during the cooking processes. Typical losses of calcium and magnesium from frozen fruits and vegetables are shown in Figure 49.

Mineral losses in refining, all minerals are lost to some extent during the refining of natural foods into the processed variety, but losses of trace minerals are the most significant. Some of these are shown in Figure 50.

Gross minerals too are lost (*see* Figure 51). In the US, iron is replaced in white flour to the level of 20 mg per pound of flour. Calcium is not required to be replaced,

Figure 49: Percentage losses of calcium and magnesium from frozen fruits and vegetables

Fruits and vegetables	Calcium	Magnesium
Apricots	33	12
Asparagus	0	30
Blackberries	56	48
Black-eyed peas	7	0
Blueberries	53	0
Brussels sprouts	33	9
Cherries	22	0
Corn	57	53
Green beans	19	34
Green peas	4	31
Lima beans	33	28
Peaches	33	40
Potatoes	0	38
Spinach	0	23
Strawberries	39	31

Figure 50: Percentage losses of trace elements in the refinement of foods

	Co	Cr	Cu	Fe	Mg	Mn	Mo	Se	Zn
White flour from whole wheat	89	98	68	76	85	86	48	16	78
Polished rice from brown rice	38	75	25	—	83	27	—	—	50
White sugar from raw cane sugar	88	90	80	99	99	89	—	75	98
Refined oils from cold-expressed oils	—	—	—	—	99	—	—	—	75
Butter production from milk	—	—	—	—	94	—	—	—	50

Figure 51: Percentage losses of gross minerals by refining of wheat and sugar

	Ca	Cl	K	Na	P	S
White flour from whole wheat	60	0	77	78	71	32
White sugar from raw cane sugar	96	99	98	99	99	99

but when it is, it must be to the level of 960 mg per pound of flour.

Mineral relationships,   The minerals in the body are all in balance with one another so that an excess of one will affect the levels of others. Their relationships are summed up in the mineral wheel shown in Figure 52.

On this wheel, an arrow pointing to a particular mineral means that a deficiency of that mineral may be caused by an excess of the mineral from whence the arrow comes. For example, a high calcium intake may reduce the amount of zinc, and high cadmium intakes will cause copper levels to drop. When the line between two minerals contains two opposing arrows, each mineral may influence the other. A low potassium intake will allow sodium to accumulate, and conversely an excess of sodium in the diet will lower potassium levels in the body.

The wheel allows other relationships to be worked out. Calcium and/or phosphorus deficiency may allow an excess of manganese to develop. This high level can cause depression of potassium, which allows sodium to accumulate. There is no direct line between calcium and sodium and potassium, but calcium levels can indirectly affect those of the other two elements. Hence calcium deficiency may have an effect upon blood pressure. In another example, calcium and/or phosphorus in excess will depress zinc levels, leading to a skin disease called parakeratosis. This condition can therefore be caused by excessive intakes of calcium and phosphorus as well as by a reduced dietary intake of zinc.

Mineral waters, when sold in bottles or drunk at the source, as at spas, have been popular for centuries as a remedy for various conditions, particularly those of

Figure 52: Mineral relationships

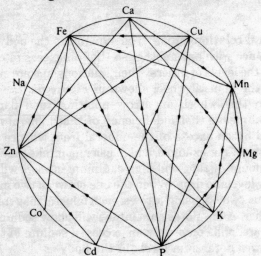

Ca - Calcium, Cd - Cadmium, Co - Cobalt, Cu - Copper,
Fe - Iron, K - Potassium, Mg - Magnesium, Mn - Manganese,
Na - Sodium, P - Phosphorus, Zn - Zinc

the rheumatic kind. With modern knowledge that such diseases may be associated with mineral imbalance, there would appear to be some logic in increasing mineral intakes for their diuretic, laxative, and replacement effects. Many people prefer mineral waters because the water has not been softened, chlorinated, or fluoridated, and has had the minimum of pipe feeding before they drink it.

Minerals in soil, humans derive their food from plants or from animals that have eaten plants, or from fish that have eaten plants. All plants, whether growing on land or in water, must derive their minerals from the soil or the sea. These are the ultimate source of all minerals. The richness of a soil as well as depending on the macro-elements nitrogen, phosphorus, and potassium must also

have present other less abundant but just as essential
trace minerals. Deficiency of macroelements does exist.
Some lands are low in phosphate, hence the importance
of the natural phosphate-rich fertilizer guano. Potassium
is lacking in some areas and deficiency is made up by
treating the land with potassium, often obtained from rich
inland lakes like the Dead Sea. Nitrogen is usually supplied in the form of nitrates. Zinc deficiency is not unknown and it reflects in the health of the farm animals who
live off plants grown on the soil. Supplementation of
animal feeds with zinc is more usual than treating the soil.

Mineral deficiencies in the soil can produce disease in
localized areas. Lack of iodine in the soil causes goiter.
Magnesium deficiency of the soil in certain areas of France
has been associated with a particular type of cancer. Some
regions in Poland had a high incidence of leukemia. The
causative agents were found to be toxins produced by the
soil microorganism *Aspergillus flavus.* This fungus flour-
ishes in soil that is deficient in iron, copper, and magnesium and has excessive concentrations of silicon and
potassium. When this imbalance was corrected by correct
fertilization of the soil (extra trace elements plus dolomite
to supply calcium and magnesium), the fungus was controlled and the incidence of leukemia dropped. Low levels
of manganese and chromium in the soil appear from
epidemiological studies to increase the chances of heart
disease and atherosclerosis in those living in the area. In
South Africa, molybdenum, copper, and iron deficiencies
in the soil have led to esophageal cancer.

Mineral excesses of a toxic element in the soil can also
produce disease. In Japan, faulty treatment of waste water
from a mine led to pollution of a river with cadmium. The
mineral was deposited in the soil from which plants absorbed it. When the rice was eaten, the local population
accumulated cadmium in the body and, combined with a

low calcium and vitamin D intake, a concentration was
reached that resulted in a bone disease that caused ex-
cruciating pain. *See* Itai-itai. Adjustment of the diet to
give the correct balance of the essential minerals cured the
condition. In the Netherlands, some areas of high silicon
content in the soil had a high incidence of all types of
cancer that was reduced by treating the soil with calcium.
This inhibited the uptake of silicon by plants. Excessively
high soil concentrations of zinc and chromium have been
associated with gastrointestinal cancer in some parts of
the world. In India, a raised water table made the topsoil
in one area more alkaline. This increased the uptake of
molybdenum and fluoride by sorghum plants (the staple
diet). These uptakes led to copper deficiency. The population eating these plants were thus copper deficient, but
had excessive intakes of molybdenum and fluoride. The
result was a crippling bone disease called genu valgum,
which was only remedied by balancing the intake of the
essential minerals.

Uptake from the soil can be affected by:
1. High levels of humic acid, which can bind minerals,
making them unavailable.
2. The presence of other minerals, e.g., low levels of potassium or high levels of phosphate, will render iron insoluble.
3. pH. This is a measure of acidity or alkalinity of the soil.
From pH 0 to 6 is acid, from pH 8 to 14 is alkaline; pH
7 is neutral. At neutral pH, most minerals are fully available to the plant. In highly acid soils, only potassium, iron,
manganese, copper, and zinc can be absorbed. In highly
alkaline soils, phosphorus, potassium, sulfur, and boron are
freely available for absorption. *See also* Mulder's chart.

Molybdenum,　chemical symbol Mo. Atomic weight 95.9.
Essential in soil and plants for processes "fixing" or utiliz-

ing nitrogen from the air. Essential trace element for animals and humans.

Best Food Sources in μg per 100 g

Buckwheat	485
Beans—canned	350
Wheat germ	200
Liver	200
Soybeans	182
Whole-wheat grains	120
Cereals	90
Organ meats	75
Eggs	50
Cocoa	50
Vegetables	26
Fruits	16
Alcoholic beverages	10

Symptoms of Excess Intake

Gout (at intakes of 10-15 mg daily)
Increased excretion of copper causing deficiency. In animals this can give rise to loss of hair color

Deficiency Symptoms

Irritability
Irregular heartbeat
Lack of uric acid production
Coma

Functions

Prevention of dental caries
Iron metabolism
Uric acid excretion (nitrogen excretory product)
Maintains normal sexual function in male

Body Content

Adult content is 9 mg with most in the liver
Fifty percent of dietary mineral is absorbed
Excretion is mainly in the urine

Deficiency Results in

Dental caries
Sexual impotence in men
Cancer of the esophagus

Deficiency Caused by

Eating foods from molybdenum deficient soils
High intakes of refined and processed foods

Molybdenum cont.

Therapeutic Uses	Recommended Daily Intake
May be of benefit in those conditions resulting in deficiency, but no clinical trials carried out yet Has been used to remove excess copper from body	Suggested only by the US Food and Nutrition Board, at 500 μg

Monosodium glutamate, a food additive that functions as a flavor enhancer. Also known as MSG and sodium hydrogen L-glutamate. Acceptable daily intake is up to 120 mg per kg body weight. Not to be given to infants under 12 weeks old. Provides 12.3 mg sodium per 100 mg. Not used in foods especially made for babies and young children. *See also* Chinese restaurant syndrome.

Morning sickness, *see* nausea.

Mouth ulcers, acute painful ulcers on the movable oral mucosal lining, occurring singly or in groups. Also known as canker sores, aphthous ulcers, and aphthous stomatitis. There are reports of the successful prevention of mouth ulcers by taking oral zinc supplement equivalent to 20-25 mg element daily. Existing ulcers may respond to directly applied zinc creams, preferably with the mineral as zinc gluconate, or mouthwashes containing zinc. *See also* ulcers.

Mucous membranes, wet surfaces of the body including the nose, eyes, mouth, respiratory system, digestive tract, anus, and genital tracts.

     Vitamin A protects all mucous membranes and maintains their health. Deficiency of the vitamin leads to drying out of the membranes, resulting in ulceration and liability to infection. *See* keratinization.

Inflammation can result from deficiency of nicotinic acid and riboflavin. Polluted atmosphere can destroy the membranes. They are best protected by vitamins A and E. Tobacco smoking irritates the mucous membranes of the respiratory tract. They are best protected by beta-carotene.

Mulder's chart, in soil a complicated mixture of minerals is presented to a plant. The uptake of a particular mineral is under the influence of other minerals which can either stimulate or antagonize the absorption of that mineral. Zinc absorption by a plant is dependent upon phosphorus, iron, and calcium. High phosphorus levels antagonize the uptake of zinc, copper, and potassium; they also stimulate the uptake of magnesium. Inter-relationships are shown in Figure 53.

Muscle cramps, prolonged painful contractions of a muscle. May appear as spasms where the muscles cannot perform a specific task but allows the use of them for other movement. Known as occupational cramp, an example of which is "writer's cramp." Can be caused by an imbalance of certain minerals, and as a result of stress, bad posture, or fatigue. May respond to extra calcium in the diet, usually between 640 and 800 mg of the element daily. This therapy has been found to relieve "growing pains" in children; night cramps; aching legs; and muscle cramps of pregnancy. Night cramps may also respond to extra potassium in the diet. *See* fatigue.

Muscle pain, may be related to biotin deficiency. Treat with 2 to 5 mg daily by mouth.

Figure 53: Plant uptake of minerals

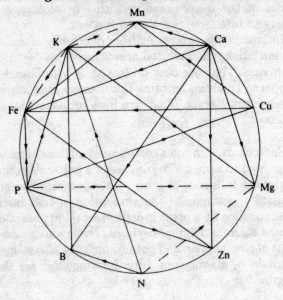

B - Boron, Ca - Calcium.
Cu - Copper, Fe - Iron.
K - Potassium, Mg - Magnesium.
Mn - Manganese, N - Nitrogen.
P - Phosphorus, Zn - Zinc.

———— Antagonism

- - - → Stimulation

Muscle spasms,   also known as restless legs. Often occurs during sleep and relieved by walking or moving the affected leg. Treated with vitamin E (100 IU with each meal or 400 IU in one dose daily).

Muscles,   need a good blood supply and efficient conversion of nutrients into energy for maximum performance. Vitamin E (400 IU daily) is essential to maintain healthy blood vessels. Vitamin C (500 mg daily) is essential for the production of carnitine, needed for muscle energy. *See carnitine.*

Muscular dystrophy, a muscle disease characterized by progressive weakness and degeneration of muscle fibers, but without evidence of nerve degeneration. A symptom of vitamin E deficiency in many animal species that can be cured by vitamin treatment. No evidence of a relationship between vitamin E and human muscular dystrophy, but occasionally cases have responded to high doses of vitamin E, preferably with the trace mineral selenium.

Benefit in rare cases has been claimed with ubiquinone, a natural vitamin-like substance, produced in the body under the influence of vitamin E.

Muscular tics, repeated and largely involuntary movements of muscles varying in complexity. Also known as tremors and twitches. May become prominent under conditions of emotional stress. Caused by an impulse conductance abnormality at the junction of the nerve and muscle, possibly due to a mineral imbalance. Most likely deficiencies are potassium and magnesium. Supplementation with these minerals can often relieve persistent tics, tremors, and twitches. May also be caused by excess toxic minerals like lead, in which case the condition is relieved by removal of the toxic mineral with the agents calcium, zinc, and vitamin C.

Myelin, the fatty sheath that covers nerves and the spinal cord and acts as an insulator. Composed of cholesterol, PUFA, and phosphatidyl choline complexed with a lipid called sphingosine. Myelin loss due to degeneration is a factor in multiple sclerosis. Vitamin B_{12} and PUFA are essential for a healthy myelin sheath.

Myocardial infarction, *see* heart disease.

Myoinositol, *see* inositol.

Myxedema, a condition caused by thyroid hormone deficiency in the adult. Also known as hypothyroidism. Symptoms and signs may be subtle and insidious at onset. The facial expression is dull; there is puffiness and swelling around the eyes; the eyelids droop; the hair is sparse, coarse, and dry; the skin is coarse, scaly, dry, and thick; memory is poor; there is intellectual impairment with gradual change in personality; sometimes this leads to a psychosis commonly called "myxedema madness." Often carotene is deposited in the palms and soles causing yellow coloration. The tongue may be enlarged. The heart rate is slow and the heart is often enlarged. Tingling in the hands and feet is often present. The reflexes are quick to contract but slow to relax. There may be excessive bleeding at menstrual periods. Constipation, low body temperature, and anemia are often present. Vitamin B_{12} absorption is adversely affected because of decreased intrinsic factor synthesis.

Treatment is replacement therapy with a variety of thyroid hormone preparations including: synthetic thyroxine; synthetic triiodothyronine; combinations of both; and desiccated animal thyroid. An average maintenance dose of 150-200 μg L-thyroxine daily is the preferred treatment. At least 60 percent of this is absorbed. In infants and young children, the maintenance dose is 2.5 μg per kg body weight per day. Triiodothyronine tends to be used to initiate therapy because it has a rapid action and turnover, but this detracts from its use in long-term therapy, where thyroxine is preferred.

Iodides cannot be used since the thyroid does not have the ability to convert them to the thyroid hormones. *See also* cretinism.

N

Natural vitamins, are those that are:

1. Derived from natural sources (e.g., d-alpha-tocopherol).
2. Produced by fermentation (e.g., vitamin B_{12}).
3. Presented in a natural environment (e.g., vitamin E in wheat germ oil or soybean oil).
4. Presented in a food (e.g., vitamin B complex in yeast).
    Advantages are:
1. Biologically more active (e.g., d-alpha-tocopherol).
2. Better absorbed (e.g., fat-soluble vitamins need fats or oils present as well).
3. Better utilized in the presence of other factors (e.g., vitamin C and bioflavonoids occur in foods together and function in the body together).
4. Retained by the body longer (e.g., natural vitamin E).

Nausea, a feeling of discomfort in the region of the stomach with aversion to food and a tendency to vomit. A side effect of many medications.

Morning sickness: Nausea of the early stages of pregnancy. Has been treated with pyridoxine (but seek medical advice).

Travel sickness: Nausea associated with various forms of travel. Has been treated with pyridoxine (25 mg) and ginger (160 mg) before the trip and, if necessary, during it. Half the dose is effective for children.

Neomycin, an antibiotic. Prevents absorption of vitamin D.

Nervous system, health depends upon adequate vitamin B complex and vitamin E. Thiamin at intakes between 50 and 600 mg daily has relieved sciatica, trigeminal neuralgia, facial paralysis, optic neuritis, and peripheral neuritis. Psychosis and mental deterioration have responded to vitamin B_{12}, preferably by injection.

Choline is of benefit in some cases of Alzheimer's disease and senile dementia. A combination of vitamin E and inositol has helped in some nerve diseases associated with muscle degeneration. High potencies of whole vitamin B complex have relieved the mental deterioration of Huntington's chorea. Mild depression will often respond to vitamin B_6 therapy alone.

Nicotinic acid in high doses (1-3 g daily) has been used successfully in schizophrenia. Paresthesia has been relieved by 50 mg pyridoxine daily.

Deficiencies of thiamin, riboflavin, nicotinamide, pyridoxine, and vitamin B_{12} all cause damage to the nervous system. It is preferable therefore to treat any mild mental or nervous condition with a high potency of whole vitamin B complex.

Neuritis, a general term for degeneration and inflammation of one or more nerves. A symptom rather than a disease.

Optic: Inflammation of the eye nerve.

Peripheral: Affecting simultaneously several nerves, usually those of the limbs. Caused by thiamin deficiency, diabetes, alcohol, and heavy metal poisoning. Also known as polyneuritis.

Treatment: See nervous system.

Niacin, a water-soluble member of the vitamin B complex. Synonymous with nicotinic acid. Presented also as niacinamide, synonymous with nicotinamide. Generally accepted as vitamin B$_3$. Also known as vitamin PP (pellagra-preventing) or PP factor. Nicotinic acid has been known since 1867, but was demonstrated to be a vitamin only in 1937 by Dr. Conrad Elvehjem.

Best Food Sources in mg per 100 g

Yeast extract	67.0
Dried brewer's yeast	37.9
Wheat bran	32.6
Nuts	21.3
Pig liver	19.4
Chicken	11.6
Soy flour	10.6
Meats	10.5
Fatty fish	10.4
Wheat grains	8.1
Cheese	6.2
Dried fruits	5.6
Whole wheat bread	5.6
Brown rice	4.7
Wheat germ	4.2
Eggs	3.7

Stability in Foods

Usually stable. *See* losses in food processing

Recommended Daily Intake

Should be at least 19 mg. *See* recommended daily intake

Functions

Acts as coenzymes NAD (nicotinamide adenine dinucleotide) and NADP (nicotinamide adenine dinucleotide phosphate) in cell respiration

Produces energy from sugars, fats, and protein

Maintains healthy skin, nerves, brain, tongue, and digestive system

Significant amounts produced in the body from the amino acid L-tryptophan—60 mg L-tryptophan makes 1 mg niacin

Deficiency Results in

Pellagra characterized by:
rashes
dry scaly skin
wrinkles
coarse structure of skin
loss of appetite
nausea and vomiting
inflamed mouth
inflamed digestive tract

Niacin cont.

Deficiency Results cont.	**Symptoms of Excess Intake**

insomnia
irritability
stress
depression
	Niacinamide (more than 3 g):
	   depression
	   liver malfunction
	Niacin:
	   flushing of face
	   sensation of heat
	   pounding headache
	   dry skin
	   abdominal cramps
	   diarrhea
	   nausea

Deficiency Symptoms
Summed up as 3 Ds:
   dermatitis
   diarrhea
   dementia	

Deficiency Caused by: Alcohol Antileukemia drugs	**Avoid** High doses during pregnancy (both types of vitamin) and when suffering from gastric and duodenal ulcers (niacin).
Therapeutic Uses Childhood schizophrenia Alcohol addiction Tobacco addiction Arthritis Reducing blood cholesterol (niacin only)	

Niacinamide, the active form of nicotinic acid. Known also as nicotinamide.

Nickel, chemical symbol Ni. Atomic weight 58.7. Occurs in nature as chalcopyrite, penthandite, garnierite, nicollite, and nillerite. Abundance in the earth's crust is 180 mg per kg. It is an essential trace mineral for rats, chicks, and swine, but its functions are not known.

Deficiency in animals impairs iron absorption, leading to low iron levels in the tissues and organs, and to iron-deficiency anemia.

Not known to be essential for humans but traces of the mineral are found in all human tissues.

Functions in animals include: an antagonistic action to the hormone adrenalin; intensifying the action of insulin; increasing blood fats; and stabilizing RNA and DNA in the tissues.

High blood levels are found in those who have suffered a heart attack; those with serious burns; those who have suffered a stroke; women with toxemia of pregnancy; women with cancer of the uterus; and those with lung cancer.

Low blood levels are found in those with cirrhosis of the liver, and those with chronic kidney failure.

Food sources are provided by contamination, such as: from the alloys used to line cooking utensils; from machines used to process and refine food; from pasteurization equipment; from margarine, where it is used as a catalyst in its production; and from cigarette smoke. In tobacco, some nickel combines with carbon monoxide to form the toxic nickel carbonyl, a known carcinogen (cancer-producing substance) for rats.

Toxic effects of excess oral nickel intakes in humans are unknown. Nickel carbonyl from tobacco smoke may be a factor in causing lung cancer in humans. Acute toxic effects of nickel carbonyl are frontal headache; vertigo; nausea; vomiting; chest pain; and cough. Nickel, when in contact with the skin of sensitive people, can cause dermatitis.

Excess oral intakes in young chicks cause pigmentation changes in the skin; swelling in the legs; dermatitis;

a fat-depleted liver; and an oxygen-depleted liver. The mineral accumulates in the liver, bones, and aorta.

Nicotinamide, the active metabolic form of nicotinic acid. Known also as niacinamide and vitamin B_3.

Nicotinic acid, *see* niacin (vitamin B_3).

Night blindness, the inability to see in the dark, due solely to vitamin A deficiency.

Nitrates, *see* nitrosamines.

Nitrites, *see* nitrosamines.

Nitritocobalamin, vitamin B_{12}. *See* B complex.

Nitrofurantoin, a urinary anti-infective. Impairs folic acid utilization.

Nitrosamines, toxic substances associated with certain types of cancer. Readily formed in the digestive tract from amines and nitrites, both present in food, drugs, cosmetics, and the environment. Nitrites are used extensively as food preservatives and are readily formed from nitrates. Nitrosamines are more likely to be produced in the stomach in the absence of acid.

Vitamin C prevents formation of nitrosamines and neutralizes the preformed variety, so this vitamin should be taken at every meal.

Nucleic acids, comprise both ribonucleic acids (RNA) and deoxyribonucleic acids (DNA). Essential components of all living cells, they are necessary for cell growth and hereditary information. Reduced synthesis leads to consequences of aging, including poor memory. They have been used to slow down the aging process, usually by injection.

The vitamins needed for healthy RNA and DNA production in humans include vitamin A, vitamin E, pyridoxine, folic acid, vitamin B_{12}, and choline.

They are present in dried yeast to the extent of 12 percent of weight.

Nuts, include almonds, Barcelona, Brazil, chestnuts, hazel, walnuts, and pecans. The kernels of all nuts are completely devoid of carotene and in the ripe state contain only traces of vitamin C. They provide good quantities of vitamin E but of only two types: alpha-tocopherol and gamma-tocopherol. Brazil nuts, chestnuts, peanuts, and walnuts contain mainly gamma-tocopherol. Individual figures for all kernels are total tocophrols. All kernels

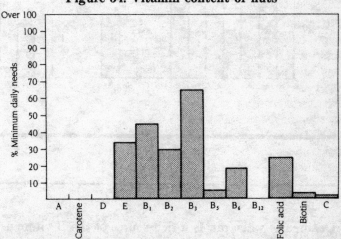

Figure 54: Vitamin content of nuts

supply good quantities of the B vitamins. *See* the entries for the individual nuts; Figure 54.

In the raw state, nuts are a sodium-free food that supplies useful amounts of all other minerals, particularly manganese. *See* Figure 55.

Figure 55: Mineral content of nuts

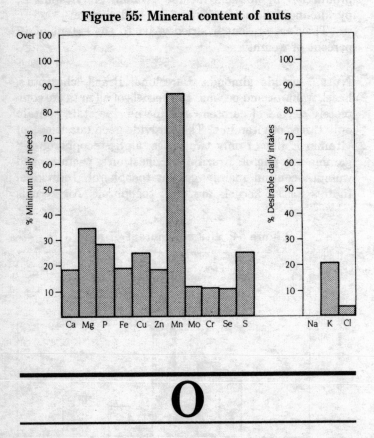

O

Oatmeal, when raw is a rich source of the B vitamins providing (in mg per 100 g): thiamin—0.50; riboflavin—

0.10; nicotinic acid—3.8; pyridoxine—0.12; folic acid—0.060; pantothenic acid—1.0; biotin—0.020; and vitamin E—0.9. It is devoid of vitamins A, D, C, and carotene.

Minerals

A low-sodium food, rich in potassium, magnesium, sulfur, and phosphorus. An excellent source of the trace minerals iron, zinc, and copper. Raw, it gives the following mineral levels (in mg per 100 g): sodium—33; potassium—370; calcium—55; magnesium—110; phosphorus—380; iron—4.1; copper—0.23; zinc—3.0; sulfur—160; and chloride—73.

Oil of evening primrose, a seed oil containing substantial amounts of a member of the essential fatty acid family, gamma linolenic acid (GLA). Usually produced in the body from linoleic acid, but there are claims that in some conditions synthesis is blocked or not sufficient. There are reports that GLA is beneficial in: multiple sclerosis; premenstrual syndrome; skin disorders; alcoholism; hyperactivity in children; arthritis and other inflammatory conditions; and disorders of the immune system. GLA functions as a precursor of the hormones, known as prostaglandins. Usual intakes are 3 to 6 capsules per day (500 mg oil containing 40 mg GLA per capsule.)

Okra, an African plant known also as gumbo. Provides 90 μg carotene per 100 g in the raw state. B vitamins present are (in mg per 100 g): thiamin (0.10); riboflavin (0.10); nicotinic acid (1.3); pyridoxine (0.08); and pantothenic acid (0.26). A good source of folic acid at 100 μg per 100 g. A good source of vitamin C at 25 mg per 100 g.

Minerals

Practically devoid of sodium, it supplies good levels of potassium, calcium, magnesium, and phosphorus, and useful quantities of the trace minerals iron and copper. In the raw state, it supplies the following minerals (in mg per 100 g): sodium (7); potassium (190); calcium (70); magnesium (60); phosphorus (60); iron (1.0); copper (0.19); sulfur (30); and chloride (41).

Onions,   contain no carotene and only traces of vitamin E. A poor source of B vitamins, made poorer by boiling. Levels for raw and boiled respectively are (in mg per 100 g): thiamin—0.03 and 0.02; riboflavin—0.05 and 0.04; nicotinic acid—0.4 and 0.2; pyridoxine—0.10 and 0.06; and pantothenic acid—0.14 and 0.10. Folic acid levels (in μg per 100 g) are 16 and 8; and biotin levels are 0.9 and 0.6 for raw and boiled onions, respectively. Vitamin C content is reduced from 10 mg to 6 mg per 100 g in boiling. Frying virtually destroys the B vitamins and vitamin C; only 0.4 mg nicotnic acid per 100 g survives.

Minerals
A low-sodium food providing good levels of potassium and sulfur. Green onions are a good source of calcium, iron, and copper. The mineral levels for raw and boiled onions, respectively, are (in mg per 100 g): sodium—10 and 7; potassium—140 and 78; calcium—31 and 24; magnesium—8 and 5; phosphorus—30 and 16; iron—0.3 and 0.3; copper—0.08 and 0.07; zinc—0.1 and 0.1; sulfur—51 and 24; and chloride—20 and 5.

Levels in fried onions are (in mg per 100 g): sodium—20; potassium—270; calcium—61; magnesium—15; phosphorus—59; iron—0.6; copper—0.16; zinc—0.1; sulfur—88; and chloride—38.

Raw, green onions contain (in mg per 100 g): sodium—13; potassium—230; calcium—140; magnesium—11; phosphorus—24; iron—1.2; copper—0.13; sulfur—50; and chloride—36.

Organ meats,   supply vitamin C in addition to all other vitamins, unlike other meat products. Liver and kidney are particularly rich in vitamin A, nicotinic acid, pantothenic acid, and vitamin B_{12}. *See* liver; kidney.

Orotates, a synthetic complex of minerals with orotic acid. There is some evidence that orotates are absorbed more efficiently than mineral salts from the intestine and they may act as carriers of certain minerals across cell membranes. Orotic acid has been named vitamin B_{13} in the past but, as ample quantities are produced within the body as an intermediate in nucleic acid metabolism, it is no longer regarded as a vitamin. Mineral orotates have been claimed to be beneficial in many clinical conditions. They are useful in replacing mineral deficiences, but some of the benefits in other conditions may be related to the orotic acid moiety.

Orotic acid, known also as whey factor, animal galactose factor, and vitamin B_{13}. No longer regarded as a vitamin.

    Richest food sources are liquid whey and root vegetables, but traces are usually present in all foods containing the vitamin B complex.

    Stable in food processing methods.

    Functions as an intermediate in the metabolism of RNA and DNA in humans and is produced in adequate quantities under normal circumstances.

    An essential growth factor for microorganisms.

    Deficiency in humans has not been reported.

    Deficiency in animals has not been reported.

    Recommended daily intake not set because need in the diet is not established.

    Toxicity is low. Up to 4 g orotic acid daily by mouth has caused no harm over many days of treatment.

    Therapy with orotic acid has been claimed beneficial in: multiple sclerosis (given by injection); chronic hepatitis (given as calcium orotate over many months); and gout (4 g daily of orotic acid for six days).

Orthomolecular medicine,   *see* megavitamin therapy.

Osteomalacia,   a disease characterized by softening of the bones and low body levels of calcium, due specifically to vitamin D deficiency in the adult. *See* D (vitamin).

Osteoporosis,   a honeycombing of the bones due to loss of calcium that is not replaced. Associated mainly with the postmenopausal period of life, and long-term corticosteroid treatment. Symptoms are bone pain and ease of fracture. Treated with high intakes of calcium (1,000 mg daily), plus fluoride, plus adequate vitamin D to ensure absorption (400 IU) or hormone replacement therapy in the postmenopausal state.

Minerals

The bones most commonly affected are the spinal vertebrae, the femur (thigh bone), and the radius (shorter arm bone). The condition is associated with: menopausal and postmenopausal females; prolonged use of oral corticosteroid drugs; excessive excretion of calcium on some medicinal drug treatments; overproduction of adrenal cortex steroid hormones; multiple myeloma; gastrectomy; and prolonged immobilization. Dietary causes include: insufficient intake of calcium over long periods; nonreplacement of lost calcium in poorly fed women with multiple births over many years; nonreplacement of calcium lost in breast-feeding; increased effect of fluoride on copper deficiency, inducing osteoporosis of the legs; increased overnight loss of calcium after the menopause; and increased urinary loss of calcium on high-protein diets. Symptoms may be absent until bone fracture occurs. Sometimes there is aching pain in the bones, particularly the back. X-ray analysis and biochemical measurements of the blood and urine are essential for correct diagnosis and to differentiate the condition from osteomalacia.

During the menopause and postmenopausal periods, medical treatment of osteoporosis is confined to hormone replacement therapy (HRT) with female sex hormones. This therapy is still being assessed for possible long-term, serious side effects. Dietary treatment involves supplementation with calcium; with vitamin D to help absorb the calcium; and sometimes with added fluoride to stimulate calcium resorption into the bones. Typical supplementary regimens are: 1,000-1,500 mg calcium daily, preferably with 400 IU vitamin D; and 1,000-1,500 mg calcium daily with 400 IU vitamin D plus 45 mg per day sodium fluoride. In view of the toxicity of sodium fluoride, this regimen should be taken only under medical supervision. Regular exercise is also an important factor in preventing and in treating osteoporosis. Adequate intake of calcium during life before the menopause also contributes to prevention of the disease once the menopause starts.

Decreased mineral density in the lumbar vertebrae of female athletes who have a reduced number of menstrual periods has been observed. Similar findings were noted in young women whose periods had stopped for reasons other than pregnancy. In all cases, calcium intake was suggested to be increased, by 800-1,500 mg per day.

Otosclerosis,   *see* deafness.

Oxygen,   occasionally causes eye problems (retrolental fibroplasia) in premature babies in oxygen tents. Prevented by administration of vitamin E, usually by injection.

P

PABA, *see* para-aminobenzoic acid.

Paget's disease, a chronic degenerative disease of the bones occurring in the elderly and most frequently affecting the skull, backbone, pelvis, and long bones. Also called osteitis deformans. In the early stages of the disease, calcium is lost from the bones. Characterized by deep, dull, aching bone pain that can cause headache, deafness, and blindness when the skull is affected, and bowing of the legs when these limbs are affected. The usual medical treatment is a prolonged course of the hormone calcitonin, but this may be complemented by extra calcium. Supplementary treatment consists of 500-1,000 mg calcium three times daily between meals, preferably in a form that does not supply phosphorus. Bone pain was relieved by this treatment, which is believed to stimulate the body's own production of calcitonin.

Pangamic acid, from *pan* meaning everywhere and *gami* meaning family. A water-soluble factor present in vitamin B complex. Also known as B_{15}; vitamin B_{15} (incorrectly); and D-gluconic acid 6-[bis (1-methybethyl)] amino acetate. First isolated from apricot pits in 1951 by the father and son team of Drs. E.T. Krebs and E.T. Krebs, Jr. Present in supplements as calcium pangamate and sodium pangamate. May also be dimethylglycine.

Richest food sources are (in µg per 100 g): rice bran (200); corn (150); dried brewer's yeast (128); oat flakes (106);

wheat germ (70); apricot pits (65); wheat bran (31); pig liver (22); barley (12); and whole wheat flour (8).

Unstable to food processing. Lost and destroyed during cooking methods.

Doubt existed as to the correct structure of pangamic acid. It is now generally accepted as D-gluconic acid 6-[bis (1-methybethyl)] amino acetate.

Functions as: a stimulator of the carriage of oxygen to the blood from the lungs and from the blood to the muscles and vital organs; a lipotropic agent to keep fat in solution; a detoxifying agent on poisons and free radicals; and a stimulator of antistress hormone production.

Deficiency in humans has not been reported. Symptoms are not specific, but may be related to the above functions.

Deficiency in animals has not been reported.

Recommended daily intake has not been set by any authority.

Toxicity is low. Safe in doses up to 300 mg daily but produces occasional transient flushing of the skin. Calcium pangamate is better tolerated than sodium pangamate.

Therapy with pangamic acid is claimed to be beneficial in: heart disease; atherosclerosis; bronchial asthma; and diabetes.

Pantothenic acid, from *panthos* meaning everywhere. A water-soluble member of the vitamin B complex. Usually presented in oral supplements as calcium pantothenate; in cosmetics and toiletries as dexpanthenol and pantothenol. Generally accepted as vitamin B_5. Also known as chick antidermatitis factor. An antistress vitamin.

Isolated from rice husks by Dr. R.J. Williams of the University of Texas in 1939. Occurs naturally as D-pantothenic acid.

Pantothenic acid cont.

Best Food Sources in mg per 100 g

Dried brewer's yeast	9.5
Pig liver	6.5
Yeast extract	3.8
Pig kidney	3.0
Nuts	2.7
Wheat bran	2.4
Wheat germ	2.2
Soy flour	1.8
Eggs	1.8
Poultry	1.2
Meats	1.1
Whole grains	0.9
Legumes	0.8
Whole wheat bread	0.6
Vegetables	0.3

Deficiency Symptoms

Aching, burning, throbbing feet
Loss of appetite
Indigestion
Abdominal pain
Respiratory infections
Fatigue
Insomnia
Depression
Psychosis
Headaches

Functions

As coenzyme A in:
  production of energy
Production of antistress hormones
controlling fat metabolism
formation of antibodies
maintaining healthy nerves
detoxifying drugs

Stability in Foods

Easily destroyed, even at deep-freeze temperatures
See losses in food processing

Therapeutic Uses

Rheumatoid arthritis
Paralytic ileus
Allergic skin reactions
Reduction of mucous secretion in respiratory allergies
Stress situations

Pantothenic acid cont.

Deficiency Caused by	Recommended Daily Intake
Stress	Should be at least 10 mg.
Antibiotics	*See* recommended daily intakes
Symptoms of Excess Intake	Difficult to assess because of production by intestinal bacteria
None have been reported	

Para-aminobenzoic acid, a member of the vitamin B complex, but not a true vitamin for humans. Known also as PABA, vitamin Bx, bacterial vitamin H, and anti-gray hair factor. A growth factor for bacteria that is blocked by sulfonamide drugs, first reported by D.D. Woods at Oxford in 1942. PABA is present as part of the structure of folic acid, but there is no evidence that humans can make folic acid from it. It is likely that intestinal bacteria can, but the body is unable to utilize the folic acid produced.

Richest food sources are liver, eggs, molasses, brewer's yeast, and wheat germ. Few figures are available, but baker's yeast contains 6 mg per kg; brewer's yeast up to 100 mg per kg.

Stability in food processing unknown.

Functions in humans not known.

Deficiency in humans gives no specific symptoms.

Functions in animals in synthesis of body protein and in red blood cell production, possibly after conversion to folic acid. Helps utilization of pantothenic acid. May act as skin cancer preventative.

Deficiency in animals causes anemia, premature graying of hair.

Recommended daily intake not set by any authority. In some countries, the maximum dose in medicines is

restricted, but there are no specified legal limits on its
amount in food, as long as that amount is regarded as
safe.

   Toxicity is low but high intakes can cause nausea,
vomiting, itching, skin rash, and liver damage.

   Therapy with oral PABA has been used in vitiligo. As
a lotion or cream, it is effective as a sunscreen agent to
prevent sunburn. May also prevent skin cancer. Has been
used in digestive disorders, nervousness, and depression.
Contraindicated when on sulfonamide treatment.

Para-aminosalicylic acid,   an antituberculosis drug. Impairs absorption of vitamins A, D, E, and K, and of B_{12}.

Paralytic ileus,   *see* surgery.

Parathyroid hormone,   a polypeptide hormone containing 84 amino acids, synthesized in the parathyroid glands
(adjacent to or embedded in the thyroid gland), that control the distribution of calcium and phosphate in the body.
Also known as parathormone. Secretion of the hormone
is stimulated by a decrease in blood calcium. A high concentration of the hormone causes transfer of calcium from
the bone reservoirs to the blood; a deficiency lowers blood
calcium levels, causing tetany. The hormone also functions
by promoting the formation of the active form of vitamin
D within the kidney. This is probably how the hormone
mediates in its action of increasing the absorption of
calcium from the intestine. The hormone also decreases the
kidney reabsorption of phosphate, allowing the mineral to
be excreted.

Paresthesia,   tingling or pricking feeling, or sometimes
numbness in the skin. A symptom of multiple sclerosis,

nerve disease, and blood vessel disease. Relieved by pyridoxine (50 mg daily), but very high doses (2,000 mg) may cause it.

Parkinson's disease, a chronic disease of the central nervous system characterized by slowness and poorness of purposeful movement, rigid muscles, and tremor. Also known as Parkinsonism and shaking palsy.

The drug levodopa, used to bring symptomatic relief, is neutralized by pyridoxine; therefore supplements of this vitamin should *not* be taken while on this drug. The side effects of levodopa may be lessened by taking vitamin C (500 to 1,000 mg daily).

Peanut butter, supplies good quantities of vitamin E and the B vitamins. Vitamin E content is 7.6 mg per 100 g. B vitamins present are (in mg per 100 g): thiamin (0.17); riboflavin (0.10); nicotinic acid (19.9); pyridoxine (0.50); and pantothenic acid (2.1). Folic acid level is 53 μg per 100 g. Traces only of vitamin C. Similar vitamin contents are in both smooth and crunchy peanut butter.

Minerals

An excellent source of potassium, magnesium, phosphorus, and chloride; also the trace minerals iron, copper, and zinc. High in sodium because of added salt. It supplies the following minerals (in mg per 100 g): sodium (350); potassium (700); calcium (37); magnesium (180); phosphorus (330); iron (2.1); copper (0.70); zinc (3.0); and chloride (500).

Peanuts, the kernels supply good quantities of vitamin E and the B vitamins. Some B vitamins are reduced when the peanuts are roasted and salted. Vitamin E contents of fresh kernels and those that have been roasted and

salted are identical at 16.9 mg per 100 g. B vitamins present for fresh kernels and those that have been roasted and
salted, respectively, are (in mg per 100 g): thiamin (0.90 and
0.23); riboflavin (0.10 and 0.10); nicotinic acid (21.3 and
21.3); pyridoxine (0.50 and 0.40); and pantothenic acid (2.7
and 2.1). Folic acid level in fresh kernels is 100 μg per 100
g, but is not detectable in the roasted and salted variety.
Traces only of vitamin C in fresh and roasted peanuts.

Minerals

An excellent source of potassium, calcium, magnesium,
phosphorus, and sulfur; also the trace minerals iron, copper, and zinc. Fresh nuts are low in sodium, but roasting
and salting them increases the sodium content significantly. Fresh and roasted-salted nuts, respectively, contain
(in mg per 100 g): sodium (6 and 440); and chloride (7 and
660). Both varieties also contain: potassium (680); calcium
(61); magnesium (180); phosphorus (370); iron (2.0); copper
(0.27); zinc (3.0); and sulfur (380).

Pears,   *eating varieties:* The edible portion has poor content of all vitamins both in the raw state and canned. There
is a loss of B vitamins and vitamin C during canning.
Carotene content is 10 μg per 100 g; traces only of vitamin
E in both eating and canned pears. B vitamins present for
eating and canned pears respectively are (in mg per 100
g): thiamin (0.03 and 0.01); riboflavin (0.03 and 0.01);
nicotinic acid (0.3 and 0.2); pyridoxine (0.02 and 0.01); and
pantothenic acid (0.07 and 0.02). Folic acid content is 11
μg per 100 g for the fresh, edible portion of the fruit and
5 μg per 100 g for canned fruit. Biotin is 1 μg per 100 g
and a trace, respectively. Vitamin C is reduced from 3 mg
to 1 mg per 100 g when the fruit is canned.

Cooking varieties have concentrations of vitamins
similar to eating pears with only slight losses on stewing,

with and without sugar. Carotene levels for raw, cooking pears, stewed without sugar and stewed with sugar, respectively, are (in μg per 100 g): 10, 9 and 8. Traces only of vitamin E. B vitamins present for raw, cooking pears, stewed without sugar and stewed with sugar respectively are (in mg per 100 g): thiamin (0.03, 0.03, and 0.02); riboflavin (0.03, 0.03, and 0.02); nicotinic acid (0.2, 0.2, and 0.2); pyridoxine (0.02, 0.02, and 0.02); and pantothenic acid (0.7, 0.05, and 0.05). Folic acid levels are respectively 11, 5, and 5 μg per 100 g, biotin levels are stable at 0.1 μg per 100 g for all three states of cooking pears.

Minerals
   Virtually free of sodium with useful potassium levels. Small amounts of all the other minerals are present.
   Eating varieties: The raw, edible portion contains these levels (in mg per 100 g): sodium—2; potassium—130; calcium—8; magnesium—7; phosphorus—10; iron—0.2; copper—0.15; zinc—0.1; sulfur—5; and chloride—only a trace.
   Cooking varieties: Stewed without sugar and with sugar respectively contain these levels (in mg per 100 g): sodium—3 and 2; potassium—85 and 78; calcium—6 and 5; magnesium—3 and 3; phosphorus—13 and 12; iron—0.2 and 0.2; copper—0.09 and 0.09; zinc—0.1 and 0.1; sulfur—3 and 2; and chloride—2 and 2.
   Canned: Provides these levels (in mg per 100 g): sodium—1; potassium—90; calcium—5; magnesium—6; phosphorus—5; iron—0.3; copper—0.04; sulfur—1; and chloride—3.

Pellagra,   a specific disease associated with deficiency of nicotinic acid, and characterized by skin, mucous membrane, central nervous system, and gastrointestinal symptoms. The symptoms may appear alone or in combination. Treatment is 300 to 1,000 mg nicotinamide daily in divided doses.

A similar disease in dogs is known as canine black tongue.

Penicillamine, an antiarthritic drug. Enhances excretion of pyridoxine.

Pentamidine isethionate, an antiprotozoal drug. Impairs folic acid utilization.

Pernicious anemia, a particular type of anemia characterized by nonspecific symptoms, loss of appetite, constipation alternating with diarrhea, and vague abdominal pains. More specific is "burning of the tongue" or glossitis. Considerable weight loss. Later, there is nervous involvement with tingling in the extremities, irritability, depression, delirium, and paranoia. Loss of sensation in lower extremities.

Only treatment is vitamin B_{12} by injection, which continues throughout life.

PGA, *see* folic acid.

Phagocytes, white blood cells that engulf and destroy invading microorganisms. *See* leucocytes.

Pheneturide, an anticonvulsant drug. Reduces conversion of vitamin D to 25-hydroxyvitamin D.

Phenformin, an antidiabetic drug. Prevents absorption of vitamin B_{12}.

Phenylbutazone, an antiarthritic drug. Impairs folic acid utilization.

Phenytoin, an anticonvulsant drug. Reduces body levels of folic acid and 25-hydroxyvitamin D.

Phlebitis, the presence of a thrombosis in a vein that causes a painful, tender, and swollen lump, usually in the leg. Daily intake of 200 IU vitamin E is believed to prevent condition. Treatment needs a daily intake of at least 600 IU vitamin E.

Phosphorus, chemical symbol P. Atomic weight 30.9. Present in the body (combined with oxygen) as phosphates and is a constituent of all plant and animal cells. With daily intakes between 1.5 and 2.0 g from a wide variety of food, deficiency is highly unlikely. A greater problem may be excessive intakes of phosphates from soft drinks, processed foods, and junk foods.

Best Food Sources in mg per 100 g

Yeast extract	1,900
Dried brewer's yeast	1,753
Dried nonfat milk	950
Wheat germ	930
Soy flour	600
Hard cheeses	520
Canned fish	520
Nuts	370
Cereals	290
Evaporated milk	250
Whole wheat bread	240
Eggs	218
Meats and poultry	200
Fish (fresh)	170

Best Food Sources cont.

Yogurt	140
All high protein foods	

Functions

Functions only as phosphates in the body

Structural components of bones and teeth

In the production of energy

In the "burning" of sugar for energy

As a cofactor for many enzymes

Phosphorus cont.

Functions cont.

Deficiency Symptoms

As activators for the
vitamin B complex

To aid absorption of
dietary constituents

To maintain the blood at
slightly alkaline
conditions (pH 7.39-7.41)

As components of
ribonucleic acids (RNA)
and deoxyribonucleic
acids (DNA), the basic
constituents of life
processes

Debility
Loss of appetite
Weakness
Bone pain
Joint stiffness
General malaise
Osteomalacia
Irritability
Numbness
"Pins and Needles"
Speech disorders
Tremor
Mental confusion

Deficiency

Considered highly unlikely
in view of widespread
distribution in foods, but
many medical conditions
can induce low blood
phosphate levels

Phosphorus Supplements
in mg per 100 mg

Bone meal (18.5); sodium
phosphate (8.7); effervescent
sodium phosphate (21.8);
potassium phosphate (17.8);
calcium phosphate (18.7);
calcium glycerophosphate
(14.7); magnesium glycerophosphate (15.9); and
sodium glycerophosphate
(9.8).

Deficiency Results in

Shortened red blood cell
life (leading to anemia)
Subnormal white blood
cells leading to reduced
resistance to infection

Phosphorus cont.

Relationship with Calcium

Contrary to previous beliefs that phosphate content of diet had crucial influence on calcium absorption, it is now accepted that dietary relationship between the two is not important. However, for babies, the calcium: phosphorus ratio of 2:1 in human milk is considered more desirable than that of 1.2:1 in cow's milk. Dried milks are now adjusted to the more favored ratio of 2:1 and the levels of both minerals reduced to those of human breast milk

Symptoms of Excess Intake

Diarrhea
Calcification in organs and soft tissues
Prevents absorption of iron, calcium, magnesium, and zinc

Body Content

Person weighing 154 lbs. (70 kg) contains between 550 and 770 g phosphorus, of which 90 percent is in the bones and teeth as calcium phosphate (hydroxyapatite) Muscles (9 percent), and nerves (1 percent), account for rest of body phosphorus

Absorption

Depends upon vitamin D for absorption from food and into bone from blood

Therapeutic Uses

Low phosphate levels induced by disease must be treated by medical practitioner who can monitor response.

Simple supplementation to ensure adequate dietary intakes can be carried out using supplementary forms listed below.

Phylloquinone, *see* K_1 (vitamin).

Phytic acid, also known as inositol hexaphosphate. Provides 28.2 mg phosphorus per 100 mg. Has long been known to be a constituent of cereals, vegetables, and most plant materials. It can combine with metals of nutritional importance to form phytates that are stable in the normal digestive system and so cannot be absorbed. Those most affected are calcium, iron, and zinc. There is some evidence that animals, including humans who have high phytic acid intakes can induce an enzyme called phytase which hydrolyses the phytic acid-metal complexes, liberating the mineral. The phytic acid content of a normal, balanced diet is unlikely to affect the essential minerals to a significant extent. Problems may arise in those eating high-cereal, high-vegetable diets where these foods are the sole source of minerals. Examples were seen in young children on a poor diet in Ireland in the 1940s. Phytic acid is concentrated in the aleurone layer of the wheat grain and is present in high concentration in high-extraction flours and in the bran. Phytic acid contents are (in mg per 100 g): bran—4,225; whole wheat flour—805; and white flour—200. These Irish children lived on whole wheat flour products with little dairy produce for three years. The reduced absorption of calcium as a result caused high rates of the incidence of rickets. Reducing the extraction rate of flour to 85 percent, combined with more milk and dairy products in their diets, caused the incidence of rickets to drop. Similar problems have been encountered with Asian immigrants in the UK. Although a low vitamin D level in the body was the main cause of the increased incidence of rickets and osteomalacia, high intakes of phytic acid in chapatis and low intake of calcium from dairy sources were also factors.

In the preparation of bread, much of the phytic acid content of the flour is destroyed. The traditional slow-rising technique of breadmaking causes 50 percent of the phytic acid of whole wheat bread to be destroyed. Techniques that use shorter rising times, like those utilizing vitamin C, give rise to losses of phytic acid totalling one-third of that in the original whole wheat flour. Most destruction is due to the enzyme phytase present in wheat and in yeast. Once this is inactivated by the baking process, further destruction is initiated by high oven temperature.

Problems with phytic acid are more likely to arise with high intakes of raw bran, cereals, and vegetables. The main source is high extraction flours but oats, high-bran breakfast foods, soy, and other beans also contribute meaningful quantities of phytic acid. When the phytate:zinc ratio in these diets exceeds 15:1, the availability of zinc decreases drastically. The zinc in whole wheat bread is 3.0 mg per 100 g but is less readily available than that in white bread which is only 0.9 mg per 100 g. This is less important in the US and UK where three-quarters of the zinc in the diet comes from animal, fish, and dairy-based foods than in those countries where cereals and vegetables supply the greater part of dietary zinc.

Figure 56 indicates the zinc, phytic acid, and dietary

Figure 56: Zinc, phytic acid, and dietary fiber contents of cereal foods

Cereal food	Zinc mg/100 g	Phytic acid mg/100 g	Phytic acid: zinc	Dietary fiber g/100 g
Whole wheat flour	2.4	850	35:1	9.6
White flour	1.5	200	13:1	7.5
Whole wheat bread	1.8	610	33:1	8.5
Brown bread	1.8	440	25:1	5.1
White bread	0.6	90	15:1	2.7
Bran-based cereals	3.6	2,200	60:1	26.7
Cornflakes	0.3	60	21:1	11.0
Wheat-based cereals	2.8	820	29:1	12.3
Oatmeal	3.4	940	27:1	7.0

fiber contents of cereal foods. Ratios of greater than 15:1 reduce zinc bioavailability.

Meat extenders and replacers derived from soybeans can also provide phytic acid which can bind zinc. This is illustrated in Figure 57. Ratios of greater than 15:1 decrease zinc bioavailability.

Figure 57: Phytic acid produced from meat extenders and replacers

Product on a dry weight basis	Zinc mg/100 g	Phytic acid g/100 g	Phytic acid:zinc
Meat extender	4.3	1.6	37:1
TVP (textured vegetable protein) beef	4.2	1.3	31:1
TVP pork	4.1	1.8	43:1
TVP unflavored	4.4	1.9	43:1
Beef	17.0 (av.)	0	—
Pork	6.6 (av.)	0	—

Phytomenadione,   see K_1 (vitamin).

Phytonadione,   see K_1 (vitamin).

Plummer's disease,   see hyperthyroidism.

Pollution,   the addition to the atmosphere of carbon monoxide and lead from exhaust fumes, ozone, nitrogen dioxide, sulfur dioxide, and dust.

Vitamin C protects against carbon monoxide and lead. Vitamin E protects against ozone and other oxidizers, and also protects vitamin A against destruction by ozone and nitrogen dioxide. A polluted atmosphere prevents ultraviolet light from reaching the skin so vitamin D is not synthesized and dietary intake must be increased.

Polymixin, an antibiotic. Prevents formation of vitamin K by intestinal bacteria.

Polyunsaturated fatty acids, originally called vitamin F, applied to linoleic, linolenic, and arachidonic acids. Now unofficially applied to linoleic acid alone since this is the precursor of the other two in the body. Known also as PUFA, and as essential fatty acids (EFA). Essentiality first demonstrated by G.O. Burr and M.M. Burr in 1929, who found these acids were needed by rats for health and survival. The main sources of linoleic acid are vegetable and seed oils. Recently PUFA from fish body oils called EPA (eicosapentaenoic acid) and DHA (docosahexaenoic acid) was found to be essential.

Richest food sources of linoleic acid are (in g per 100 g): oil of evening primrose (72.70); safflower oil (71.63); soybean oil (49.66); corn oil (47.75); wheat germ oil (41.54); peanut oil (27.70); and olive oil (10.51). Oil of evening primrose contains, in addition to linoleic acid, gamma-linolenic acid (average 8 percent).

Functions: constituents of cell membranes and myelin sheath of nerves; precursors of hormones called prostaglandins; constituents of cholesteryl esters; and constituents of triglycerides (body fats).

Deficiency in animals and humans causes mild skin conditions, including scaly dermatitis. May cause infantile eczema.

Recommended daily intake: None has been laid down by any authority, but many recommend that most of fat intake (25-35 percent of total calorie intake) should be as PUFA oils.

Therapy has proved beneficial in: mild skin conditions; atopic eczema; infantile eczema; premenstrual tension; multiple sclerosis; thrombosis prevention; and reducing high blood cholesterol levels. EPA and DHA appear to be beneficial in increasing blood clotting time (i.e., thinning the blood); angina pectoris; reducing high blood fat concentrations; and preventing thrombosis formation.

Potassium,   chemical symbol K, from the Latin *kalium*. Atomic weight 39.1. An alkali metal that is found mainly as sylvite (potassium chloride), in the aluminosilicates orthoclase and microcline, and as carnallite. Occurrence in the earth's crust is 2.59 percent.

The body potassium content of a person weighing 145 lbs (65 kg) is about 140 g. Of this, only 3.1 g is present in the extracellular fluid. The remaining 137 g occurs inside body cells and of this, four-fifths is present in skeletal muscles. The quantity in the skeleton is negligible.

Dietary intakes of potassium are between 1,960 and 5,870 mg daily, with a usual intake of 2.54 g equivalent to 4.85 g potassium chloride.

Food sources of potassium are widespread but very variable in content. The best sources are (in mg per 100 g): dried fruits (710-1,880); soy flour (1,660-2,030); molasses (1,470); wheat bran (1,160); raw salad vegetables (140-1,080); chipped potatoes (1,020); nuts (350-940); breakfast cereals and mueslis (100-600); savory biscuits (140-500); fresh fruits (65-430); boiled vegetables (50-400); fish (230-360); meat and poultry (33-350); fruit juices (110-260); whole wheat flour (360); whole wheat bread (220); white bread (100); eggs (140); cheese (100-190); brown rice (190); and polished rice (110). Beverages are particularly rich sources, e.g., instant coffee (4,000); Indian tea (2,160); roasted coffee (2,020); cocoa powder (1,500); and hot chocolate (410). For other levels, *see* the entries for individual foods.

Absorption of potassium from the diet is passive, requiring no specific mechanism. Absorption takes place throughout the small intestine and is dependent upon the potassium concentration within the intestinal contents.

Absorption takes place as long as this concentration is greater than that of the blood. Secretion of potassium probably takes place in the large bowel. Rapid movement of intestine contents through the small and large intestine is unfavorable to absorption. Under conditions such as persistent diarrhea, low body potasssium can develop.

Excretion of potassium reflects its dietary intake. Out of a daily intake of 2.35 g, 2.15 g is excreted in the urine with 0.39 g in the feces. The negative balance of 0.19 g is due to normal cellular breakdown, which releases potassium eventually into the urine. Such breakdown of cellular proteins increases in diabetes, underfeeding, and after injury. Potassium can also be displaced from the cells by hydrogen ions. Any condition giving rise to acidosis is thus liable to cause cellular depletion of potassium.

Diuretic drugs, particularly the thiazide variety, act by increasing the output of sodium and water from the kidneys, but at the same time potassium excretion is increased. Supplementation with potassium is therefore usual. In severe kidney failure, potassium is not excreted in the urine and excessive levels build up in the blood and tissue. The consequences are discussed below.

Fecal excretion is low in a healthy person, probably not exceeding 200 mg daily. The digestive juices contain significant amounts, but these are usually reabsorbed in the lower gut. Diarrhea can cause large losses in the feces, in amounts up to 3.52 g in 24 hours. This is particularly serious in infants suffering from diarrhea induced by protein-energy malnutrition, who may lose as much as 10-30 percent of their total body potassium. Heart failure may result. Similar losses may appear in infants or adults with chronic diarrhea brought on by other causes (e.g., infection), and it is important in these cases that potassium as well as water losses are replaced by supplementation.

Sweat losses of potassium are usually negligible, since

sweat contains only about 352 mg per liter. Excessive perspiration can lead to more significant losses, but these do not approach those of sodium in importance.

Functions of potassium are:

1. In maintaining a normal balance of water within body cells as the major positively charged ion within these cells.
2. As an essential activator in a number of enzymes, particularly those concerned with energy production.
3. To help stabilize the internal structure of body cells.
4. In assisting specialized cell particles to synthesize proteins.
5. In nerve impulse transmission in conjunction with sodium.
6. To increase the excitability of the heart and skeletal muscle to make them more receptive to nerve impulses.
7. In preserving the acid-alkali balance of the body in conjunction with bicarbonate, phosphate, and protein, as well as with sodium, calcium, and magnesium.
8. In stimulating the normal movements of the intestinal tract.

Causes of potassium deficiency are:

1. Drug therapy with: thiazide and other diuretics including frusemide, chlorthalidone, ethacrynic acid, mercurials, and carbonic anhydrase inhibitors; long-term use of corticosteroids and ACTH; overuse of laxatives; excessive intake of licorice and the drug carbenoxolone from licorice; high-dose sodium penicillin and carbenicillin; intravenous infusions of glucose and salt solutions not containing potassium; ion-exchange resins used to reduce blood cholesterol; and low-sodium diets.
2. Surgical operations: ileostomy, colostomy; extensive bowel resection; gastric drainage. Other deficiency causes are: extensive burns; extensive injury; diabetes mellitus; Cushing's syndrome; excessive excretion of aldosterone;

diabetes insipidus; periodic familial paralysis; chronic diarrhea; persistent vomiting; influenza; megaloblastic anemia; ulcerative colitis; kidney disease; severe heart disease; chronic respiratory failure; prolonged fasting; therapeutic starvation; bizarre diets, especially in the elderly; anorexia nervosa; alcoholism; clay eating; cystic fibrosis; and alkalosis.

Symptoms of deficiency include: vomiting; abdominal distension; paralytic ileus; acute muscular weakness; paralysis; paresthesia ("pins and needles"); loss of appetite; low blood pressure; polydipsia (intense thirst); drowsiness and confusion leading to respiratory failure; coma; an inability to concentrate urine; and increased toxicity of digitalis.

Treatment of low potassium levels is with:

1. Oral or intravenous potassium chloride solutions.
2. Increased dietary intake of potassium-rich foods.
3. Drugs such as triamterene or spironolactone taken with potassium-losing diuretics.

Potassium phosphate may be given by injection as an alternative to potassium chloride in the presence of acidosis.

Excess intake of potassium causes effects first on the muscles of the skeleton and of the heart, giving rise to muscular weakness and mental apathy. Intravenous potassium in excess may stop the heart. High oral doses can cause ulceration of the small bowel, particularly if the tablets are of the enteric-coated type (i.e., treated to prevent dissolution in the stomach to ensure they dissolve in the small intestine), which produce a localized high concentration of potassium. Lower doses of salts may cause nausea, vomiting, diarrhea, and abdominal cramps.

Excess caused by: kidney failure; insufficient production of adrenal gland hormones; and shock after injury in which condition potassium leaks out of the damaged cells into the blood. Treatment is withdrawal of potassium salts and of foods; in serious cases, medical expertise is necessary.

Potassium supplements are usually potassium chloride which provides 52.4 mg potassium in 100 mg chloride, but potassium acetate, bicarbonate, citrate, gluconate, sulfate, acid tartrate, tartrate, and phosphates have also been used. Amino acid or protein complexes are also available, which are claimed to be better absorbed than potassium salts. These complexes also replace protein losses, which may accompany excessive potassium excretion.

Food additives that contain potassium are: potassium acetate; potassium alginate; potassium benzoate; potassium bromate; potassium carbonate; potassium chloride; tripotassium citrate; tetrapotassium diphosphate; potassium ferrocyanide; potassium gluconate; potassium bicarbonate; potassium dihydrogen citrate; potassium hydrogen glutamate; potassium dihydrogen orthophosphate; dipotassium hydrogen orthophosphate; potassium hydroxide; potassium lactate; potassium malate; potassium metabisulphite; potassium nitrate; potassium nitrite; tripotassium orthophosphate; potassium pectate; potassium persulfate; potassium polyphosphates; potassium propionate; potassium salts of fatty acids; potassium sodium tartrate; potassium sorbate; potassium sulfate; dipotassium tartrate; monopotassium tartrate; and pentapotassium triphosphate.

Potassium sorbate,   a food additive used as a preservative. Provides 26.1 mg potassium per 100 mg.

Potatoes,   all potatoes, old and new, cooked in every way, contain only traces of carotene and vitamin E per 100 g.

A poor source of B vitamins, but regarded as an important provider of vitamin C in the Western diet.

As they are an important item in the Western diet because of the amount eaten, potatoes in all forms are regarded as supplying significant quantities of potassium, phosphorus, sulfur, and chloride, plus the trace minerals iron, copper, zinc, chromium, and selenium. For amounts of nutrients present, *see* vegetables.

Substantial losses of vitamin C occur from potatoes when they are stored (*see* Figure 58) and during all cook-

Figure 58: Vitamin C remaining in potatoes after storage

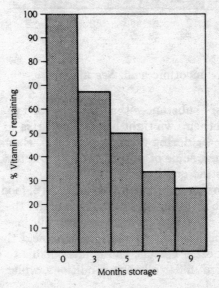

ing methods (*see* Figure 59). Keep water volume low to minimize losses in boiling; much can be recovered by utilizing cooking water.

Figure 59: Vitamin C remaining in potatoes after cooking

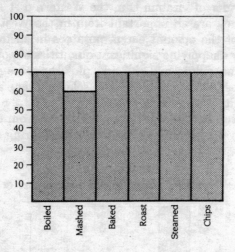

PP factor,   nicotinic acid. *See* niacin.

Precursors,   substances that occur in food that are not vitamins in their own right but can give rise to vitamins in the body, or during cooking processes. Examples are:

Carotenes, some of which are converted to vitamin A in the intestine and liver.

L-tryptophane, an essential amino acid of food proteins, converted to nicotinic acid in the liver under the influence of thiamin, riboflavin, pyridoxine, and biotin.

Niacytin, a bound form of nicotinic acid that occurs in corn and other cereals, and is unavailable to the body unless cooked under alkaline conditions, which liberates nicotinic acid.

7-dehydrocholesterol in the skin is converted to vitamin D by the action of sunlight or particular wavelengths of ultraviolet light.

Vitamin D itself is inactive, but is a precursor of 25-

hydroxy D and 1,25-dihydroxy D, which are its active forms in the body.

Pregnancy, all authorities recognize that dietary intake of all vitamins and some minerals must be increased during pregnancy, but there is no agreement on extent of increase. Blood levels of vitamin A, nicotinamide, pyridoxine, vitamin B_{12}, and ascorbic acid markedly decrease in pregnant women, suggesting all should be supplemented. There is some evidence that low vitamin levels may lead to some birth defects. Daily supplementation with a good general multivitamin preparation is recommended throughout pregnancy, since availability from the diet is highly unlikely. Folic acid is a special case. Amounts required may be above those on general sale, so should be obtained from a medical practitioner.

High levels of any vitamin should not be taken during pregnancy, apart perhaps from folic acid. Vitamin A supplements should not be more than 7,500 IU (250 μg) daily; vitamin B_6 (pyridoxine) supplementary intakes should not rise to more than 25 mg daily.

Prickly heat, known also as miliaria, characterized by small pimples on the skin surface that irritate, cause scratching, and eventual bleeding of the affected area. Induced by retained sweat. Treated and prevented by daily dose of 1,000 mg vitamin C for adult weighing 150 lbs: proportionally less for children, depending upon weight.

Primidone, an anticonvulsant drug. Reduces conversion of vitamin D to 25-hydroxyvitamin D.

Processed meats, such as canned meats, pastes, sausages, hamburgers, and meat pies, all supply significantly fewer vitamins than the meats from which they were made. Reduced levels are due to processing losses and dilution of the meats with fat and flour.

Prostaglandins, hormones produced within the body that control many metabolic processes. All prostaglandins are made from certain polyunsaturated fatty acids, which are in turn derived from the dietary polyunsaturated fatty acids, linoleic acid, and alpha-linolenic acid. Each acid is the starting material for a separate series of prostaglandins.

Prostaglandins can make blood thick, and so increase the chances of thrombosis, or thin, and so prevent thrombosis. Production of "thinning" prostaglandins is stimulated by vitamin E. PUFA from fish body oils, called EPA and DHA, also thin the blood, reducing its ability to form thrombosis, because they are precursors of "thinning" prostaglandins.

Prostate gland, the male accessory gland that rests just below the bladder and completely surrounds the bladder's narrow neck, called the urethra. When it is enlarged, the prostate pinches off the urethra, restricting the flow of urine. When the prostate is inflamed, prostatitis is the result, requiring antibacterial treatment. Enlarged prostate, for whatever reason, is usually treated by surgery. Maintaining a healthy prostate appears to require adequate zinc intakes. Both the healthy prostate and the semen usually contain high concentrations of zinc. Those with prostate problems almost invariably had low zinc levels in the gland and in their semen. Supplementation with an average of 25 mg elemental zinc daily relieved the symptoms in some men with enlarged prostates. More importantly, adequate intakes of the mineral throughout life may cut down the chances of developing an enlarged prostate.

Low saturated-fat diets combined with high-fiber intakes may also contribute.

Prostate problems, usually due to inflammation or enlargement. Supplement needs include PUFA (safflower oil, oil of evening primrose, 3 g daily) plus the mineral zinc (25 mg daily).

Protein, a nutrient that is supplied in the diet, digested to amino acids, and absorbed in the gastrointestinal tract, then rebuilt by the body into its own proteins which are required for growth and repairing of body cells, tissues, muscles, and organs.

Synthesis by the body requires vitamin A, so high protein intakes require concomitant vitamin A intake. Also needed is pyridoxine. Blood clotting proteins require vitamin K for synthesis. Nucleoproteins are complexes of protein and nucleic acids, and need vitamin B_{12} for synthesis. *See* nucleic acids.

Psoriasis, a common chronic and recurrent skin disease characterized by dry, silvery, scaling eruptions and plaques of various sizes, due to overproduction of epithelial cells. Has been treated with oral and topical (applied to skin) vitamin A, retinoic acid, and synthetic vitamin A derivatives.

Psoriatic arthritis, a particular form of arthritis that is associated with the skin condition psoriasis. Occurs in a minority of those with psoriasis, but is very painful and disabling. May occur in the spine, toes, and fingers as a spondylitis; and in the back joints as sacroiliitis. Studies in Denmark indicate that some cases respond to the mineral zinc, taken as zinc sulfate (220 mg, three times daily). Stiff joints became mobile; the grip strengthened;

swelling was reduced; and pain and morning stiffness disappeared. Benefit may be due to the activity of zinc in the body's own immune system which attacks the inflammatory response in arthritis. The skin condition psoriasis may also respond to this treatment.

Pteroyglutamic acid, *see* folic acid.

Pteroylmonoglutamic acid, *see* folic acid.

PUFA, *see* polyunsaturated fatty acids.

Purpura, hemorrhages under the skin that occur without definite cause, or due to slight injury. Has been treated with oral vitamin E (400-600 IU daily) until the purpura disappeared. *See also* bruises.

Pyridoxal, *see* B_6 (vtiamin).

Pyridoxamine, *see* B_6 (vitamin).

Pyridoxine, *see* B_6 (vitamin).

Pyrimethamine, an antimalarial drug. Impairs folic acid utilization.

R

RDA, recommended dietary allowances. Established by the Food and Nutrition Board, National Academy of Sciences—National Research Council, to indicate the amounts of vitamins and minerals that will help maintain good nutrition in healthy persons living in the United States. Safety factors are added to deal with three variables.

1. To take account of individual variations in requirements. Safety factor covers 95 percent of population.
2. To take account of possible increases caused by minor stresses of life, but extra needs during infections, injuries, and other illnesses are ignored.
3. To take account of the different availability of vitamins in various foods.

Figures vary among countries, reflecting variation in how they are arrived at. Also the number of vitamins with reommended intakes differ among several authorities, (*see* Figure 60).

Minerals
    See Figure 61.

Regional enteritis, *see* Crohn's disease.

Retinal, vitamin A aldehyde, retinaldehyde. The active form of vitamin A in sight process.

Retinene, an old name for retinal.

Retinoic acid, vitamin A acid. The active form of vitamin A in growth. Used on the skin in treating skin conditions, including skin cancer.

Retinoid, a term to describe vitamin A and its derivatives, both natural and synthetic.

Retinol, *see* A (vitamin).

Figure 60: Recommended daily intakes of vitamins for adults

		Au	Ca	Dn	FDR	Fl	CDR	H	I	Ne	No	Nz	Ro	Sp	Sw	UK	US	USSR	WHO/FAO
VITAMIN A	Female (μg)	750	800	800	900	750	800	750	750	850	750	750	1,500	750	900	750	800	1,500	750
	Male		1,000	1,000													1,000		
THIAMIN	Female (mg)	1.1	1.0	1.0	1.4	0.8	0.9	1.0	1.0	0.8	1.0	1.0	1.8	0.9	1.0	0.9	1.0	1.5	0.9
	Male		1.5	1.1	1.6	1.6	1.5	1.2	1.2	1.0	1.4	1.2	2.1	1.2	1.4	1.2	1.4	1.8	1.2
RIBOFLAVIN	Female (mg)	1.4	1.7	1.2	1.6	1.3	1.5	1.5	1.2	1.2	1.5	1.7	2.0	1.3	1.5	1.3	1.2	2.0	1.3
	Male		1.2	1.6	2.0	1.4	1.6		1.6	1.4	1.7		2.4	1.8	1.7	1.7	1.6	2.4	1.8
NIACIN	Female (mg)	13	15	15	16	17	18	15	16	15	15	13	15	16	14	15	13	18	15
	Male	18	20	18	19	19	20	18	18	19	18	18	18	20	18	18	18	20	20
PYRIDOXINE	Female (mg)	1.5	2.0	2.0	1.6	–	–	–	–	–	–	2.0	1.7	–	–	–	2.0	1.8	–
	Male		1.5		1.8													2.1	
PANTOTHENIC ACID	mg	–	–	–	8.0	–	–	–	–	–	–	–	–	–	–	–	4-7	10	–
VITAMIN B₁₂	μg	2.0	3.0	3.0	5.0	–	–	–	2.0	–	–	3.0	–	2.0	–	–	3.0	–	2.0
VITAMIN C	Female (mg)	30	30	45	75	30	70	30	45	50	30	60	75	30	55	30	60	64	30
	Male												85		60			75	
BIOFLAVONOIDS	Female (mg)	–	–	–	–	–	–	–	–	–	–	–	16	–	–	–	–	17	–
	Male												18					20	
VITAMIN E	Female	–	8	12	12	–	–	–	–	–	–	13.5	10	–	–	–	8	–	–
	Male		6	15													10		
VITAMIN D	μg	10	2.5	2.5	2.5	2.5	2.5	2.5	2.5	2.5	2.5	10	2.5	2.5	2.5	2.5	5.0	–	2.5
																	7.0		
FOLIC ACID	μg	200	200	100								200				300	400		200

Figure 61: Recommended daily intakes of minerals for adults

		Au	Ca	Cz	Dn	FDR	Fi	GDR	H	I	Ne	No	NZ	Po	Ro	Sp	Sw	UK	US	USSR	WHO/FAO
CALCIUM mg	Female	700	700	800	800	700	600	800	500	600	800	800	600	800	900	400	800	500	800	800	400
	Male	800	800	800	800	800	700	800	500	600	800	800	600	800	900	500	800	500	800	800	500
IODINE µg	Female	120	100	-	225	-	-	-	-	-	-	-	200	-	-	-	-	140	150	-	-
	Male	150	150	-	225	-	-	-	-	-	-	-	200	-	-	-	-	140	150	-	-
IRON mg	Female	15	14	14	18	18	12	15	18	18	12	18	15	12	20	28	18	12	18	15	28
	Male	12	10	12	10	12	8	10	12	10	10	10	12	12	12	14	10	10	10	15	14
MAGNESIUM mg	Female	-	250	350	300	220	-	-	-	300	-	-	300	300	-	-	-	-	300	400	-
	Male	-	300	400	350	260	-	-	-	350	-	-	350	400	-	-	-	-	350	600	-
ZINC mg	Female	16	9	8	15	-	-	-	-	15	-	-	-	-	-	-	-	-	15	-	-
	Male	16	12	8	15	-	-	-	-	15	-	-	-	-	-	-	-	-	15	-	-

Key:

Au:	Australia	H:	Hungary
Ca:	Canada	I:	Italy
Cz:	Czechoslovakia	Ne:	Netherlands
Dn:	Denmark	No:	Norway
FDR:	West Germany	NZ:	New Zealand
Fi:	Finland	Po:	Poland
GDR:	East Germany	Ro:	Rumania

Sp:	Spain
Sw:	Sweden
UK:	United Kingdom
US:	United States of America
USSR:	Russia
WHO:	World Health Organization
FAO:	Food and Agricultural Organization

Retrolental fibroplasia, an eye problem in premature babies. *See* oxygen; E (vitamin).

Rheumatism, a general term indicating diseases of muscle, tendon, joint, bone, or nerve, resulting in discomfort and disability. Often used to include rheumatoid arthritis, osteoarthritis, spondylitis, bursitis, fibrositis, myositis, lumbago, sciatica, and gout. Vitamin therapy is as for rheumatoid arthritis. *See also* gout.

Rheumatoid arthritis, *see* arthritis.

Riboflavin(e), *see* B$_2$ (vitamin).

Ribonucleic acid (RNA), *see* nucleic acids.

Rickets, a disease in children characterized by lack of mineralization of the bones, and due to deficiency of vitamin D.

Symptoms are restlessness, poor ability to sleep, and constant head movement. Infants do not sit, crawl, or walk early, and the closing of the soft joints in the head bones is delayed. Weight-bearing eventually bends the bones causing bowlegs, knock-knees in the legs, and pigeon breast.

Therapy is doses of up to 20,000 IU daily of calcium and phosphorus.

Rose hip syrup, in undiluted form is a very rich source of vitamin C. Traces of vitamin E are present. Traces only of thiamin, riboflavin, nicotinic acid, pyridoxine, pantothenic acid, folic acid and biotin. Vitamin C content is 295 mg per 100 ml.

Rutin, a bioflavonoid, particularly rich in buckwheat.

Used to treat bleeding gums and strengthen capillary walls at daily intakes of 60 to 600 mg. Preferably taken with vitamin C (up to 500 mg daily).

S

Salt, strictly speaking, a salt is a combination of a metallic element or ammonia with an acid group. Examples are sodium sulfate, potassium chloride, magnesium acetate, calcium phosphate, ammonium chloride, postassium iodide, zinc carbonate, sodium bicarbonate, sodium citrate, and postassium tartrate. In these cases, the part of the salt of most interest to the body is the metallic or ammonia part, but chloride, iodide, and phosphate can also be utilized because they contain chlorine, iodine, and phosphorus, respectively.

In common parlance though, salt has come to mean sodium chloride or table salt, since this is the most widespread in our diet. When dissolved in water, sodium chloride splits into postively charged sodium ions (cations) that are electrically neutralized by negatively charged chloride ions (anions). Hence salt is neutral because there are equal numbers of sodium and chloride ions. All other water-soluble salts split when in solution into positively charged metal or ammonia ions and negatively charged acid group ions.

Each 100 mg of sodium chloride contains 39.3 mg sodium and 60.7 mg chloride. Salt is the main source of both sodium and chloride in the diet. Other sodium salts present in the diet include sodium bicarbonate, sodium nitrite, monosodium glutamate, sodium benzoate, sodium alginate, and sodium sulfite. Like sodium chloride, these too are commonly added to foods. All foods contain an inherent amount of sodium in them, but there are wide variations in the quantity. *See* the entries for individual foods for their sodium content.

Salt requirements are relatively low. It is doubtful if salt need be added to any food for its nutritional value. There is evidence that early humans managed, and some primitive communities today manage, to survive on a diet to which no salt was or is added. Intakes of natural sodium expressed as sodium chloride are as little as between 30 and 600 mg salt per day and these primitive communities have adapted to such small quantities. As civilization progressed, humans discovered that salt evaporated from sea water or mined from the ground could be used to preserve food. This assumed importance for storing food out of season, so salt became highly valued. Roman soldiers were paid partly in salt, hence the word "salary" for remuneration. As methods for isolating salt improved, and as its transport became easier, the mineral became cheaper and available to all. Its consumption increased, not because it was needed but because of its flavor-enhancing qualities. Today the population in the West consumes between 8 and 14 g salt daily. They could equally well manage on 3.5-7.0 g salt daily. High salt consumption leading to high blood levels can be harmful in several conditions (*see* sodium), but the most important is the effect on blood pressure, which is a factor in the development of heart attacks, strokes, and kidney failure.

Dietary salt and high blood pressure appear to be related on the basis of animal experiments and epidemiological studies. In animals with inherent forms of high blood pressure and in rats bred in stock colonies, an increased salt intake raises the blood pressure. This rise can be partly offset by increased potassium intake. Once high blood pressure is established in these species, lowering the salt intake will not always result in decreased blood pressure.

In human epidemiological studies, it was concluded that sodium intake and blood pressure are not always related within any particular community. There is, however, a direct relation between potassium excretion, the sodium/potassium ratio in the urine, and blood pressure. The higher the bood level of potassium, the lower the blood pressure. In Africa, tribespeople who move from rural areas to the cities develop higher blood pressure that is in part related to an increased salt intake. In one study, where Africans were deliberately given an extra 16 g salt in their daily diets, their blood pressure rose. One reason for this effect of salt is that people who have some inherent abnormality in their kidneys cannot excrete the excess sodium.

Prevention of high blood pressure by reducing salt intake has been proved to be effective in animal experiments. No parallel work is available on human beings, but babies fed a low-salt diet for the first year of life had lower blood pressure levels than those fed normal salt intakes.

Treatment of high blood pressure by reducing salt intake is effective in some individuals. Very low salt-containing diets were found to reduce high blood pressure before the introduction of diuretics and other drug treatments. Simply halving salt intake to 3.5 g (1 level teaspoon) daily can reduce blood pressure by the same amount as that obtained with one tablet of blood pressure-lowering drugs. These drugs are more effective if salt intake is reduced at the same time. The higher the blood pressure, the more effective are the drugs on a salt-restricted diet. Those people with only mildly raised blood pressure can sometimes reduce their blood pressure to normal values and maintain it by simple salt restriction.

The positive effect of salt restriction and restriction of sodium from other sources is enhanced if the intake of potassium is increased at the same time. It is likely too that adequate intakes of calcium and magnesium are also important in reducing high blood pressure to normal values, or in maintaining these values.

Salt retention is also associated with other conditions:

1. Premenstrual edema. Many women gain weight and experience a bloated feeling a few days before their periods. Symptoms include swelling of the abdomen, ankles, and fingers, and they are due to retention of water. This edema can be prevented or reduced by cutting down on the salt intake, and at the same time increasing the potassium intake by eating more fresh fruits and vegetables and by drinking fresh fruit and vegetable juices.

2. Crash dieting. Fasting and the severe calorie-restricted diets that are favored for rapid weight loss are effective in the short term, but resumption of normal meals after several days can result in sodium retention and hence edema.

3. Heart failure. When the arteries of the body, including those of the heart, become constricted, the heart works harder to pump out blood, and its muscle may become damaged. The kidneys respond by retaining sodium in an attempt to assist the heart, but the result is retention of water in many parts of the body, including around the heart. A vicious circle results because the heart works harder when edema is present, and the usual consequence is heart failure. Diuretic drugs help remove this excess water, but their action is improved if salt (i.e., sodium) intake is restricted at the same time.

4. Liver disease. The kidneys may respond to liver damage as they do to heart muscle damage by retaining sodium and hence water. Salt and sodium restriction in the diet can complement conventional medical treatment, but the

possibility of abnormally low body levels of sodium must be considered.

5. Kidney disease. In some kidney conditions, the organ has lost the ability to rid the body of excess salt, so high blood pressure results. Some salt and sodium restriction is therefore necessary, but the extent of this is the province of the medical practitioner, since in severe kidney disease sodium reduction may exacerbate the condition. In nephrotic syndrome, where massive amounts of protein are lost in the urine, there is often retention of water and sodium. This is one kidney disease where dietary salt restriction can safely be undertaken in conjunction with diuretic and other drug treatments. Sometimes in rare cases the kidney is unable to retain sodium and excessive quantities are lost in the urine. Here sodium restriction is undesirable and extra salt may have to be eaten; this should only be done under professional advice.

Restricted salt regimen is a diet in which dietary sodium is reduced to about one-third of normal by eliminating salt added at table; reducing that added during cooking processes to a minimum; and selecting foods with low sodium levels. Foods that are rich sources of sodium should be avoided. On this regimen the intake of sodium is 2.3 g, equivalent to 5.9 g salt. General guidelines are:

1. No table salt is allowed.
2. Salt added during cooking and baking powder must be reduced to a minimum.
3. Ham, bacon, sausages, canned meats, canned fish, shellfish, cheese, sauces, cookies, and baked goods must not be eaten.
4. Bread of any type is restricted to five thin slices per day; butter intake must not exceed 30 g (1 ounce).
5. Meat and fish in small helpings are allowed.
6. Sodium-containing vegetables like beets, celery, carrots,

radish, turnip, and watercress are allowed in small quantities as long as no extra salt is added to them. Potatoes cooked in their skins without added salt are allowed.

7. One egg per day is allowed, as is a total of 250 ml (half pint) of milk.

8. Intake of fruits and nuts (unsalted) is unlimited.

9. There is no restriction on sugar, honey, jams, and rice.

10. Salads without added salt are allowed but dressings are not permitted unless they are of the low-sodium type.

Low sodium diets are more difficult to organize at home without expert dietary instructions and supervision. One important aspect is that salt-free bread and butter are essential. This is easier when both are homemade, but they are available in some shops, as are salt-free polyunsaturated margarines. The sodium intake on the following daily regimen is no more than 1.2 g equivalent to 3.1 g salt.

Daily allowance of milk is 250 ml (half pint), preferably of the low-sodium variety; that of low-sodium butter or margarine is 30 g (1 ounce). *Breakfast:* fruit or fruit juice; low salt cereal; milk from allowance and sugar; one egg (unsalted); low-sodium bread or toast; butter from allowance; jam or marmalade; coffee or tea with milk from allowance. *Lunch:* fruit or fruit juice; 90 g (3 ounces) unsalted meat, poultry, or fresh white fish, either grilled or fried in vegetable oil; potato or rice or pasta; permitted vegetable; salad with low-sodium dressing; low-sodium bread and butter from allowance; fruit sweetened with honey or sugar; tea or coffee with milk from allowance. *Dinner:* fruit or fruit juice; 60 g (2 ounces) meat or fish or one egg; permitted vegetable and salad with low-sodium dressing; low-sodium bread with butter or margarine from allowance; tea or coffee with milk from allowance. *Bedtime:* remainder of milk allowance.

The following must be avoided: all cured, canned and

pickled meats and fish; canned vegetables and soups; cheeses; bottled sauces; pickled vegetables; sausages; any foods with the ingredients bicarbonate of soda, baking powder, sodium benzoate, monosodium glutamate, or any sodium salt listed under sodium-food additives. Potassium chloride may be substituted to flavor some foods, but the taste will be different from that when sodium chloride is used.

Schilling test, specific for detecting a vitamin B_{12} deficiency induced by malabsorption of vitamin from diet. Small amount of radioactive vitamin B_{12} is given by mouth, followed some time later by a high dose given intravenously to flush out the absorbed vitamin. Radioactivity in the urine is then measured over 24 hours. The test is repeated with radioactive vitamin plus intrinsic factor. The differences in the two amounts excreted in the urine allows the diagnosis to be made.

Schizophrenia, a group of mental disorders in people who exhibit: disturbance of logical associations; limited range of emotional response; autism; and mixed feelings to an incapacitating degree. Has been treated with folic acid and pyridoxine, or folic acid alone at high potencies. Others respond to nicotinamide plus vitamin C. Occasionally vitamin B_{12} injections may help. *See* megavitamin therapy.

Scurvy, a disease specific to vitamin C deficiency. The symptoms are lassitude, weakness, irritability, vague muscle and joint pains, loss of weight, bleeding gums, gingivitis, and loosening of the teeth. Minute hemorrhages under the skin are followed by large hemorrhages in the thigh muscles. Therapy is with vitamin C at oral doses of 200-2,000 mg daily.

Sea salt, mainly sodium chloride, but contains significant quantities of other salts. A typical composition is (in g per 100 g): sodium chloride—77.82; magnesium chloride—9.44; magnesium sulfate—6.57; calcium sulfate—3.44; potassium chloride—2.11; magnesium bromide—0.22; and calcium carbonate—trace.

Seafood, *crustacea* include crab, lobster, prawns, crayfish, scampi, and shrimps that provide meaningful quantities only of vitamin E among the fat-soluble vitamins. All contain moderate amounts of the vitamin B complex but are relatively rich in B_{12}.

Mollusks include cockles, mussels, oysters, scallops, whelks, and winkles. Their vitamin content is similar to that of crustacea. Some oysters provide vitamin C, but most seafoods contain virtually none (*see* Figure 62).

Figure 62: Vitamin content of seafood

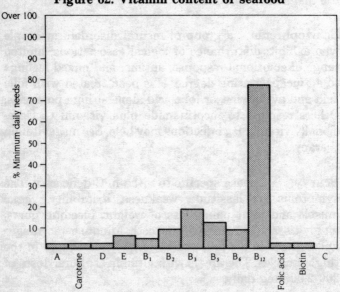

All seafoods are important providers of the essential trace minerals as well as the gross minerals (*see* Figure 63).

Figure 63: Mineral content of seafood

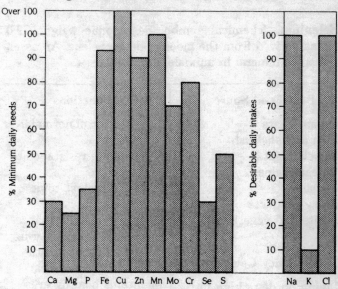

Seasonal supplementation, extra vitamin A is required during winter because of low environmental temperatures. Extra vitamin D is required during winter because sunshine is shorter-lasting and weaker, and the body is more covered. Extra vitamin C is required during winter because of prevalence of respiratory infections, and intake of fresh fruits and vegetables in diet is decreased. Extra vitamin B complex should be taken during winter to help overcome the stress of low environmental temperatures.

Seborrheic dermatitis, chronic, reddish, scaling inflammation of the skin, often occurring with acne, rosacea, and psoriasis. In infants, responds to biotin therapy (5 mg daily until cured). In adults, sometimes responds to pyridoxine therapy with an ointment of 10 mg pyridoxine per base in addition to biotin given orally.

Selenium, chemical symbol Se. Atomic weight 79.0. Name derived from the moon goddess Selene. An essential trace mineral in animals and humans.

Best Food Sources		Functions
Organ meats	40	Preservation of normal liver function
Fish and shellfish	32	Maintaining resistance to disease
Muscle meats	18	Protects against toxic minerals
Wheat grains	12	Promotes male sexual reproductive capacity in production of prostaglandins (hormones)
Cereals	12	
Dairy products	5	
Fruits and vegetables	2	Maintains healthy eyes and sight

Deficiency Caused by

Living on diets high in refined and processed foods

Living on foods grown on selenium-deficient soil

Has been seen in babies fed on dried milk rather than breast milk

No specific symptoms of deficiency, but conditions induced include Keshan disease and white muscle disease

Maintains healthy hair and skin

Act as anti-inflammatory agent

Maintains healthy heart

Protects against toxic substances produced in body

May protect against cancer

Works together with vitamin E in production of ubiquinone (*see*

Selenium cont.

Functions cont.

   ubiquinone)
Protects the body as an
   antioxidant

Recommended Daily Intake

Suggested only by the US
Food and Nutrition Board
as no more than 200 μg
from food. Supplementary
selenium should not
exceed this.

Therapeutic Uses

Arthritis
High blood pressure
Angina
Keshan disease (*see* Keshan
   disease)
Hair, nail, and skin
   problems
Detoxification of arsenic,
   cadmium, and mercury
Cataracts
In animals it has been
successful in treating:
   nutritional muscular
      dystrophy (white
      muscle disease)
   liver disease
   infertitility in males
   cancer

Selenium Supplements

Selenium-rich yeast (up to
   1,000 μg per g); sodium
   selenite (45.7 μg per
   100 μg)
Total selenium supplemen-
   tation should not
   exceed 200 μg daily

Body Content and Absorption

Adult content is about 20
   mg with most of it in
   kidneys, liver, and, in
   the male, testes
Absorption is more efficient
   from organic selenium
   (as found in growing
   yeast) than from the inorganic variety

Symptoms of Excess Intake

Dental caries in children
Hair loss
Skin depigmentation
Abnormal nails
Lassitude
Garlic odor on breath (in
   absence of garlic)

Selenium cont.

Relationship to Vitamin E

Selenium can spare vitamin E (it can partly replace it)

Selenium is 50 to 100 times more active an antioxidant than the vitamin

Protective enzyme glutathione peroxidase requires both selenium and vitamin E

Combined selenium and vitamin E gives better relief from angina than either one alone

Both trace mineral and vitamin needed for efficient resistance to infection

Cancers (experimental) in animals were inhibited by both selenium and vitamin E, preferably also with vitamin C

Skin cancers induced by excessive ultraviolet light were inhibited by selenium plus vitamins E and C

Best ratio is 100 IU vitamin E: 25 μg selenium

Beneficial effect of combined selenium and

Relationship to Vitamin E cont.
vitamin E is greater than additive effect of each alone, i.e., they are synergistic

Geographical Distribution

Irregular distribution occurs in soils of various countries and areas within the same country

Reflected in the selenium contents of the food grown in those areas

Low levels in Europe; US; Australia; New Zealand

High levels in Taiwan; Japan; Thailand; Philippines; Puerto Rico; Venezuela; Costa Rica

Within UK, Norfolk has high levels

Within US, Wyoming and the Dakotas have high levels

Epidemiological studies indicate that those who live in areas of low-selenium soils have more cancer and heart conditions than those living in areas of high-selenium soils

Selenium sulfide, used only as a shampoo in the treatment of dandruff and seborrheic dermatitis of the scalp. It is highly toxic if taken internally. If swallowed, the stomach should be emptied by aspiration and lavage and a purgative such as sodium sulfate (30 g in 250 ml water) given as a solution. Vitamin C (10 mg per kg body weight) given by mouth assists the removal of selenium sulfide through the kidneys.

Hair levels of selenium are increased after the application of shampoos containing selenium sulfide.

Selenium yeast, provides up to 1,000 μg selenium per g of yeast. Produced by adding inorganic selenium salts to growing yeast, which incorporates the trace mineral into its protein. This involves replacement of the sulfur in the sulfur-containing amino acids by selenium. The main protein constituent is selenomethionine. Selenium in yeast protein is better absorbed, better utilized, and less toxic than inorganic selenium salts.

Senile dementia, is due to a degenerative process with a large loss of cells from certain brain areas. The condition is more common in women and appears usually in the seventh or eighth decade of life, i.e., later than Alzheimer's disease. For treatment, *see* Alzheimer's disease.

Shingles, an acute infection of the central nervous system caused by a virus and characterized by skin blisters and pain in the nerve endings of the skin. Also known as herpes zoster.

Has been treated with vitamin C by injection at a dose of 3 g every twelve hours plus 1 g orally every two hours. Pain was relieved and blisters dried up within 72 hours. Some people respond to injections of vitamin B_{12} (500 μg daily), and are clear by third day. High oral doses of whole vitamin B complex are recommended in all cases to help clear up nerve lesions. Continue treatment after blisters have dried up. May also respond to high daily intakes (up to 3 g daily) of the amino acid L-lysine in addition to vitamin supplementation.

Silicon, chemical symbol Si. Atomic weight 28.1. Found in nature as silica (silicon oxide) in quartz, sand, and sandstone; as silicates in feldspar, kaolinate, and anorthite. The second most abundant element on earth (next to oxygen), constituting about 27.6 g per 100 g in the earth's crust.

Silicon and silicon salts are so insoluble that only trace amounts are found in body tissues. It has been shown to be an essential trace element for the growing rat and chick; deficiency in these species leads to abnormalities in the bones. In addition, it is an essential component of cartilage where it is important for the strength and elasticity of the gristle. Silicon helps keep arterial walls elastic, an important feature of blood pressure control. All connective tissue of the body contains silicon. All studies have been carried out on animals but similar functions probably apply to human beings also.

Toxic effects of silicon are confined to the inhalation of silica as dust from coal, glass manufacture, ceramics production, and sandblasting of rocks. The resulting disease is silicosis where particles of silica are deposited in the lungs, setting up irritation and eventually loss of elasticity.

Silicon compounds used in tablets include silicon dioxide.

Silicon dioxide, also known as silica and colloidal silica. Provides 46.8 mg silicon in 100 mg.

Skin cancer, *see* cancer.

Skin color, dark pigmentation of skin reduces the effect of ultraviolet light in producing vitamin D in the skin. Hence a long exposure to sunlight is necessary to produce sufficient vitamin D, or ensure enough by eating D-rich foods or by supplementation.

Skin depigmentation, *see* vitiligo.

Skin diseases, are sometimes related to mild deficiency of vitamins and some will respond to oral intakes of vitamins plus direct application to the skin. Vitamins particularly important to healthy skin are: A, riboflavin, nicotinic acid, pyridoxine, biotin, C, and E. Adequate polyunsaturated fatty acids are also important. *See* acne; dermatitis; eczema; seborrheic dermatitis; and psoriasis.

Smell, a sense that can be reduced by vitamin A deficiency; and restored by intramuscular injection of high potencies of the vitamin. Zinc deficiency may also cause loss of the sense of smell.

Smoking, *see* acetaldehyde, and cancer, lung.

Sodium, chemical symbol Na, from the Latin *natrium.* Atomic weight 23.0. An alkali metal that occurs naturally as sodium chloride, sodium bromide, sodium silicates, and sodium carbonates. Abundance in the earth's crust is 2.8 percent.

The adult body content (143 lbs or 65 kg weight) of sodium in a healthy individual is about 92 g, equivalent to 234 g sodium chloride. More than half the sodium is in the fluids that bathe the cells (extracellular); 34.5 g is present in the bones; and less than 11.5 g is retained within the cells (intracellular). Bone sodium is not generally available as an immediate reserve since it is enmeshed in the crystals of the insoluble bone minerals. If sodium is injected into the body as common salt, it quickly equilibrates with both intracellular and extracellular sodium, but exchange with bone sodium is almost negligible. The total exchangeable sodium in the body is therefore about 64.4 g and it is this sodium that changes rapidly, depending upon its intake from the diet and the excretion of the mineral.

Daily intakes of sodium from the food are from 1.61-6.90 g, which corresponds to 4.10-17.55 g common salt. The food eaten contributes only 4.6 g sodium daily (corresponding to 11.7 g common salt), the remainder being added as table salt.

In babies, the ideal sodium content of food is that of human breast milk (180 mg per liter). Unmodified cow's milk contains 770 mg per liter, so it should not be fed to babies in the first three months of life. Animal experiments indicate that too much salt in a baby's diet can cause high blood pressure and even death. US and UK health authorities recommend that salt should not be added during the processing and preparation of infant foods.

Foods as they occur in nature do not generally have high amounts of sodium, but the mineral is added in large amounts as sodium chloride (common salt) during cooking, refining, processing, and preservation of foods, as sodium bicarbonate in baking powder, or as monosodium glutamate. Bakers, for example, add salt to bread at a level of about 1 percent; butter, bacon, processed meats, and canned foods in general are all salted in preparation. Thus an ordinary diet without salt supplementation will provide ample sodium for body needs; added salt at the table is simply an acquired taste.

Rich sources of sodium are (in mg per 100 g): yeast extract (4,640); bacon (1,900); smoked fish (1,000-1,800);

salami (1,800); sauces (1,100-1,400); cornflakes (1,200); canned or boiled ham (1,200); savory biscuits (610-1,200); processed cheese and cheese spread (1,360); Danish blue cheese (1,420); Camembert cheese (1,410); Stilton cheese (1,150); corned beef (910); Edam cheese (980); salted butter (870); margarine (800); sausage (780); Cheddar and other hard cheeses (610); cottage cheese (450); bread (560); fresh and canned shellfish (210-550); and canned vegetables (230-330).

Moderate sources of sodium are (in mg per 100 g): sweet cookies (200-500); self-rising flour (350); cream cheese (300); root vegetables (60-140); eggs (140); fresh fish (100); raw meats (60-90); yogurt (64-76); legumes (30-60); corn flour (52); oatmeal (33); light cream (42); and dried fruits (30).

Poor sources of sodium are (in mg per 100 g): fresh fruit (1-30); unsalted nuts (1-20); green vegetables (2-13); fruit juices (1-4); rice (6); flour (2-4); and lard (2). For other levels *see* the entries for individual foods.

Foods of animal and fish origin usually contain more sodium than whole grains, fruits, vegetables, unsalted nuts, and fruits. Poultry supplies only moderate amounts.

Absorption of sodium as common salt or in any soluble form from the intestines is passive, so excess intakes are as easily absorbed as moderate ones. There is no control of absorption, as with most other minerals, so the gastro-intestinal tract plays little part in controlling body levels.

Excretion of sodium is mainly via the kidneys and the resulting urine usually contains from 920-2,300 mg sodium per liter. Increased intake of the mineral leads to increased excretion, and normal healthy kidneys have no difficulty in excreting the excess as long as there is sufficient water excreted. There is a limit to the amount by which the kidneys can concentrate urine (specific gravity of about 1.035 is the maximum), so high intakes of sodium, usually as salt, must be accompanied by large volumes of water.

Excessive salt intakes usually induce thirst which, when satisfied, compensates for the increased requirements of water. The highest excretion of sodium occurs about midday, with the lowest at night.

Control of urinary excretion of sodium is under the influence of hormones. These act upon the kidney tubules by stimulating or slowing the reabsorption of sodium within the kidney. One hormone is aldosterone, which is elaborated in the adrenal cortex. When the body sodium is depleted, e.g., by excessive sweating or by starvation, aldosterone is secreted; this stimulates the kidney to reabsorb and thus conserve the sodium in the urine. In Addison's disease, aldosterone is no longer produced because the adrenal cortex is destroyed, and sodium is excreted in large, uncontrolled amounts. The result is muscular weakness and low blood pressure. Treatment is to give sufficient sodium in the form of salt to replace the losses, and to supply the hormone by injection. Diseased kidneys, as in renal failure, are unable to conserve sodium, and the individual becomes markedly depleted.

Excessive amounts of aldosterone and other adrenal cortex hormones will cause increased retention of sodium. This also happens in congestive heart disease and in certain types of kidney disease. The usual result is high blood pressure.

Fecal excretion of sodium is very small, usually only about 115 mg daily. All the digestive juices contain large amounts of sodium, but most of this is reabsorbed in the large intestine. In diarrhea, reabsorption is inefficient and significant daily losses of sodium up to 2,070 mg are possible in the feces. These must be replaced in chronic diarrhea to prevent body depletion.

Excretion through the skin is usually negligible, but when sweating is excessive, losses can be significant. Sweat contains from 460 to 1,840 mg sodium per liter, but in those who are acclimatized to heat, this is maintained at 960 mg per liter. In tropical climates or while indulging in heavy manual work, excretion of sweat can reach up to 14 liters, so sodium loss then becomes serious and more significant than urinary sodium loss. Without supplementary salt in these conditions, sodium depletion soon follows. Miner's cramp is one such condition.

Sodium balance in a healthy individual should be zero. For example, with a good intake of 3,105 mg and no salt added at the table, excretion should be 2,990 mg in the urine plus 115 mg in the feces; sweat excretion is negligible if the individual is sedentary. Under conditions of hard exercise or manual work, sweating can induce a negative balance, i.e., more sodium is excreted than eaten. Excessive intakes and certain diseases can cause a positive balance where the extra sodium in the diet is not excreted. A negative balance is usually treated by increased oral intake of sodium; a positive balance by diuretic drugs.

Deficiency of sodium is highly unlikely on any diet but it can be associated with dehydration, as in heat exhaustion brought on by high temperatures, hard exercise, and manual work; in babies, it can be caused by diarrhea. The extracellular fluid volume is reduced, as is the blood volume. The blood thickens, veins collapse, blood pressure is reduced, and the pulse becomes rapid. These changes cause dryness of the mouth, even though thirst may be absent. There is usually mental apathy, loss of appetite, and sometimes vomiting. Muscle cramps are usually present. Dehydration is also indicated by sunken features—particularly the eyes, which recede—and a loose, nonelastic skin.

Deficiency of sodium may occur without water depeletion; the condition is called water intoxication. It occurs: after heavy sweating when the thirst is quenched with water to which no sodium has been added; in the treatment of sodium deficiency, if too much water is given by mouth or intravenously; and in the treatment of dehydration if only water is given. Symptoms include loss of appetite; weakness; mental apathy; muscular twitchings; convulsions; and coma induced by excessive retention of water by the brain. Treatment is to ensure that salt is added to replacement fluids in the above conditions.

Causes of low blood sodium levels may also be kidney failure; hormonal imbalance, e.g., excess production of antidiuretic hormone or vasopressin; lung cancers; lung infections; meningitis; myxedema; lack of adrenal and pituitary hormones; edema as in heart failure, liver cirrhosis, nephrotic syndrome, nephritis, and toxemia of pregnancy; high blood glucose levels; and porphyria. Treatment of low blood sodium in these conditions is salt replacement, hormones, and successful correction of the underlying disease.

Excess sodium in the body accumulates primarily in the extracellular fluids. As the concentration rises the body responds by passing more water into the extracellular fluids to dilute the sodium, so edema results. Consequences of high salt intake that is not excreted are therefore high blood pressure; enlarged heart; abnormal ECG tracings; and enlarged kidneys, leading to nephritis. Epidemiological evidence shows that high blood pressure in some countries is associated with habitual high salt intakes. Elevation of the blood serum sodium concentration is indicative of a deficit in body water relative to sodium.

Causes of high blood sodium levels include diabetes insipidus where vasopressin is deficient; kidney failure; high blood calcium; low blood potassium; excessive sweating without access to water (e.g., infants, bedridden or comatose patients); excessive diarrhea, especially in children; and grossly excessive intakes of sodium with limited access to water. Treatment is water replacement usually accom-

panied by drug diuretic treatment; restriction of sodium
in the diet; and occasionally kidney dialysis.

Functions of sodium are:

1. In maintaining a normal balance of water between body
cells and the surrounding fluids. Potassium also contributes to this.
2. In nerve impulse transmission, where the flow of sodium
into the nerve cell and the opposite flow of potassium out
of the cell sets up an electrical impulse that travels down
the nerve to the muscle.
3. In all muscle contraction, including that of the heart,
where the correct balance of sodium and potassium is
essential for a smooth response.
4. In preserving the acid-alkali balance of the body in close
relationship with bicarbonate, phosphate, and protein, and
the minerals potassium, calcium, and magnesium.
5. As a constituent of ATPase, the enzyme responsible
for splitting adenosine triphosphate in the production of
energy.
6. The active transport of the nutrients, amino acids, and
glucose into body cells.

Supplementary sodium is sodium chloride, which provides 39.3 mg sodium in 100 mg chloride.

Recommended daily intake has not been suggested by
any authority since insufficiency in the diet is highly
unlikely.

Food additives of sodium, apart from those found in
natural foods, include sodium acetate; sodium alginate;
sodium aluminium phosphate, acidic and basic; sodium
ascorbate; sodium benzoate; sodium bicarbonate; sodium
carbonate; sodium caseinate; sodium chloride; sodium
hydrogen citrate; trisodium citrate; tetrasodium diphosphate; trisodium diphosphate; sodium ferrocyanide; sodium
gluconate; sodium hydrogen glutamate (monosodium

glutamate); sodium hydrogen sulfite; sodium metabisulfite; sodium nitrate; sodium nitrite; sodium polyphosphates; sodium propionate; sodium 5-ribonucleotide; soaps or sodium salts of fatty acids; sodium sesquicarbonate; sodium sorbate; sodium stearoly-2-lactate; sodium sulfate; sodium sulfite.

Drugs containing sodium include sodium alginate—suspending agent; sodium bicarbonate—antacids; sodium acetate and sodium lactate—electrolyte replenishers; sodium phosphate, sodium sulfate and sodium tartrate—purgatives; sodium ascorbate—vitamin; sodium calcium edetate—treatment of heavy metal poisoning; sodium carboxymethylcellulose—bulking and swelling agent; sodium citrate—cough mixtures; sodium cromoglycate—asthma; sodium fusidate—antibacterial; sodium hyaluronate—eye preparation; sodium lauryl sulfate—laxative; sodium lauryl sulfoacetate—laxative; sodium nitroprusside—angina treatment; sodium oleate—hemorrhoid treatment; sodium perborate—gingivitis; sodium picosulfate—laxative; sodium pyrrolidone carboxylate—skin cleanser; sodium ricinoleate—gingivitis; sodium saccharin—sweetener; sodium salicylate—pain and fever; sodium valproate—epilepsy.

Sodium pump, the mechanism whereby potassium levels inside the body cells and sodium levels outside them are kept constant. Cell membranes are permeable to both minerals when in solution; the concentration gradients are such that potassium tends to flow out of cells and sodium tends to flow in. To maintain the balance of high levels of potassium inside and sodium outside the cells, energy is required, which is provided by the splitting of high-energy phosphate bonds of adenosine triphosphate. The minerals are transported on the backs of glucose and some unknown carrier. Certain factors can affect the efficiency of the sodium pump, causing it to slow down. One is ouabain, a plant drug that acts like digitalis; the other is phlorizin, the toxic principle of apple, pear, plum, and cherry trees (but not their fruits). Vasopressin, the sodium-excreting hormone from the adrenals, slows down the sodium pump. This increases the blood pressure and it has been shown recently that the sodium pump is slower in those people with high blood pressure.

Soups, all soups provide some B vitamins but little else, apart from lentil and tomato soups, which also provide vitamin A, carotene, and vitamin D. Canned, condensed as eaten, and dried as eaten, soups contain these B vitamins (in mg per 100 g): thiamin (0.01-0.07); riboflavin (0.01-0.05); nicotinic acid (0.1-0.8); and pyridoxine (0.01-0.07). Folic acid is detected only in soups based on tomatoes and mushrooms and at levels of 2-12 μg per 100 g. Thiamin level of dried oxtail soup as eaten is 0.8 mg per 100 g, which is mainly derived from the flavoring agent.

Lentil soup also provides 40 μg vitamin A per 100 g; 430 μg carotene per 100 g; and 0.28 μg vitamin D per 100 g, due mainly to ham ingredient plus traces of vitamin C.

Tomato soup also provides 210 μg carotene per 100 g and traces of vitamin C.

Minerals

All provide high sodium levels (except specific low-sodium varieties) but are good sources of potassium, calcium, magnesium, phosphorus, chloride, and the trace elements depending upon type.

Canned, condensed as eaten, and dried as eaten soups contain the following (in mg per 100 g): sodium (350-6,120); potassium (16-920); calcium (3-140); magnesium (3-48); phosphorus (10-260); iron (0.2-4.3); copper (0.02-0.33); zinc (0.1-2.4); and chloride (290-9,030).

Soy flour, an excellent source of B vitamins that is even better when defatted. Devoid of sodium but rich in potassium, calcium, magnesium, phosphorus, and iron. *See* Figures 64 and 65.

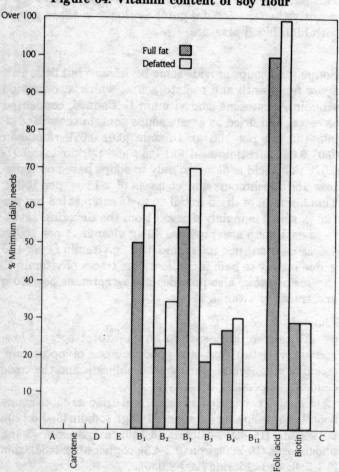

Figure 64: Vitamin content of soy flour

Figure 65: Mineral content of soy flour

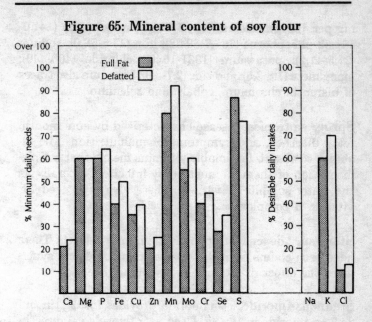

Spirits, all alcoholic spirits (liquors) are completely devoid of all vitamins.

Spironolactone, a diuretic. Reduces the availability of vitamin A.

Spirulina, a blue-green alga, used as a staple food by the Aztecs of Mexico and now being developed as a high-protein food supplement rich in vitamins and minerals. The vitamins present are (in mg per 100 g): carotene (250); vitamin E (19.0); thiamin (5.5); riboflavin (4.0); nicotinic acid (11.8); pyridoxine (0.3); pantothenic acid (1.1); inositol (35.0); folic acid (0.05); biotin (0.04); and vitamin B_{12} (0.2).

Minerals
    The range of mineral contents of dried material is (in

mg per 100 g): calcium (104.5-131.5); magnesium (141.0-191.5); phosphorus (761.7-894.2); iron (47.5-58.0); sodium (27.5-41.2); potassium (1331-1540); chloride (400-440); manganese (1.8-2.5); and zinc (2.7-3.9). There are also traces of bismuth, chromium, cobalt, and selenium.

Sprue, a tropical disease characterized by sore mouth, fatty diarrhea, and symptoms of malnutrition. The inability to absorb fat-soluble vitamins means that supplementation of them all must be by injection, or orally as the water-solubilized variety. There also is a need for vitamin B complex.

Stamina, dependent upon blood vitamin E levels. There have been claims from Russia that pangamic acid synergizes the effect of vitamin E. *See* endurance.

Stannous fluoride, tin fluoride. Provides 75.8 μg tin and 24.2 μg fluoride in 100 μg. Used as a fluoride gel directly applied to the teeth to prevent dental caries. Also added to fluoride toothpastes, but may stain the teeth.

Sterility, *see* fertility.

Steroids, *see* corticosteroids.

Stilbestrol, a synthetic estrogen. Reduces body levels of pyridoxine. Shown to be a health hazard, its use has been banned from livestock production in the US.

Stomatitis, an inflammatory condition of the mouth that may occur as a primary disease or as a symptom of some other disease, e.g., sprue. May respond to daily intake of 300 mg nicotinamide orally. *See also* glossitis; gingivitis.

Stress, increases the body's requirements for vitamin B complex and particularly pantothenic acid because of its role in producing antistress hormones. Also vitamin C for the same reason. During stressful periods, increase vitamin B complex and C intakes to at least ten times the minimum daily requirements.

Oxidative stress: Also increase vitamin E intake to at least 400 IU daily. *See* E (vitamin).

Physical stress: See athletes.

Stretch marks, also known as striae. Apply vitamin E cream as soon as possible and supplement the diet with 400 IU daily in divided doses.

Stroke, a cerebrovascular disease due to atherosclerosis of brain blood vessels and high blood pressure.

Prevention or post-stroke treatment should include high intakes of vitamin E (400-600 IU), vitamin C (500-1,000 mg), safflower oil or evening primrose oil (3 g), lecithin (5-15 g), and fish oils containing EPA and DHA (3 g), all daily, and a switch from saturated dietary fats to poly-unsaturated oils.

Strontium, chemical symbol Sr. Atomic weight 87.6. An alkaline earth metal, named from its discovery in the ore from the lead mines of Strontian in Scotland.

No evidence that it is essential for animal and human life. It behaves as calcium and accompanies it in foods rich in calcium, e.g., milk, grains, and fresh vegetables. Dietary strontium in biological material is usually about one-thousandth that of calcium.

Cow's milk is richer in both strontium and calcium than human milk. Bottle-fed babies tend to receive intakes of strontium some four times greater than those breast-fed. Some of it is retained. Breast-fed babies excrete more than they receive because their urinary volume is increased. In all babies, the ratio of strontium to calcium is higher in the urine and feces than in the bones. These results suggest that in infants at least the body discriminates against strontium in favor of calcium.

Some epidemiological evidence shows that strontium may have a protective effect against dental caries. One study suggests it may be helpful in the treatment of osteoporosis. It may also protect the energy-producing apparatus of body cells.

Strontium-90, a radioactive form of strontium produced by the effect of nuclear explosions. It can be dispersed over wide areas, and so finds its way into plants and thence into animals and humans. Like calcium, it accumulates in the bones where it can continue to radiate radioactivity. With a half-life of 28 years, such effects can eventually become dangerous. Strontium-90 represents the only toxic form of strontium. The nonradioactive mineral appears to be perfectly safe.

Sugar, the refined white variety is completely devoid of all vitamins.

Turbinado sugar contains the following B vitamins (in mg per 100 g): thiamin, (trace); riboflavin (0.01); nicotinic acid (2.0); pyridoxine (0.1); and pantothenic acid (0.20). Contains also choline (2.8 mg per 100 g), and inositol (24.0 mg per 100 g).

Minerals

Demerara sugar provides significant quantities of all minerals; white sugar is practically devoid of minerals. Demerara and white varieties respectively, provide (in mg per 100 g): sodium (6 and trace); potassium (89 and 2); calcium (53 and 2); magnesium (15 and trace); phosphorus

(20 and trace); iron (0.9 and trace); copper (0.06 and 0.02); sulfur (14 and trace); and chloride (35 and trace).

Sulfa drugs, anti-infection drugs that function by inhibiting the uptake of PABA by harmful bacteria. PABA should not be taken as a supplement while taking sulfa drugs. They prevent the synthesis of vitamin K by destroying intestinal bacteria.

Sulfur, chemical symbol S. Atomic weight 32.1. Occurs in nature in the free state and in combination as sulfates and sulfides. Constitutes 0.05 percent of the earth's crust.

As it is a constituent of all proteins, it is an essential element for humans, animals, plants, and microorganisms. The sulfur content of an adult body is about 100 g. The greater part occurs in the three amino acids cysteine, cystine, and methionine. Some is present in the amino acid taurine. The rest appears as sulfate within body cells, either free or attached to body constituents like the anti-blood clotting substance heparin and the structural component chondroitin sulfate.

Sulfur is also present in the two vitamins thiamin and biotin; in vitamin D of milk, where it occurs as a water-soluble sulfate; in fatty acid sulfates; and in the enzymes that contain glutathione and coenzyme A. Sulfur-containing compounds are often prefixed by the term "thio," derived from the Greek word for sulfur, *theion*. Thiosulfates and thiocyanates are present in body fluids in very small amounts where they are produced in the detoxification of the cyanide present in foods, polluted atmospheres, and tobacco smoke.

Body content of sulfur resides mainly in: keratin, the horny layer of the skin; the fingernails; the toenails; the skin; and the joints. The characteristic smell of burning

hair is due to its high sulfur content. The curliness of hair
depends upon the sulfur—sulfur bonds of cystine. To
straighten hair, these bonds must be opened up. During
permanent waving the bonds are opened with one agent,
then closed again to the desired shape or pattern with
another agent. Sheep's wool, which is very curly, can contain 5 percent of its weight as sulfur.

Food sources of sulfur are (in mg per 100 g): mustard
powder (1,280); dried egg (630); scallops (570); lobster (510);
shellfish (250-450); crab (470); nuts (150-380); garlic (370);
prawns (370); poultry (200-340); meats (200-330); kidney
(170-290); liver (220-270); white fish (200-300); nonfat milk
(320); fatty fish (150-260); cheese (230-250); dried peaches
(240); roe (240); horseradish (210); organ meats (140-200);
mung beans (190); whole egg (180); Indian tea (180); kidney
beans (170); mustard and cress (170); peas (130-180); dried
apricots (160); oatmeal (160); whole wheat flour (150); water
cress (130); lentils (120); coffee (110); barley (110); whole
wheat bread (81). For other foods *see* individual entries.

Protein supplies most of the sulfur in the diet, but
some comes in the form of sulfates. A good diet will provide 800 mg sulfur daily. Little is known about its intermediate metabolism, but excretion parallels that of nitrogen. There is no evidence of any deficiency states in animals
or humans.

Medicinal uses of sulfur include: a mild laxative when
taken orally; a mild antiseptic in ointment form to treat
acne; a parasiticide in lotion form, used to treat scabies;
with lead acetate to darken gray hair; and as a depilatory
agent to remove body hair.

Medicinal forms include: precipitated sulfur or milk of
sulfur, dose 1-4 g; sublimed sulfur or flowers of sulfur, dose
1-4 g; sulfurated potash, a mixture of potassium poly-
sulfide, potassium sulfite, and potassium thiosulfate containing 42 percent sulfur, used as a lotion on the skin.

Sulfasalazine,   used to treat Crohn's disease and ulcerative colitis. Prevents absorption of folic acid.

Sulfitocobalamin,   *see* B_{12} (vitamin).

Sulfonamides,   *see* sulfa drugs.

Sunburn,   responds to vitamin E cream applied directly and 600 IU (200 IU 3 times daily) taken orally to help healing and prevent scarring. Vitamin C (1,000-1,500 mg daily) will help healing and prevent infection. In addition 15 mg zinc daily will benefit.

Sunscreen agent,   the most effective is PABA, which is incorporated at 5 percent in creams and lotions. It may also be the best protectant against skin cancer induced by ultraviolet light.

Sunshine vitamin,   *see* D (vitamin).

Surgery,   of the intestinal tract may cause paralytic ileus (paralysis of the intestine) characterized by gas pains and abdominal distension. Doses of calcium pantothenate (50-100 mg per day), preferably by injection, are used in prevention and treatment. Supplementary intakes of all vitamins, but especially vitamin C (1,000 mg daily) and the mineral zinc (20 mg daily), before and after surgery, may help accelerate healing process. Postsurgical hemorrhage can be controlled by vitamin K given under medical supervision.

Symptoms of mineral deficiencies in plants,   when the minerals required by a plant are not in sufficient concentration in a soil or they are prevented from being absorbed by certain factors, specific symptoms appear. Plants in deficient soil may grow, but are far from healthy. Typical symptoms are shown in Figure 66.

Figure 66: Symptoms of mineral deficiencies in plants

Deficient minerals	Symptoms
Nitrogen	Lack of growth and yellowing leaves. Entire plant affected.
Phosphorus	Dark green stunted plants. Delayed maturity. Entire plant affected.
Potassium	Mottled yellowing. Spots of dead areas. Weak stalks. Roots more susceptible to disease.
Sulfur	Yellowing of young leaves. Veins remain green.
Magnesium	Mottled or yellow leaves. Leaf tips turned upwards. Older leaves most affected.
Calcium	Inhibition of root development with death of shoot and root tips. Young leaves and roots most affected.
Iron	Yellowing of veins in young leaves. Stems short and slender. Buds remain alive.
Chlorine	Wilted leaves, yellowing, spots of dead areas. Stunted, thickened roots.
Manganese	Yellow, dead areas between veins. Smallest veins remain green.
Boron	Death of stem. Leaves twisted, pale at base. Swollen, discolored root tips.
Zinc	Reduction in leaf size. Yellowing. Older leaves most affected.
Copper	Young leaves dark green, twisted, wilted, misshapen.
Molybdenum	Yellowing or twisting and death of young leaves.

T

Talc, purified, native hydrated magnesium silicate containing a small amount of aluminum silicate. Also known as French chalk. A food additive used as a release agent; also used as a lubricant in tablet making. Excessive inhalation of talc can cause lung disease (pneumoconiosis).

Tea, the dried leaf of black tea (Indian), has a useful content of some vitamins but these are drastically reduced when it is infused. Traces only of carotene and vitamin C are in the dried leaf, but not detectable in the drink. B vitamins present for the dried leaf and infusion, respectively, are (in mg per 100 g): thiamin (0.14 and trace); riboflavin (1.2 and 0.01); nicotinic acid (7.5 and 0.1); and pantothenic acid (1.3 and trace).

Minerals

The dried leaf is rich in minerals, but infused tea contains only traces of most minerals with a high content of manganese (about 1 mg per cup). Levels for dried leaf and infusion, respectively, are (in mg per 100 g): sodium—45 and trace; potassium—2,160 and trace; calcium—430 and trace; magnesium—250 and 1; phosphorus—630 and 1; iron—15.2 and trace; copper—1.6 and trace; zinc—3.0 and trace; sulfur—180 for dried leaf; and chloride—52 and trace.

Teeth, pyridoxine may help prevent tooth decay, particularly in children, when taken at a daily dose of 10 mg. Vitamins A and D are essential during childhood for the normal development of healthy teeth. Vitamin C, at intakes of 100 mg with each meal, has been used as an orthodontic supplement in children. *See also* bruxism.

Temperature, *see* seasonal supplementation.

Tetany, a condition resulting from a severe low blood calcium or a reduction in the serum ionized calcium when total blood calcium is normal. It is characterized by sensory symptoms of tingling (pins and needles) of the lips, tongue, fingers, and feet; muscular spasms of the hands and feet; and spasm and twitching of the face muscles. May be indicative of low body calcium or respiratory or metabolic alkalosis (excess alkali in the body). Treatment is supplementary calcium, orally in mild cases; by intravenous infusion in severe cases.

Tetracycline, an antibiotic. Prevents the formation of vitamin K by intestinal bacteria.

Thiamin(e), *see* B_1 (vitamin).

Thrombophlebitis, *see* phlebitis.

Thrombosis, *see* blood clot.

Thymus, a gland concerned with the development of immune system and resistance to infection. It is fully developed at two years of age, then slowly regresses after a period of stagnation. Full activity requires adequate vitamin A, choline, folic acid, vitamin B_{12}, and amino acid. Methionine is essential in pregnant mothers for full, efficient development of the thymus in babies.

Thyroid, an endocrine gland found in the neck in front

of and partially surrounding the thyroid cartilage and the upper end of the trachea. *See* hyperthyroidism.

The term also applies to the thyroid gland of slaughtered animals when it is freed from connective tissue and fat and then dried and powdered. Contains not less than 1.70 mg and not more than 2.30 mg iodine in combination per dried gland. One dried thyroid equals 5 g fresh gland. In humans, it is used as a source of thyroid hormone in hypothyroidism. In animals, it has been used in obesity; kidney failure; chronic skin conditions; and to increase spermatogenesis, libido, and milk production.

Thyrotoxicosis, *see* hyperthyroidism.

Thyroxine, known also as L-thyroxine; T4. First isolated from the thyroid gland by E.C. Kendall of the US in 1919. It is a natural thyroid hormone containing four atoms of iodine per molecule of thyroxine. Can also be obtained by chemical synthesis. Used in the treatment of hypothyroidism, particularly for long-term therapy. D-thyroxine has been used to decrease high fat levels in the blood serum. L-thyroxine has been used to treat some cases of obesity. *See* hypothyroidism; iodine; and triiodothyronine.

Tin, chemical symbol Sn, from the Latin stannum. Atomic weight 118.7. Occurs in nature as cassiterite, stannite, and tealite; abundance in the earth's crust is 6 mg per kg.

It has been considered to be an essential trace mineral for some animals since the 1960s, when rats reared on a tin-free diet were found to have retarded growth. The addition of 1 mg tin sulfate to each kg of their diet restored normal growth.

Functions of tin in animals are believed to reside in:

1. Its stimulating the transcription of RNA and DNA, which determine genetic characteristics.
2. Protein synthesis through RNA.
3. Growth, probably a result of (1) and (2). No functions of tin have been discovered in humans.

Food sources of tin are unknown because of the difficulty in measurement, but canned foods contain higher levels than fresh or frozen foods due to contamination from the container. Even this is reduced because the insides of tins are now lacquered. Human diets can provide between 3.5 and 17 mg per day, but only when some of the food is of the canned variety. The toxic level is believed to be about 6.0 mg per kg body weight, so fresh-food diets have a high safety margin. As the toxic amount for a 154 lb (70 kg) adult is 420 mg tin, excessive intakes of canned food can approach this level. A concentration of 300 mg tin in 100 g food causes toxic effects in experimental animals.

Excess intakes in animals cause anemia, which can be reversed by feeding extra iron and copper; and depressed growth.

Absorption of tins and its salts from the gastrointestinal tract is very poor and most is excreted in the feces.

Acute toxic effects in humans include colic; distension of the abdomen (tympanites or meteorism); and constipation.

Chronic toxic effects in humans include nausea; colic; headache; weakness; fever; muscle pain; joint pain; and tinnitus (ringing in the ears).

Inhalation over prolonged periods can cause pneumoconiosis (lung disease). The maximum permissible concentration in the atmosphere is 2 mg per cubic meter.

Medical uses of tin and tin oxide in tablet form include the treatment of boils, carbuncles, and acne; also tapeworm infestation.

Tinea versicolor, a skin infection characterized by multiple patches of lesions varying in color from white to brown. Also known as pityriasis versicolor. It is common in young adults. Tan, brown, or white, slightly scaling areas are seen on the chest, neck, abdomen, and occasionally on the face. These areas do not tan, but appear as white "sun spots". Treatment is the application of undiluted selenium sulfide shampoo or a 2.5 percent lotion to affected areas (avoiding the scrotum) for three or four days at bedtime, washing it off in the morning.

Tissue salts, inorganic mineral salts, specific deficiency of which is believed to be associated with particular diseases. Also known as biochemic tissue salts. Tissue salt therapy is based upon the homeopathic principles first put forward by a German doctor, Wilhelm H. Schuessler of Oldenburg, and tested by him from 1872 until his death in 1898. Dr. Schuessler believed that the disease process was always associated with a deficiency of one or more tissue salts that are normally present, in correct balance, in body tissue cells. By supplying the deficient mineral salts a healthy balance is restored. The twelve tissue salts of Dr. Schuessler are: calc. fluor. (calcium fluoride); calc. phos. (calcium phosphate); calc. sulf. (calcium sulfate); ferr. phos. (ferric phosphate or iron phosphate); kali. mur. (potassium chloride); kali phos. (potassium phosphate); kali. sulf. (potassium sulfate); mag. phos. (magnesium phosphate); nat. mur. (sodium chloride); nat. phos. (sodium phosphate); nat. sulfph. (sodium sulfate); and silica (silicon dioxide).

True deficiency of a particular mineral is not overcome by sole treatment with a tissue salt, since the quantity in its preparation is minute, based upon homeopathic principles of dilution. At this dilution, the biochemic tissue salt is more likely to influence the way in which the deficient mineral is distributed throughout the body, and hence rectify imbalances in that way. Biochemic tissue salts can also influence minerals when they are present in excess in body cells and tissues. Biochemic remedies may therefore be regarded as having a regulatory function on body minerals by influencing the distribution of anions and cations within body cells, and in the extracellular fluids bathing those cells.

The preparation of biochemic tissue salts is based upon homeopathic principles of serial dilution and trituration. One part of the appropriate salt is mixed with nine parts of lactose (milk sugar) and the resultant mixture is vigorously ground and mixed to ensure a completely homogeneous blend. This is termed "trituration" and comprises the first decimal potency called 1X. One part of this potency is mixed with a further nine parts of lactose and the resulting mixture is exhaustively blended to produce the homogeneous second decimal potency 2X. One part of this potency is further diluted with nine parts of lactose in the same manner as before and the resulting mix is termed the third decimal potency 3X. The process, which is known as "serial dilution" (the X simply means that each stage of the dilution is ten-fold) is carried on until the sixth decimal potency. At this stage the tissue salt has been diluted one million times and is known as potency 6X, the most commonly utilized homeopathic potency. Further dilution to 12X is sometimes carried out but it is seldom necessary to continue beyond this. This constant serial dilution combined with exhaustive blending (trituration) is known as potentization, a term also applied to homeopathic preparations. The potentized powder is finally highly compressed into small tablets that readily dissolve on or under the tongue.

For best effect the following precautions should be taken:

1. No food or drink should be consumed within 15 minutes of taking a biochemic remedy.
2. Teeth should not be cleaned within the same time restraint.
3. All tissue salts should be kept in containers that will not let in daylight or odors from other substances.
4. Avoid handling the tablets apart from those to be immediately consumed.
5. Transfer to other containers from those in which they are supplied should not be carried out. This is to avoid contamination of the minute amounts of salt left in the biochemic remedy.

The following observations are also important to any-one contemplating biochemic tissue salt remedies:

1. The remedies may be used to treat acute disease (usually infections) and chronic disease (inflammatory and degener-ative conditions).
2. Sometimes the condition appears to worsen after tak-ing tissue salts. If it happens during treatment of an acute illness, like an infection, administration of the remedy should cease to allow the body to enter a healing phase. Improvement should then follow. If not, the services of a practitioner, preferably a homeopathic one, should be sought. Similar considerations apply to treatment of a chronic condition, except that worsening may occur several weeks after therapy is initiated. In the same way, therapy should cease to allow the healing phase to come into opera-tion. If necessary when the condition persists, continued therapy at the recommended dose should be restarted.
3. All biochemic tissue salt therapy is safe but those un-duly sensitive to lactose should be aware of its presence in these remedies.
4. No other complementary therapy is affected by tissue

salts, but the effectiveness of the latter may be reduced
and professional advice should be sought.

Properties and applications of the twelve tissue salts
are:

Calc. fluor.: Calcium fluoride. Indicated where tissues
have lost their tone, e.g., varicose veins; leg ulcers; eczema;
piles; poor blood circulation; constipation; backache; and
chronic synovitis (arthritis). May be used to treat diseases
of the teeth, bones, skin, and nails where a surface lesion
exists.

Calc. phos.: Calcium phosphate. Promotes healthy cells
in organs and tissues; assists digestion, absorption, and
assimilation of foodstuffs; improves poor blood circulation;
relieves chilblains; relieves generalized pruritus (itching) in
the elderly; and helps shrink enlarged tonsils and nose
polyps. In conjunction with ferr. phos., treats simple
anemia; and in alternation with kali. phos., produces more
rapid results in relieving pruritus.

Calc. sulph.: Calcium sulfate. Cleanses the blood and
tissues by removing toxic and waste products. Is used in
mild skin conditions; mucous membrane infections; and
catarrhal complaints where it supplements the action of
kali. mur. On its own, calc. sulph. helps relieve head pains
and neuralgias in the elderly.

Ferr. phos.: Ferric phosphate (or iron phosphate). Maintains healthy, strong blood vessel walls; ensures the blood
is rich in oxygen to maintain health; complements other
treatments for anemia; and relieves congestion, inflammation, high temperature, and rapid pulse. Should be given
as a standard in the early stage of all acute disorders at
frequent intervals. Is an excellent general remedy for illnesses associated with aging and with children. Can be
regarded as a first-aid treatment for any sort of muscular
or joint injury.

Kali. mur.: Potassium chloride. Indicated for any

soft glandular swelling, or those associated with chronic rheumatic conditions. Should be used in conjunction with calc. sulph., which complements its action by purifying the blood. Specific for infantile eczema. When used alternatively with ferr. phos., is particularly beneficial in all children's ailments. Kali. mur. is specific for any sort of thick, white, gelatinous discharges; for a sluggish, underactive liver; and for reduced bile production. When alternated with ferr. phos., it is indicated for inflammatory conditions of the respiratory system like coughs, colds, sore throats, tonsillitis, and bronchitis. Problems associated with the digestive system may respond to kali. mur.

Kali. phos.: Potassium phosphate. Is indicated for mild nerve conditions that cause headaches; dyspepsia; sleeplessness; depression; lethargy; reduced vitality; and edginess. Regarded as a general tonic. May also help in nerve-related conditions like shingles (infection of nerve endings with herpes zoster); nervous asthma; and nervous insomnia. In these conditions its beneficial action is accentuated by taking mag. phos. in conjunction with it.

Kali. sulph.: Potassium sulfate. Acts primarily on the skin and mucous membranes of all the internal organs. It treats the feelings of extremes of cold and of heat; pain in the limbs; and vague, generalized pains. Any abnormal condition of the skin and mucous membranes, particularly where there is discharge or scaling, will respond to kali. sulph. Specific for catarrh, a condition of the respiratory mucous membranes. Also treats psoriasis of the skin and the fungal infections of athlete's foot. In conjunction with silica, it restores brittle nails to health; with silica and nat. mur., it helps maintain healthy hair.

Mag. phos.: Magnesium phosphate. The antispasmodic tissue salt. Like kali. phos., it maintains a healthy nervous system; in conjunction with this tissue salt, it relieves cramping, shooting, darting, and spasmodic pains. On its own, mag. phos. is indicated for the painful conditions of neuralgia, neuritis, sciatica, and headache. Muscular twinges, cramps, hiccoughs, fits of coughing, and any sudden, sharp pains will respond to mag. phos. It acts more rapidly when the biochemic salt tablets are taken with a sip of hot water.

Nat. mur.: Sodium chloride. Restores to normal any part of the system that is too wet or too dry, where the water balance is upset. Typical conditions include headache; constipation; hard feces; soreness of the anus; watery discharge of colds; dry nose and throat; sluggish digestion; thirst, excessive flow of tears and saliva as in neuralgia and toothache; watering eyes; hay fever; respiratory allergies; dryness of the skin; tiredness on waking; and craving for salt and salty foods. Nat. mur. stimulates the flow and production of hydrochloric acid in the digestive system. It controls water distribution throughout the body. Has been used to make salt-free or low-salt diets more acceptable to the individual. Relieves insect bites and stings when applied directly to the affected area.

Nat. phos.: Sodium phosphate. An acid neutralizer. Excess acid can give rise to rheumatic conditions; digestive upsets; intestinal disorders; and inefficient assimilation of nutrients. Nat. phos. relieves all of these states. It also helps regulate the bile content and flow and so is indicated in the treatment of jaundice, colic, sick headaches, and gastric disturbances. It helps promote the absorption of water and so with nat. mur. and nat. sulph., serves to control body water balance. Nat. phos. helps emulsify fatty acids in the digestive system, so it is indicated where fat digestion and absorption is difficult. Specific for relieving gouty and allied conditions due to the deposition of uric acid in the joints. Remedies any condition giving rise to yellow exudates and discharges.

Nat. sulph.: Sodium sulfate. Controls the density of the extracellular fluids (which bathe the cells) by eliminating excess water. Essential for the healthy functioning of the liver by ensuring an adequate supply of bile to assist in fat digestion. Toxins from body cells are excreted through the cell membrane to the extracellular fluid from where they are eliminated through the kidneys. Nat. sulph. is concerned with this disposal, so it is essential to prevent accumulation of toxins in the cells and water. For this reason it is indicated in rheumatic conditions; in biliousness; in treating influenza; in sluggish kidneys; in conditions causing a coated tongue; and when there is excess bitterness in the mouth.

Silica: Silicon dioxide. Acts upon the organic tissues of the body including the bones, joints, glands, and skin. It is indicated for any condition where there is pus formation like abscesses, stys, and boils. An inflamed throat, as in tonsillitis, needs biochemic silica. It is also of benefit in nail and hair conditions. Silica restores a healthy skin and normalizes the perspiration. When rheumatic conditions are related to excess uric acid, as in gout, silica functions by dissolving the crystals and excreting them. The mild mental aberrations observed in old people (senile dementia) may respond to silica.

Often a combination of tissue salts is more effective in relieving a variety of related symptoms. Examples are mag. phos., nat. mur., and silica for migraine; ferr. phos., kali. mur., and nat. mur. for coughs, colds, and influenza; calc. fluor., calc. phos., kali. phos., and nat. mur. for backache and lumbago; calc. fluor., ferr. phos., and nat. mur. for varicose veins and blood circulation problems; kali. mur., kali. sulf., calc. sulf., and silica for minor skin ailments; ferr. phos., kali. phos., and mag. phos. for sciatica, neuralgia, and neuritis; calc. phos., kali. phos., and ferr. phos. for general debility and nervous exhaustion.

Tobacco amblyopia, *see* eyes.

Tocopherol, *see* E (vitamin).

Torula yeast, *torulopsis utilis.* A strain of yeast less bitter than baker's and brewer's varieties containing the following vitamins (in mg per 100 g dried product): carotene (trace); thiamin (15.0); riboflavin (5.0); pyridoxine (3.5); nicotinic acid (50.0); pantothenic acid (10.0); biotin (0.1); folic acid (3.0). A rich source of RNA and DNA; together they account for 12 percent of dried yeast.

Toxemia of pregnancy, may be related in some cases to lack of pyridoxine and, more importantly, folic acid.

Toxic reactions, the undesirable effects of vitamin therapy are rare in the West but they have been observed, usually as a result of excessive intake of vitamins when self-administered as supplements.

For the water-soluble vitamins, it is difficult to produce high tissue levels because the kidneys readily excrete the excess when blood concentrations are above a certain threshold. There is no evidence that the body is able to convert excessive quantities of the B complex into their metabolically active forms above those normally present.

Fat-soluble vitamins, however, tend to be stored both in the liver and in the fatty tissues of the body. When these vitamins spill over into the tissues, toxic reactions occur and certain symptoms become apparent, summarized as follows:

Vitamin A: First indications of acute vitamin A toxicity were reported when seamen and Arctic explorers ate polar bear liver, which is a particularly rich source of the vitamin. Symptoms include drowsiness, increased cerebrospinal fluid (which bathes the spinal column and brain) pressure, vomiting, and extensive peeling of the skin.

Vitamin A quantities measured in millions of units were eaten.

At least twenty cases of children under three years of age with vitamin A poisoning have been described in the US medical literature. The cause was usually misguided enthusiasm on the part of the mothers, who gave their offspring from 30 mg (90,000 IU) to 150 mg (450,000 IU) of vitamin A daily for several months. The symptoms of these chronic intakes included loss of appetite; irritability; a dry, itching skin; coarse, sparse hair; and swellings over the long bones. Usually an enlarged liver was present.

Much of our knowledge of vitamin A toxicity comes from India and the Philippines, where doses of 200,000 IU are given to deficient patients in outlying villages once every six months. From 3-4 percent of them suffer loss of appetite, nausea, vomiting, and headache within 24 hours. These side effects last only a few days; then as the body distributes the vitamin, deficiency symptoms disappear and the beneficial effects of the vitamins are felt.

Severe overdosage gives rise to generalized itching; redness of the skin; dry scaling of the skin and mucous membranes; cracking of the corners of the mouth and lips; inflamed tongue and gums; ulceration of the mouth; and loss of hair. In addition there is fatigue; hemorrhages; retention of water; tenderness of the long bones; and a tender, enlarged liver. If intake is continued there is mental irritability; sleep disturbance; loss in weight; and rises in the blood enzyme alkaline phosphatase, which leads to calcium deposition in the blood vessels.

Toxicity is unlikely if the daily intake is kept below 5,000 IU per kg body weight (i.e., 350,000 IU for a 154 lb. (70 kg) individual) for not more than 200 days. Intervals of four to six weeks between courses of treatment are recommended. These levels of intakes apply only when the vitamin is being used therapeutically and under medical supervision. There is now an increased tendency to give large daily doses of vitamin A and its analogs for skin diseases and for cancer. The symptoms mentioned above apply mainly to vitamin A alcohol (retinol), because it is stored in the liver. Retinoic acid is not stored and is used where high blood levels are needed quickly.

Synthetic retinoic acid analogs (retinoids) can induce toxicity symptoms but at intakes higher than those of vitamin A. The widely used 13-cis-retinoic acid used to treat acne gives side effects confined to the skin, the mucous membranes of the mouth, the nose, and the eyes. Toxic symptoms rapidly abate when treatment with the analogs is stopped. Reducing the intake of vitamin A and its analogs is the only treatment for overdosage.

Vitamin D: There is a narrow gap between the nutrient requirement and the toxic dose. As little as five times the recommended intake (50 μg daily) taken over prolonged periods can lead to high blood calcium levels in infants and calcium deposition in the kidneys of adults.

Toxicity is more likely in children, either because of excessive doses administered by over-zealous mothers or because of increased sensitivity of some infants to fortified milk containing the vitamin. The usual signs in children are loss of appetite with nausea and vomiting. Excessive urination with consequent thirst are soon evident. Constipation often alternates with diarrhea. Frequently there are pains in the head and in the bones. The child becomes thin, irritable, and depressed, eventually becoming stupored. Calcium deposits are laid down in the arteries, kidneys, heart, lungs, and other soft tissues and organs. Death can result.

In adults a regular intake of more than 100,000 IU (2.5 mg) of vitamin D for long periods is required to produce the typical symptoms of weakness, nausea, vomiting, constipation, excessive urination, thirst, and dehydration. Less obvious but more serious results are deposition of calcium in the soft tissues and organs and eventually kidney failure leading to death.

High doses of vitamin D are used in treating metabolic bone disease, hypoparathyroidism, malabsorption, and certain arthritic conditions. Potent preparations must be taken for long periods, so close medical monitoring is essential.

The only treatment for vitamin D overdosage is to stop taking the vitamin.

Vitamin E: The only side effect noted with this vitamin is muscle weakness in a few people taking at least 600 IU daily. Many more have taken from 400 to 1,600 IU daily with no ill-effects. In a period spanning forty years, doctors at the Shute Institute in Canada have treated over 40,000 patients with doses of vitamin E up to 5,000 IU daily with no discernible side effects. Occasionally there is a transient rise in blood pressure in susceptible people given over 800 IU daily, but no effect has been noted in those being treated for high blood pressure. Both muscle weakness and the raised blood pressure quickly disappear when the vitamin intake is stopped or reduced to 400 IU daily. Occasionally, contact dermatitis has occurred when people applied the pure oil to the skin or even an ointment or cream containing more than 100 IU per g. Reduction of the potency removes the allergic reaction.

Thiamin: Very occasionally, injections of thiamin can cause hypersensitivity reactions in susceptible people. Effects include itching and swelling at the site of injection; swelling of the tongue, lips, and eyes; generalized itching and sweating; sneezing, wheezing, difficulty in breathing, and cyanosis (where the skin becomes blue); nausea; low blood pressure; and, very rarely, death has resulted. No side effects have been reported from orally administered thiamin.

Nicotinic acid: Large doses of between 3 and 10 g daily have been prescribed to reduce blood cholesterol levels, and the toxic reactions include flushing of the skin of the face, neck, and chest, accompanied by itching in these areas. More than one-third of patients so treated continue to suffer this flushing while undergoing this therapy. In some there are rashes, dry skin, and increased pigmentation of the skin. Occasionally jaundice appears, accompanied by nausea, diarrhea, abdominal pain, and headache in as many as 20 to 40 percent of patients treated. Gastric and duodenal ulcers can worsen.

Nicotinamide in similar doses does not cause flushing, but liver damage has been recorded. Nicotinic acid must therefore be used with caution and under close monitoring in those suffering from gastric and duodenal ulcers, gout, diabetes, and liver disease, and in pregnant women.

Pyridoxine: Until recently was believed to be nontoxic, although for some time it has been known to neutralize the effect of the drug levodopa used in treating Parkinson's disease. There are cases of toxicity reported in subjects who took more than 200 mg pyridoxine daily, but the most comprehensive study was as follows:

Daily intakes of at least 2,000 mg pyridoxine taken over 2 to 40 months have given rise to peripheral neuropathy in seven subjects. Typical symptoms started with numbness in the feet and unstable gait. This led to increasing inability to walk steadily, particularly in the dark, and difficulty in handling small objects. Numbness and clumsiness of the hands followed within months, sufficient to impair typing ability; there were also changes in the feeling in the lips and tongue. Normal blood plasma levels of pyridoxine are in the range of 0.36 to 1.8 μg per 100 ml, but those patients had levels of 3.0 μg and above. After one month's abstinence from pyridoxine supplementation, the level fell to 1.7 μg per 100 ml plasma. In all cases, withdrawal of pyridoxine led to improvement in symptoms and tests indicated a marked recovery of the nervous system, but the process took several months. None of these patients experienced symptoms when their intake was below 2,000 mg pyridoxine daily. There is no evidence of harm from the more usual daily dose of 25 to 100 mg taken for PMS.

Folic acid: Antagonism has been reported between folic acid and the drug phenytoin used in treating epilepsy. Hence balance between the drug and the vitamin is critical and best left to the medical practitioner.

High folic acid intakes can deplete vitamin B_{12} stores in the body. If given to those suffering from pernicious anemia resulting from malabsorption of vitamin B_{12}, high-dose folic acid can mask the blood anemia symptoms but allow the spinal column nerve degeneration to continue. Hence the importance of diagnosing megaloblastic anemia as due to either folic acid or vitamin B_{12} deficiency.

Oral therapy has given rise to loss of appetite, abdominal distension, and flatulence. Occasionally injection of folic acid can cause a transient rise in temperature and symptoms of fever.

Vitamin B_{12}: Toxicity reactions from oral dosage have never been reported. Very rare allergic reactions have occurred following intramuscular injection of the vitamin.

Riboflavin: No reported toxicity reactions.

Pantothenic acid: No reported toxicity reactions even after long-term treatment with up to 2 g daily in cases of rheumatoid arthritis, either orally or by injection.

Carotene: Generally accepted as safe, even at intakes sufficient to impart a yellow color to the skin.

Biotin: No adverse reactions reported, even in infants given 5 mg daily, orally or by injection, for skin lesions.

Vitamin C: Generally regarded as one of the safest vitamins, even when taken in massive doses. There are

some who should avoid large (i.e., greater than 1 g daily)
intakes of the vitamin because they suffer from inherited
metabolic diseases giving rise to excess oxalic acid, cystine,
or uric acid in the blood and urine. They have a greater
tendency to form kidney stones. Such disease is rare and
most people can tolerate vitamin C intakes up to 3 g daily
and even more. Those who suffer from kidney stones and
those who are taking oral anticoagulant drugs should take
high-dose vitamin C with caution, although intakes of up
to 500 mg daily can be tolerated by these people for long
periods.

Physical signs of overdose are gastrointestinal and
include nausea, abdominal cramps, and diarrhea. The
vitamin can also act as a diuretic causing increased urination, but this can be beneficial in removing excess body
water. If a high intake causes diarrhea, reducing the
amount taken by 500 mg or 1 g daily will often reduce the
side effect. Previous claims that high vitamin C intakes
can destroy vitamin B_{12} have now been discounted.

Trace elements, are elements that occur in the body at
very low concentrations, usually less than 0.01 percent of
the body's weight. Also known as trace minerals. At least
15 trace elements are recognized as essential for warm-
blooded animals and birds. They are, in order of demonstrated need: iron, iodine, copper, manganese, zinc, cobalt,
molybdenum, selenium, chromium, tin, vanadium, fluorine,
silicon, nickel, and arsenic. Twelve of them have been
demonstrated to be needed by humans, but it is likely that
the other three—arsenic, nickel, and tin—are also essential (*see* Figure 67). Difficulty in creating deficiencies of
these three in modern diets has been conducive to lack of
knowledge of their specific roles in humans. All trace
elements can also be toxic in humans, but in most cases
the range of intakes between needs and toxicity is wide.

Some trace elements are postively harmful in humans; these include cadmium, lead, and mercury.

Figure 67: Recommended daily intakes of selected trace elements

	Age (yrs)	Cu (mg)	Mn (mg)	F (mg)	Cr (μg)	Se (μg)	Mo (μg)
Infants	0-0.5	0.5-0.7	0.5-0.7	0.1-0.5	10-40	10-40	30-60
	0.5-1	0.7-1.0	0.7-1.0	0.2-1.0	20-60	20-60	40-80
Children and	1-3	1.0-1.5	1.0-1.5	0.5-1.5	20-80	20-80	50-100
adolescents	4-6	1.5-2.0	1.5-2.0	1.0-2.5	30-120	30-120	60-150
	7-10	2.0-2.5	2.0-3.0	1.5-2.5	50-200	50-200	100-300
	11+	2.0-3.0	2.5-5.0	1.5-2.5	50-200	50-200	150-500
Adults		2.0-3.0	2.5-5.0	1.5-4.0	50-200	50-200	150-500

(For the recommended daily intakes of iodine and iron, *see* the appropriate entries.)

The functions of trace elements in the body are as integral components of many enzymes and some hormones. Unlike the macroelements, they play no part in the structural makeup of the body (with the possible exception of fluroide in bones and teeth), nor do they contribute to the electrolyte balance. An excess or a deficiency of trace elements can be wholly or partially responsible for a number of disorders. The toxic trace elements in particular may accumulate in the body and produce harmful effects in an insidious manner.

Estimated safe and adequate daily intakes of selected trace elements have been recommended by the Food and Nutrition Board, National Research Council—National Academy of Sciences, 1980, as shown in Figure 67.

Travel sickness, *see* nausea.

Tretinoin, vitamin A acid; retinoic acid. Toxic effects include transitory stinging, redness, and allergic dermatitis when applied to skin.

Triamterene,   a diuretic. Impairs folic acid utilization.

Trifluoperazine,   an antidepressant, bronchospasm relaxant, gastro-intestinal sedative, sedative, and antinausea agent. Prevents the absorption of vitamin B_{12}.

Trigeminal neuralgia,   a severe, brief, lancing pain at either side of the face. Known also as facial neuralgia. Has been relieved with large doses of thiamin (50-600 mg daily).

Triiodothyronine,   known also as liothyronine and T3. First isolated from the thyroid gland by J. Gross and R. Pitt-Rivers of the UK in 1952. A natural thyroid hormone containing three atoms of iodine per molecule triiodothyronine. Can also be obtained by chemical synthesis. Used in the initial therapy of hypothyroidism because it has a faster action and turnover rate than thyroxine.

Elevated blood levels have been found in victims of sudden-infant-death syndrome. *See* hypothyroidism; iodine; and thyroxine.

Tryptophan(e),   an essential amino acid normally supplied by the diet. Has been used to treat depression in high doses along with nicotinamide pyridoxine, and vitamin C. A precursor of nicotinic acid; 60 mg tryptophan is necessary for each mg of vitamin. Tryptophan in the diet will not be sufficient to supply all nicotinic acid needs, but conversion depends upon adequate quantities of thiamin, riboflavin, pyridoxine, and biotin. A precursor of serotonin, an essential factor for nerve and brain function. Vitamin B_6 is required for the synthesis of serotinin, lack of which produces depression.

U

Ubiquinone, a vitamin-like substance found in all body cells, but particularly rich in the heart muscle. Functions as an oxygen transfer coenzyme. Synthesis is dependent on vitamin E. A rich source is yeast. Known also as coenzyme Q.

Ulcers, loss of substance on the surface of the skin or mucous membranes. There are several types:

Decubitus: See bedsores.

Indolent: An ulcer that will not heal. May respond to oral vitamin E (400-600 IU daily) plus direct application of vitamin E cream.

Leg: Sometimes associated with diabetes. Treat as for indolent with vitamin E or folic acid (5 mg tablets three times daily) and in serious cases with additional injections of 20 mg twice weekly.

Gastric: Has responded to 150,000 IU vitamin A daily for four weeks.

Mouth: Prevented by adequate intakes of riboflavin (10 mg daily) plus vitamin A (7,500 IU daily). May be treated by same regimen.

Varicose: See indolent ulcer.

V

Vanadium, chemical symbol V. Atomic weight 50.9.

Widely distributed in ores; abundance in the earth's crust is 100 mg per kg.

An essential trace element for rats and chicks, it may also be necessary for human beings. Deficiency in animals causes reduction in red blood cell production leading to anemia; upset in iron metabolism; lack of growth of bones, teeth, and cartilage; increased blood fat levels; and increased blood cholesterol levels. It therefore functions in growth; fat metabolism; blood production; and possibly in the prevention of dental caries. Feeding vanadium to deficient animals reduces blood fat and cholesterol levels.

Excess vanadium in humans may be related to manic depression. Manic depressives, when fed a low-vanadium diet or given extra vitamin C (to remove excess vanadium) showed great improvements as their body levels of vanadium fell. Daily intakes of vanadium in the diet are probably between 100 and 300 μg. Most of this passes directly through the system, unabsorbed, but some is retained in the bones and liver.

Food sources are (in μg per 100 g): parsley (2,950); lobster (1,610); radishes (790); dill (460); lettuce (280); gelatin (250); fish bones (240); strawberries (70); calf liver (11-51); sardines (46); cucumber (38); apples (33); cauliflower (9); tomatoes (4); and potatoes (1). Most other foods contain less than 1 μg per 100 g.

Processed foods may contain more than the fresh variety because of contamination from the vanadium in the stainless steel of processing plants.

Toxic effects have not been reported except the possibility that the trace mineral may be related to manic depression.

Varicose veins, a swollen, knotted, and dilated condition of vein. Bioflavonoids (1,000 mg daily) plus vitamin C (500 mg daily) can help improve the condition. Vitamin E (400-600 IU daily) can reduce swelling and pain, and prevent phlebitis. Lecithin (5-15 g daily) complements the actions of vitamin E.

Vasopressin, a peptide hormone, produced in the pituitary gland, that increases the reabsorption of water by the kidney thus preventing excessive losses from the body. Also known as antidiuretic hormone or ADH. Used medically to treat diabetes insipidus.

Veganism, an extreme form of vegetarianism where no product of animal, fish, fowl, or insect is eaten. Vegans may be prone to vitamin B_{12} deficiency, but this can be obtained from supplements that contain the vitamin produced by fermentation. Spirulina, an alga, can supply sufficient B_{12} acceptable to vegans. Possible vitamin D deficiency is overcome by exposure of skin to sunshine or supplements containing the vitamin derived from yeast.

Vegetable oils, important sources of vitamin E and the polyunsaturated fatty acid linoleic acid. *See* Figure 68.

Soft margarine made from these oils also provides useful quantities of these nutrients plus vitamins A and D.

Vegetables, completely devoid of vitamin A, but some are a good source of its precursor carotene. They contain no vitamin D, but usually some vitamin E. Most supply all the B vitamins except for vitamin B_{12}, but concentrations vary. Some vegetables supply good quantities of vitamin C. Carotene and vitamin E are unaffected by cooking methods. Invariably, there is some loss of B vitamins when vegetables are cooked.

Green, leafy varieties include asparagus, broccoli, brussels sprouts, cabbage, chicory (endive), celery, kale, leeks, cauliflower, lettuce, parsley, spinach, turnip tops, and watercress.

Figure 68: Vitamin E content of vegetable oils

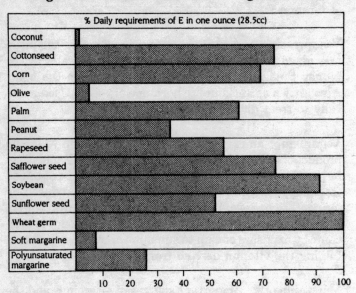

% Daily requirements of E in one ounce (28.5cc)
Coconut
Cottonseed
Corn
Olive
Palm
Peanut
Rapeseed
Safflower seed
Soybean
Sunflower seed
Wheat germ
Soft margarine
Polyunsaturated margarine

Root varieties include artichokes, beets, carrots, parsnips, potatoes, pumpkin, radishes, sweet potatoes, turnips, and yams. To these can be added surface vegetables such as beans, corn, eggplants, cucumbers, peas, squash and tomatoes.

The contributions of vegetables to vitamins and minerals in the diet are shown in Figures 69 through 72. Also shown in Figure 73 are the amounts of vitamins and minerals left in the vegetables after cooking.

See also legumes.

Minerals remaining after boiling

Minerals cannot be destroyed but they are leached from food during cooking processes. All losses can be recovered by utilizing the cooking water.

More minerals are lost from food boiled in soft water

Figure 69: Vitamin content of green, leafy vegetables

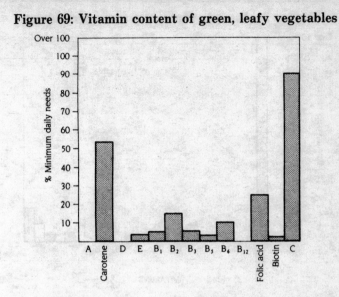

Figure 70: Mineral content of green, leafy vegetables

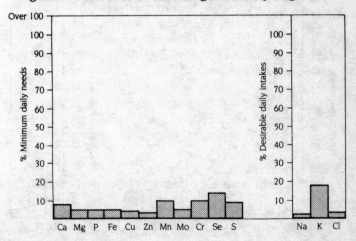

Figure 71: Vitamin content of root vegetables

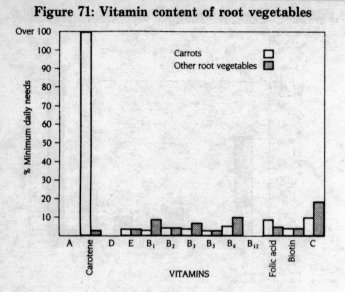

Figure 72: Mineral content of root vegetables

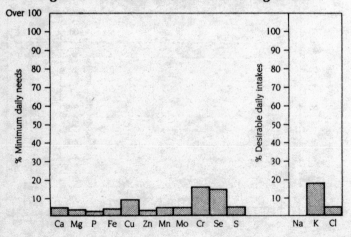

Figure 73: Vitamins remaining in vegetables after boiling

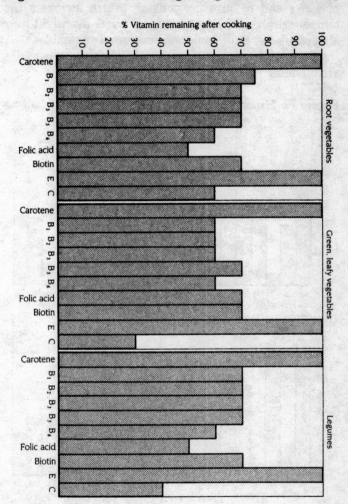

than in hard. Losses are increased by using large volumes of water and by pressure-cooking, which increases the temperature. Soaking vegetables in water overnight may also cause losses of some minerals from vegetables.

Figure 74 indicates the minerals left in the vegetables after boiling.

Figure 74: Minerals remaining in vegetables after boiling

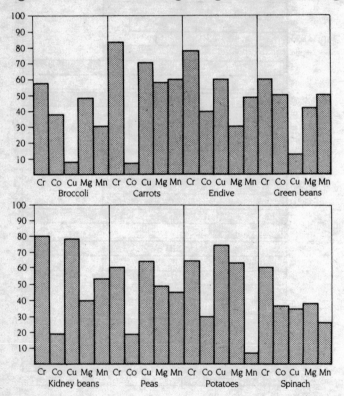

Vegetarianism, practiced by those who eat no meat, fish, or fowl. May benefit from vitamin B_{12} supplementation, but vegetarians probably obtain enough from dairy products in the diet. Same source for vitamin D. Tend to receive high intakes of folic acid and vitamin C because of dietary habits.

Veruccae, *see* warts.

Virus, the smallest of parasites. Consists of a central core of nucleic acid and an outer cover of protein. Wholly dependent on bacterial, plant, or animal cells for reproduction. Nucleic acid represents the basic infective material. Best natural defenses against viruses are adequate vitamin A and vitamin C. Viral infections are best supplemented with vitamin A (7,500 IU) and vitamin C (up to 6 g daily).

Vitamin, a micronutrient essential for health that cannot be synthesized in sufficient amounts by the animal or human body. Derived from *vita* meaning life and *amine*, a substance incorrectly assigned to all vitamins. The term was first used by the Polish chemist Casimir Funk in 1911. Divided into fat soluble—A, D, E, and K—and water-soluble—B-complex and C.

Vitamins must satisfy three criteria:

1. Adequate amounts are supplied only in the diet.
2. Deficiency produces discrete clinical symptoms and disease.
3. Disease and symptoms are cured only with specific vitamin.

Exceptions may be vitamin D (produced in skin by sunshine), and biotin and vitamin K (produced by intestinal bacterial synthesis).

Vitamin B$_3$, nicotinic acid. *See* niacin.

Vitamin B₄,   adenine (no longer regarded as a vitamin).

Vitamin B₅,   *see* pantothenic acid.

Vitamin B₇,   a growth factor for microorganisms but not for humans.

Vitamin B₈,   a growth factor for microorganisms but not for humans.

Vitamin B₉,   a growth factor for microorganisms but not for humans.

Vitamin B₁₀,   an unindentified growth and feathering factor for chicks.

Vitamin B₁₁,   an unindentified growth and feathering factor for chicks.

Vitamin B₁₃,   *see* orotic acid.

Vitamin B₁₄,   a derivative of vitamin B₁₂.

Vitamin Bc,   *see* folic acid.

Vitamin BT,   *see* carnitine (no longer regarded as a vitamin).

Vitamin Bx,   *see* para-aminobenzoic acid.

Vitamin F,   once applied to polyunsaturated fatty acids, especially linoleic acid, but now no longer used and officially not recognized.

Vitamin G,   *see* B$_2$ (vitamin).

Vitamin H,   *see* biotin.

Vitamin H$_3$,   procaine (no longer regarded as a vitamin).

Vitamin L$_1$,   ortho-aminobenzoic acid; L$_2$, adenine derivative. Factors presumably necessary for lactation. Very doubtful significance in human beings.

Vitamin M,   *see* folic acid.

Vitamin P,   old name for carotenoids, but no longer accepted as a vitamin.

Vitamin PP,   nicotinic acid. *See* niacin.

Vitamin T,   also known as tegotin, termitin, factor T, vitamin T Goetsch, and Goetsch's vitamin. A complex of growth-promoting substances, originally obtained from termites. Also present in yeasts and fungi. Probably a mixture of known vitamins and growth-promoting factors, but never characterized fully.

Vitamin U,   the antiulcer substance reported in cabbage leaves and other green vegetables. It is no longer accepted as a vitamin. Believed to be L-methionine methylsulphonium salt. Has been used to treat gastric ulcers.

Vitamin/mineral relationships,   functions where each is needed for complete utilization of the other and where both are required for a specific process. Examples are:

1. Vitamin D is essential for the absorption and assimilation of calcium and phosphate.

2. Vitamin C is essential for the absorption of iron and its incorporation into hemoglobin.

3. Vitamin C is possibly needed for the absorption of calcium phosphate.

4. Riboflavin (vitamin B_2) is essential for iron utilization in making hemoglobin.

5. Vitamin E complements the action of selenium. Selenium is a constituent of the enzyme glutathione peroxidase, but vitamin E appears to be essential for its function also.

6. Zinc liberates vitamin A from the liver stores.

7. Zinc is essential for absorption of folic acid.

8. Calcium is necessary for absorption of vitamin B_{12}.

9. Zinc and vitamin B_6 are essential and function together in the production of essential brain transmitters.

10. Magnesium and vitamin B_6 combine to prevent kidney-stone formation.

11. Manganese is needed by the intestinal bacteria for the synthesis of vitamin K.

Vitiligo, the depigmentation of areas of skin that have lost the ability to produce the natural pigment melanin. The condition worsens on exposure to sunlight, probably because nonaffected areas become darker with tanning. A harmless condition apart from cosmetic blemish.

Has been treated with PABA, 50 mg by injection twice daily plus 100 mg twice a day orally. The condition improved after six to eight months. May be complemented with additional pantothenic acid, vitamin B_6, zinc, and manganese to stimulate melanin production.

W

Warfarin, an anticoagulant drug. Acts by inhibiting the action of vitamin K.

Warts, common, benign skin eruptions caused by a virus. Known also as veruccae. Have been treated with directly applied solutions of water-solubilized vitamin A palmitate. Alternatively may respond to vitamin E oil applied directly, plus oral supplement of 400 IU daily.

Wheat flour, may be whole wheat flour in which the whole of the wheat grain is ground with nothing added or taken away. May also be white flour from which the bran and wheat germ have been removed before grinding. White flour is inferior in its contents of minerals and vitamins, but is fortified with calcium, iron, thiamin (B_1), and nicotinic acid (B_3). *See* Figures 75 and 76.

Wheat germ, the germ or embryo of the wheat grain situated at the lower end of the grain; consists of a root and shoot. Makes up 3 percent of the total weight of the grain. It is claimed that wheat germ (60 g, or 2 ounces daily) plus vitamin C (2,000 mg daily) is more effective in preventing respiratory conditions than vitamin C alone. Usually stabilized by mild heat, but the product is still an excellent source of minerals and some vitamins. *See* Figures 77 and 78.

Wheat germ oil, expressed or solvent-extracted oil from germ of wheat grain. A rich source of vitamin E (190 mg

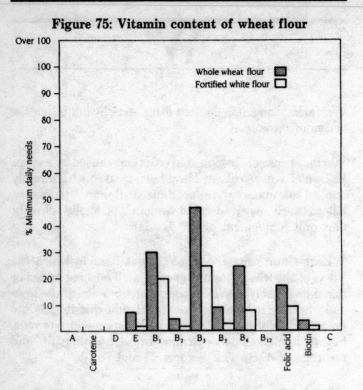

Figure 75: Vitamin content of wheat flour

per 100 g) and polyunsaturated fatty acids (41.54 g per 100 g).

Whey factor, *see* orotic acid.

Whole grains, comprise barley, oats, wheat, and corn, which are ingredients of muesli and granola. All are meaningful sources of the B vitamins and vitamin E, along with the essential minerals. *See* Figures 79 and 80.

Wilson's disease, hepatolenticular degeneration. A rare

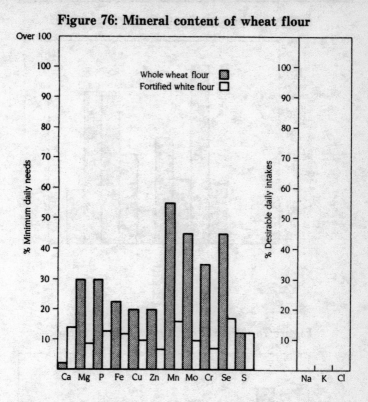

Figure 76: Mineral content of wheat flour

familial disease that occurs most often in children whose parents are blood relations. Excessive amounts of copper accumulate in the tissues, due to defective synthesis of ceruloplasmin (which carries copper in blood) in the liver, and hence allows copper to be transported in the blood plasma only loosely bound to albumin. Deposition of copper in the liver and brain leads to cirrhosis of the liver and brain disturbances. That in the kidneys causes renal dysfunction. The mineral is also deposited in the eye, causing a golden-brown or gray-green pigment ring at the

Figure 77: Vitamin content of wheat germ

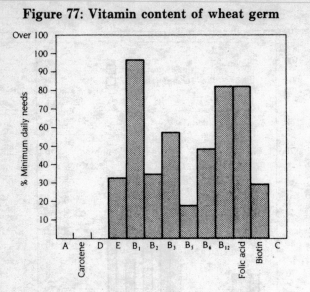

Figure 78: Mineral content of wheat germ

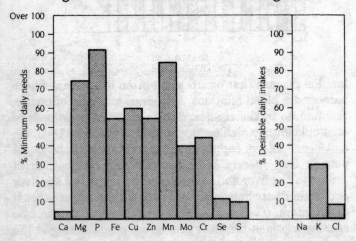

Figure 79: Vitamin content of whole grains

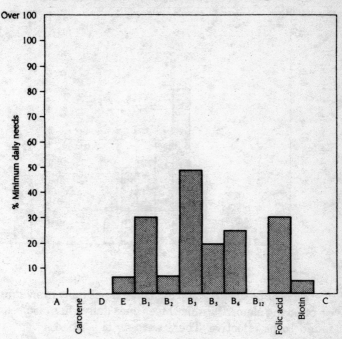

edge of the cornea. Radiating brownish spokes of copper deposits on the lens capsule form the characteristic sunflower cataract.

Treatment is by avoidance of foods high in copper; chelation of the excess copper with chelating drugs such as D-penicillamine or ethylene diamine tetraacetate; and displacement of excess copper from the body with zinc.

D-penicillamine can cause acute toxic reactions in about one-third of those treated, e.g., fever, rash, low white blood cell count, and low blood platelet count. Vitamin B_6 is given at a dose of 25-50 mg daily to prevent possible deficiency.

Figure 80: Mineral content of whole grains

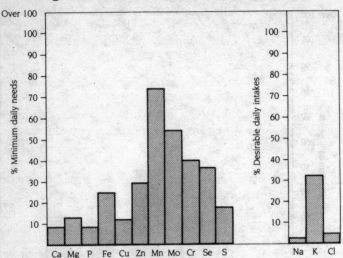

Zinc sulfate, 200 or 300 mg three times daily (providing 45 or 68 mg elemental zinc three times daily), has also been found to be effective. There were no side effects.

Women, have different vitamin and mineral needs than men because of the menstrual cycle. May have requirements for pyridoxine ten days or so before menstruation far above those supplied by the diet (usually a minimum of 25 mg daily). May also have extra needs for vitamin C, folic acid, vitamin B_{12}, and vitamin E to ensure maximum incorporation of iron into hemoglobin to replace the blood losses of the menstrual flow. Extra requirements for all vitamins and minerals while pregnant and during period of breast-feeding. Those taking the contraceptive pill have increased requirements for certain vitamins. *See also* contraceptives; menstruation.

Wound healing,   is accelerated by supplementary intakes of vitamin C, vitamin E, vitamin A, and mineral zinc. Healing needs many micronutrients including iron, zinc, vitamins A and C, with adequate protein in the diet. The key healing nutrient is zinc, which functions in:

1. Rapid cell division, dependent on DNA synthesis, which supplies new cells close to the wound.
2. Synthesis of collagen, which toughens up the newly laid-down cells by meshing them with existing old tissue cells; this process also needs vitamin C.
3. Liberation of vitamin A, which is also needed for the rapid rate of production of new tissue cells from the liver.
4. Stabilizing cell membranes, keeping them strong and resilient under stress.

To ensure maximum healing rate, supplementation should provide at least 15 mg zinc element daily and possibly twice this. Excessive quantities of zinc will not cause faster healing, so there is no point in taking more than the recommended supplement.

Xerophthalmia,   a drying and degenerative disease of the transparent part of the eye associated with vitamin A deficiency.

364

Y

Yeast, an excellent source of all minerals, but particularly rich in the trace minerals including chromium and selenium. Torula variety is similar but devoid of chromium and selenium. Useful source of B vitamins apart from B_{12}. *See* baker's yeast; brewer's yeast; and torula yeast.

Yeast extract, a very rich source of most of the B vitamins but completely devoid of carotene, vitamin E, and vitamin C. B vitamins present are (in mg per 100 g): thiamin (3.1); riboflavin (11); nicotinic acid (67); and pyridoxine (1.3). Folic acid level is 1,010 μg per 100 g; vitamin B_{12} content is 0.5 μg per 100 g, but this is probably added.

Yogurt, a useful source of some B vitamins plus the fat-soluble variety. Has higher potencies than milk because of bacterial synthesis, providing (in mg per 100 g): vitamin A—0.008; carotene—0.005; thiamin—0.05; riboflavin—0.26; nicotinic acid—1.16; pyridoxine—0.04; folic acid—0.002; vitamin E—0.03; vitamin B_{12}—trace; and vitamin D—trace.

Minerals

An excellent source of calcium, potassium, phosphorus, and chloride. Has small but useful amounts of the trace minerals and only moderate amounts of sodium. Mineral levels vary, according to variety, in the following ranges (in mg per 100 g): sodium—64-76; potassium—220-240; calcium—160-180; magnesium—17-20; phosphorus—140; iron—0.09-0.24; copper—0.04-0.10; zinc—0.60-0.69; and chloride—150-180.

Z

Zinc, chemical symbol Zn. Atomic weight 65.4. An essential trace mineral for plants, animals, and human beings.

Best Food Sources in mg per 100 g

Oysters	70.0
Liver	7.8
Dried brewer's yeast	7.8
Shellfish	5.3
Meats	4.3
Hard Cheese	4.0
Canned fish	3.0
Whole wheat bread	2.0
Eggs	1.5
Legumes	1.0
Whole grain cereals	1.0
Rice	0.4
Green leafy vegetables	0.3
Potatoes	0.3

Zinc Supplements in mg per 100 mg

Zinc amino acid chelate (10); zinc gluconate (13); zinc orotate (17); and zinc sulfate (22.7)

Functions

Growth
Insulin activity
Releases vitamin A from liver
In metabolism of pituitary, adrenals, ovaries, and testes
Development of skeleton, nervous system, and brain in growing fetus
Maintaining healthy liver function

Absorption from Food

On the average, 20 percent of zinc in food is absorbed. Zinc from animal and fish sources is better absorbed than that from vegetables and fruits. This is due to high cysteine content of animal-derived foods

Factors Limiting Absorption

Phytic acid in cereals and vegetables

High dietary fiber intakes

Polyphosphates, used as food additives

Ethylenediaminetetra-acetate (EDTA), used in food processing

TVP (textured vegetable protein) products eaten in excess

Supplementation with zinc required in all above

Factors Reducing Dietary Zinc

Two most important are:
  food refining
  food processing
Production of white flour from whole wheat causes 77 percent loss of zinc; refining of unpolished brown rice to white rice causes 83 percent loss; processing cereals from whole grains causes 80 percent loss

Body Content

Adult contains between 2 and 3 g zinc. Highest concentration in prostate, semen, and sperm, but muscle, liver and kidney also have high concentrations

Muscles and bones contain 63 percent of body zinc; skin contains further 20 percent

Some also in hair—when zinc is lacking, hair growth slows or stop

Excretion

Mainly via the feces but some lost in urine. Low intakes cause power losses; with high intakes, excess is simply excreted

Excessive loss in:
  alcoholism
  kidney disease
  liver disease

Drugs cause extra losses, e.g., diurectics of thiazide type, or lower losses, e.g., diuretics of frusemide type

Zinc cont.

Therapeutic Uses

Treating acne, eczema, psoriasis, rosacea

Prevention and treatment of prostate problems

Treating mild mental conditions

Decreasing blood fat levels

Supplementing schizophrenics

Supplementing hyperactive children

Treating the common cold with zinc gluconate in lozenge form

Treating anorexia nervosa

Deficiency

In humans, gives rise to condition characterized by lack of physical, mental, and sexual development. Can be reversed in pre-puberty girls and boys with increased zinc intakes

Causes growth failure, impaired sense of taste, poor appetite, all of which are reversed with continued zinc treatment

Deficiency cont.

Has caused impotence in men on long-term kidney dialysis.

Causes acrodermatitis enteropathica, a rare skin disease of infancy.

Deficiency Symptoms

Eczema of face and hands

Hair loss

Mental apathy

Defects in reproductive organs, particularly testes

Decreased growth rate

Impaired mental development

Postnatal depression

Congenital abnormalities in newborn

Loss of sense of taste

Loss of sense of smell

White spots on nails

Pica—eating of dirt and strange substances by children

Susceptibility to infections

Relationship to Other Minerals

Zinc accompanies calcium in the mineralization of bone and when calcium is lost from bone

High copper content of blood can depress zinc absorption from the intestine; high zinc intakes can reduce copper absorption. Increase in copper: zinc dietary ratio from normal, 4, to 14 or 20 causes increased blood cholesterol leading to atherosclerosis

Cadmium, a toxic non-essential mineral, antagonizes zinc intake from food. Zinc can help detoxify high body cadmium levels

Recommended Daily Intake

Should be between 15 and 20 mg zinc. *See* recommended daily intakes

Effects of Excess Intake

Toxic effects of supplementary oral zinc at intakes up to 150 mg daily have not been reported

Very high doses may cause mild gastric irritation and vomiting

NOTES